WORLDS BE
the 'Spirit World'

Minds never 'die':
Find out WHY you exist!
(Sequel to 'Truths, Lies & Distortions')

Knowledge dictated
by Evolved Masters

Channelled by

French Medium
BRIGITTE RIX

CON-PSY Publications

First Edition

© Brigitte RIX
2015

Published by
CON-PSY PUBLICATIONS
P.O. BOX 14, GREENFORD,
MIDDLESEX, UB6 0UF

ISBN 978 1 898680 73 4

....
Other books by Brigitte Rix:
- 'I'm Not Dead: I'm Alive Without a Body'- *Vol. 1&2-* (2011 / 2012 & 2013)
- 'Truths Lies & Distortions' (2012 & 2015)
- 'Get by in French: BBC Active' (1998 & 2007)
- 'Pas de Problème' (2003)
....

ACKNOWLEDGEMENTS

My loving and respectful thanks to my very patient 'Spirit' Guide and Teachers in the Hereafter, who not only share with me their advanced knowledge, but are also channels for Evolved Masters and Beings of refined Mind Energy, from BEYOND the vibration level of the 'Spirit World'.

Once more, they asked me to take time to listen to them on a regular basis and channel their dictations, so that they could produce **their** new book. It is an honour for me to be the recipient of their revelations and to help such Advanced Beings offer them to Mankind. Their work taught me mind-blowing, astounding and exciting facts. I feel very privileged to be their humble messenger and scribe, as I keep my promise to them to share those wonders with other Truth Seekers.

All my love and gratitude to my kind and loving daughter Anne-France for her help, patience and advice.

Of course, all my gratefulness to my very dear Stan for his patience, understanding and caring help, so that I have time to receive, type and prepare those many hundreds of pages for the publishers.

My warmest and heartfelt thanks to one of my keen readers: my special and dear friend Pauline Crossley, in Greater Manchester, who very kindly offered to help and enthusiastically devoted long hours checking my manuscript. You are a gem, my dear Pauline! Thank you for coming into my life.

My thanks to my technician Graham Barnes - from bbdimension.co.uk - for his IT skills in putting together my ideas for the cover. Also to my publisher, Candy Taylor of Con-Psy Publications, for her work to ensure the publication of this book.

Finally, all my love to my beautiful rescued cats, for their purring love as they patiently kept me company during those long hours at the computer!

WORLDS BEYOND the 'Spirit World'

Acknowledgements

CONTENTS

PART 1
CONSOLIDATING FUNDAMENTAL FACTS

PART 2
REACHING BEYOND 'THE SPIRIT WORLD'

PART 3
CONSCIOUSNESS

Please visit my website for further knowledge, or to ask me questions about the Afterlife:

www.italkwithspirits.com

INTRODUCTION
by Brigitte RIX

My readers have been waiting for this, my latest channelled book to-date, the sequel to *Truths Lies & Distortions,* also dictated by my team of Advanced Masters. HERE IT IS!

It guarantees to stretch your Mind like malleable rubber and enlighten it with even more groundbreaking and astounding revelations, answering clearly more aeons-old questions as to why and how we, our Earth and our universe have come to exist. These explanations are free from any religion, religious doctrines or dogmas. Yet to any open-minded reader, these should make far more sense than the distorted theories and ideologies thrown at us from childhood...

WHO AM I?

This book is not at all 'about me' - I do not see myself as 'the Author', but only as the messenger for these teachings dictated at high speed by knowledgeable Beings. I am a clairaudient medium who gratefully agreed to channel the dictations of a team of genuine, Advanced Beings. They wish to impart Knowledge to Mankind - as part of centuries of efforts by those in the Great Beyond, to try and bring Humanity back to its senses!

For those readers who have not yet read my other channelled books - yet wish to know more about me, my experiences and discoveries - I have included at the end of this book, the detailed Biographical Introduction from the first published volume of my diary of conversations with those in the Afterlife World: *'I'm Not Dead: I'm Alive without a Body'*. It explains in detail: who I am, my amazement when I discovered

I could communicate and develop my mediumship, my astonishment as I received unexpected evidence and wonderful knowledge and made mind-blowing discoveries - and why I was eventually asked and gently convinced by those guiding personalities in the 'Spirit World', to be their channel and scribe.

But for now here is a bit about me to show you that I am a 'normal' person, and to explain how this book evolved.

I am a French language teacher and University lecturer by profession, now retired. I am also a qualified Healer and successfully trained in several Complementary Therapies. Though born in France, I have now been living in UK for several decades: married to David Rix, (a British Russian language lecturer at the University of York), who has now 'emigrated' to the 'Spirit World' from where he keeps in touch. I have our two grown-up children and rescued cats. I live in York, UK and you can find me on Facebook and Twitter – my website is: **www. italkwithspirits.com**.

I am also a genuine (!) clairaudient medium and probably have been all my life - yet I only realised it properly in 1983! I then made sure I trained to polish my mediumship ethically and safely. This means I can give people personal messages (at no charge), that provide evidence of life after (and before) death – *but only IF their deceased loved ones have learnt how to communicate* - as not all can! But nowadays, nearly all my time is now devoted to specializing in channelling the eye-opening knowledge and 'teachings' dictated by Evolved Beings, from the World of Mind and Light – knowledge which they wish me to share with the world by publishing and promoting their books.

When I am very relaxed and 'tuned in' to their fine Energy frequencies, I have been able for decades to converse with numerous people who have lost their flesh bodies, but who are still alive! They have kept their personalities and emotions and are fully aware of who they are in that World of Mind and Light, which we tend to call the 'Spirit World', or other names such as the 'Hereafter', 'Paradise' or 'Heaven'.

I can also receive 'automatic' and inspired writing. As my communicators 'overshadow' me by blending their Minds closely with mine, I am in an altered state. I hear the words **at the very same time** as my pen *feels compelled to write them down* at high speed. I receive answers immediately to any question that I ask. Yet once the 'overshadowed dictation' is over, I hardly recall what they said! Because the answers have provided so much new information that I have never heard before, going beyond my own weak grasp of scientific knowledge — and have often been the opposite of my own beliefs and expectations — this has proved to me, time and time again, that this information is not coming from my own Mind or subconscious! I sometimes argue with my communicators, because of my own limited understanding of these astounding concepts, but they remain so patient with me, and calmly do their best to explain things in various other ways.

MY CHANNELLED BOOKS

This book is just one of many of my conversations with those in the 'Spirit World'... and BEYOND it - as this book will explain! I have channelled decades of writings that I am now able and devoted to sharing with the world. It has taken me years to type up the thousands of handwritten pages that I received!

1) Since 2011, I have published to-date 4 channelled books, starting with the first 2 volumes of a diary of conversations with several of my loved ones and my 'Spirit teaching Guide', who are alive in the Afterlife. Its title "*I'm Not Dead: I'm Alive Without a Body*" stems from my own mother's comments, days after her passing, as she marvels at the wonders of being

still alive and pain-free! She contacted me of her own accord, very unexpectedly and to my great surprise, as I was certainly not trying or thinking to reach her so early! Her detailed and enlightening 'travelogue' reveals what it's like to painlessly leave your body at 'death' of the flesh; what life is like after we die; and what activities we can do in that 'Other World', where what you think about will manifest in front of you!

Though my mother is the 'star' of that diary, other family members joined in and shared their discoveries. Among several others, five years later, my husband Dave (who, when on Earth, used to not really believe in the possibility of communications with the Other World), and eventually years later, my eldest brother who passed in very tragic circumstances, but our mum was there to receive him. She has reported to me in great detail how he was helped to settle down in that New World and adjust his thinking. He has eventually learnt to reach me too!

There will no doubt soon be a third volume of that *"I'm Not Dead"* diary series, revealing how the 'departed' can - if they wish and at their own pace - **expand their Consciousness**. Therefore it shows they are progressing well, yet have not actually 'gone somewhere else'. By learning to focus and manipulate their Mind Energy, each Being is able to discover more about the mysteries of existence, because their Minds are able to expand to accept the new information, instead of holding on to the restrictive boundaries of old beliefs that limit their knowledge.

For example, my deceased father now particularly enjoys unravelling the laws of Physics, but from a superior level of understanding than can be achieved in Earthly life. And my mother who (when on Earth) did not grasp the fact we can decide and choose to reincarnate, is now amused and intrigued to discover her so-called 'past' lives (as totally different people and genders) that she had lived, before her life with me.

She watches them like 'films', to observe how her fundamental attitude as a Being of Energy/Spirit, learnt, grew and evolved throughout those various experiences.

Doing this helps her to understand herself as a far larger many-sided Being, that has led, and will continue to experience many more lives as different personalities, than just the character she has been as 'my mum'.

The more varied our experiences, the more the diamond of our individual Higher Self/ Oversoul /Real Self, polishes its complex multi-facets and shines increasingly. This happens through the expansion of Consciousness and learning acquired by our 'various Souls as diverse Humans', by how we choose to handle a multitude of experiences.

And for those readers who wonder about this: Though my loved ones are enjoying their numerous Mind trips into higher and more refined levels of learning, they said they do *not* intend to consider tackling the tribulations of any possible reincarnation yet - certainly not before my other brothers and I have passed over to meet up with them for good. So they will be there to welcome us and 'show us round'. What's the rush? There is Eternity to achieve what one fancies doing!

2) Like its predecessor, *Truths Lies & Distortions,* this book you are now holding, *WORLDS BEYOND the 'Spirit World'* was written down **exactly as it was dictated to me** at the request of very knowledgeable and evolved Energy Personalities.

As they say, they are no longer focused on our physical world or their temporary physical form (the flesh body), as they are now back to their normal, 'original state' as Beings of Energy and Mind. They had chosen to previously live on Earth at some time or other, to temporarily experience that state, in order to be able to comprehend what it is like to be a Human and handle and link with Humans' Minds.

Over several years, these individual 'spokes-people' (or should I say 'spokes-Beings'?) came close to me to unexpectedly start dictating profound statements and facts, most of which were absolutely unknown to me! As I marvelled at the mind-boggling contents, they asked me to make sure 'their' books were made available to the public.

Not only are those Evolved Teachers extremely well-informed and have very profound and insightful knowledge to share, but they are also acting as channels for 'Beings of Pure Energy' at an even higher level of development, to pass down knowledge about the invisible Energies of this, and other Universes, and planes of existence.

Those Beings and Masters (who do not need and have chosen not to have a physical body) provide stupefying facts and astounding knowledge, which are transmitted and transmuted into easier information, so that human Minds can comprehend the science of Mind Power.

Their teachings merge the boundaries of Science and Spirituality, making more logical sense than some Humans' theories and assumptions! Yet I was rather reluctant to stick my neck out and 'go public': I told them I did not want to be 'burnt at the stake' for stepping on the toes of rigid and established man-made theories... They replied that if I wanted and enjoyed acquiring this knowledge, I had to share it and not keep it for myself.

Their book purposefully avoids obscure or complex scientific angles and jargon, as those Spiritual Masters want the information to appeal to and reach the general public. They endeavour to explain, as simply as they can, these brand new, groundbreaking concepts. If the readers keep an open-mind and let the gist of each chapter flow gently, they will pick and absorb the main points, which will help raise their own Consciousness and understanding and absorption of the next chapter.

Imagine mineral-rich water slowly dripping inside a cave - each drop over time will leave a mineral deposit on the ground, which eventually accumulates to form a stalagmite of the precious mineral. Your knowledge will grow in the same way, when you allow yourself to encounter and gradually assimilate such new concepts that will strengthen the foundational bedrock of your Consciousness.

There is no need to worry about not always grasping it all. **What matters is that you are open-minded,** to help you comprehend what is constantly going on during and behind, the Creation of the physical Universes... and where 'other worlds' exist!

Those are facts, which could not be clarified to help Mankind over previous centuries, because they were automatically crushed and denied by the 'leading authorities' of the days. Authorities who tortured or burnt alive, anyone who disagreed with their dogmas that for example, the Earth was flat, or that an invisible, old bearded man on a celestial throne, created the world and he would throw you into the eternal flames of Hell for not believing in him. Why? Because those leaders benefited from keeping populations in ignorance of the Truths.

Those eye-opening, mind-stretching revelations are now offered again to this more modern world, and provided in all sincerity for the good of Mankind. Hopefully open-minded modern cosmologists and other scientists may consider the facts, shared in this book by those Beings in the real World of Mind Power, who can see and handle the Energies forming the Cosmos. Because if those Humans do not bother, once they 'pass over' themselves, they will grasp how TRUE those given facts are! But it will be a bit late by then for them to kick themselves for not having followed up this channelled information!

15

HOW THESE TEACHINGS CAN HELP YOU

These Masters want to encourage Humanity to open its Mind, to understand where it has gone wrong, and to help itself by using its Mind Power. The profound knowledge within this book can help people who are seeking the Truth. They will get the courage to enlarge their vision of events and even **challenge** entrenched, unfounded or distorted man-made dogmas or theories.

This book does not impose any dogmas, but offers hope, a greater understanding and long-awaited answers to profound questions, which have puzzled and frustrated Mankind, who chose to create arguments, wars and religious rifts.

Ideally you will be reading it AFTER having read its first volume *'Truths, Lies & Distortions*. May you read this with an open mind so that you can: truly grasp Reality and your Life Purpose; discover your own inner strength; rid yourself of fears; improve your health; **learn how you ever started to exist, why you are on Earth and why this Earth exists**.

Above all, I hope these teachings help you to realise that you are more than what you see in the mirror - you have Free Will to choose and act accordingly. You are always free and will not be 'judged' except by your own Higher Self and conscience, which is the harshest jury!

Your Mind is a ginormous creative Power - so do not 'pass the responsibility' over to any other imaginary power to 'make things happen': **You can WILL them into becoming a reality yourself!** YOU are indeed a special Eternal Being!

****

16

"Few men are willing to brave the disapproval of their fellows, the censure of their colleagues, the wrath of their society. MORAL COURAGE is a rarer commodity than bravery in battle or great intelligence. Yet it is the one ESSENTIAL, vital quality for those who seek to change a world which yields most painfully to change."

Robert F. Kennedy 1966

**** Medium's comments or questions to her communicators are shown as *(BR + plain italics)*.

PREFACE
By the 'Real Authors'

BR- Could you please dictate your Preface for your new book? You'll do it far better and faster than I could ever do it.

'Worlds BEYOND the 'Spirit World'... This title says it all in a way. We had to put across that the limitations imposed by Mankind's narrow views of what is really gigantic Reality, have caused Humans to completely lose their way and be confused as to what to believe or not. That includes 'teachings' both as religious and scientific dictums and proclamations.

We are endeavouring to cover as much as can be taken in by someone who is reading our new book, yet who has no background in either narrow-minded physics or religions. That way we hope this open-minded person will allow themselves to discover and grasp what could be a great turning point in their life! It could be so IF they acknowledge we are talking with the best intentions in our 'hearts' and offering genuine profound knowledge – the latter coming from far higher levels of vibrations than the reader could ever hope to obtain from Humans' Minds and theories.

We are not apologizing for sounding somewhat 'conceited' yet that was not our aim. We are only here to help every one of you who is searching and wondering why they have come to existing on Earth and what's the point of it all. We have already explained a lot in our first book *'Truths, Lies & Distortions'*: from before the beginning of the Earth creation to how Humans have come to live there. And also why some want to return many times, as they feel attached or linked to the Earth life — yet that will only happen a limited number of times because, as this current book shows and explains, there is so much more available to he who seeks! The Earth is only a very puny and very temporary stage in the journey of those experimenting with different happenings and experiences.

So, please read this at your own pace, with attention to the fact that what has been dictated is NOT from the Mind of the medium who took down on paper what we were saying; it is not even all from OUR own Minds — us the temporary Teachers from the 'Spirit World'—as we are ourselves channelling knowledge from even superior Beings who never lived on Earth, yet have a great part in its conception and creation!

We are thus opening the door for you Humans to become acquainted with Real Knowledge not tainted by Humans' ideas and theories. Up to you to accept it — or leave it on a mental shelf, until your own Mind has stretched and expanded enough to absorb some new concepts.

Many thanks for paying attention to our dictated efforts.

We do not have a 'need' to provide you with all those facts, since we have a happy existence in our own worlds of Mind and Light. We are not getting any rewards or privileges for putting together those pages and ensuring they are passed over to the Earth World. But then, it is up to YOUR Free Will to use it and expand your Consciousness and Knowledge – or not! We are still there for you whenever you are ready!

§§§

"The suppression of uncomfortable ideas may be common in religion and politics, but it is not the path to knowledge: it has no place in the endeavour of science".

Carl Sagan (1934 – 1996), Cosmos, 1980

****

PART 1

CONSOLIDATING FUNDAMENTAL FACTS

****

"During times of deceit, telling the Truth becomes a revolutionary act".

(George Orwell)

CHAPTER 1

The theme today (as a continuation of our first book), is to do with the link between the Earth world and the ones around it, i.e. the planets, stars and other realms you know of and don't know of.

There is a big difference between being on the Earth plane and its inhabitants and feeling oneself out of that atmosphere and floating out in space. That is to start with. It is a totally different experience for a Human; but if you go beyond it as a 'Spirit', you'll discover even more differences! We know what it's like because we do it constantly, having to be near you and away from you.

The main point is the feel of the vibrations. We know of vibrations because we are part of them, we are made of them and are aware of that 'consistency', that state of 'being' a Reality which is totally foreign, even alien, to you all. We know what it is like because we live in a world of vibrations!

Life as a vibrational state is very different when you don't have a body of Matter, as Matter has its vibrations reduced or 'shaped' to a different rate, so that you can be aware of it and of each other.

We live in a world of HIGH vibrations, where the Mind instantaneously creates in front of you what you think of: you are far more aware of what goes on and its power and scope. When you come to this, our world, THAT is what will strike you - the difference is enormously wonderful!

But we also want to talk to you about other planets and such like. If you are on a planet, as you call them, there will be totally different ways of existing. You could not expect all planets to be the same as the Earth as this was not meant to be. The Earth is a one-off in a sense, because it was created for what it was meant to be and we've already told you about that.

The other 'worlds' as you call them but 'planets' to be specific, have their own system(s) of existence. With an inner intelligence, an aim to exist for a reason, a planet is not a dead piece of rock floating round the Earth or across the Solar System that you have worked out. It has its own 'agenda'. A schedule so well sorted out that it has been going on for millions of your years and you still do not know why they are there!

As planets were created for the stabilisation of the Earth on its orbit, it had to be done with great care and 'calculations'. It could not be done at random, anyhow, as the whole plan would collapse and the Earth would be hurtling through Space, away from its own Sun and hitting no doubt other planetary objects or stars...

It had to be done with great attention indeed: that's why the 'calculations' were made by very knowledgeable Minds here in our world, who could work out how and where everything should be placed so that the effect of rotation, the pull of vibrations, the 'magnetic' attraction as you call it, would be more effective and not destructive.

Since the results have proved successful, we can say they've done quite a good job! But that's not all: the 'secret' of their existence lies also in the gravitational pull (the attraction caused by gravity) among each other — and that pull as you know for example with the Moon, has a great effect and result on many aspects of life on each 'place'. So when the Moon loosens its attachment to the Earth, it also does so on other planetary bodies around you and itself; that will create other vibrational shake-ups, which will have a repercussion all around the 'Space' they are in.

22

That '**Space**' as you call it, is not just an expanse of vibrations. It **has a life of its own.** It is meant to exist, not as a void into which everyone or everything falls. It is meant to be **an expanse of web-like vibrations** holding you all in its 'arms' or its net, **to hold everything at the right distance, on the correct wavelengths** and most of all to support the Life System.

BR- How does it do that?

The Life system is not just a few drops of water bringing life to a planet, as some Earthly scientists seem to think. **The Life System we are talking about is a whole concoction of webs of Energy which can trigger the metamorphose, the transformation of Energies of one kind into Energies of other kinds.**

So if you think Life is just life on Earth, you are wrong because there are far more 'types of Life' we could say.

Life in itself is the Light of vibrations from the Spirit World as you'd call it (but we call it the **World of Mind and Reality**), made to activate the bodies of such creatures or Beings or anything which wishes to exist in whatever state or 'place'. But we must explain more clearly so that you can grasp properly.

Life on other planets we are talking about is not a rock being able to walk or feel or a stone growing herbs on it. It **has to do with the infinitesimal spark of the Urge to exist somewhere**, somehow, for whatever reason. That spark is not necessarily big, it can be very small; and when it exists wherever it does exist, then that 'place' has got Life on it. It won't ever be spotted by your Earthly scientists, but it will still exist!

23

That possibility of Life elsewhere is something puzzling Mankind, unfortunately they may be looking for the wrong thing or at least for the wrong 'beginnings' of Life. What we are talking about is the beginning of a spark of any kind of 'Life' on any 'place' so to speak. We have to use words you know to make sense to you all.

There is a big difference between an amoeba or microbe however invisible it may be to your instruments, and the reality of existence within another planet or world of rocks and stones or even gases.

What **you would need to look for are the differences in vibrations, in tension between electromagnetic waves**, the subtle difference perceived only by very sophisticated and sensible instruments (if they ever exist) which register that subtle feel between the vibrations of the same kind, as well as the ones between vibrations of different kinds.

That is no doubt beyond Human scope to get this right but when you have done that, then you'll know what we mean by feeling the 'Urge of living' within a tiny, microscopic, infinitesimal speck of Light wanting to exist elsewhere for a change. As that's what it is all about in the end! Why should a speck of that Life have an urge within it? Because **Life in itself is an Urge to Be,** that's all and yet that's a lot!

The Urge to Be is not squashable, never exhausted and unquenchable: **an Urge is a Life creating Power.** A Mind Creative Power has Life as an end product because it will create something and that means 'giving life' to something. It may not be a living, breathing Being, but it will be something. An Urge for Life itself to exist means it will bring a spark to anywhere, so that that spark can learn to adapt itself, to improvise, to evolve, to mature or simply to decide it isn't right for it and go elsewhere if wishes.

An interesting aspect of this potential is that whenever and **wherever a spark decides to 'have a go', the power of Life has roots if it wishes to**.

A Life spark is an Urge, remember, an Urge made more 'solid' as you'd call it, for ease of terms — so that it can test the possibilities, the feasibility and the goals it may wish to develop.

An Urge is not a Being, an Urge is an Urge, that is an 'emotion' you could call it. It is not something tangible so it will not be measured by instruments - that's why scientists in your world will never find it that way.

BR- So how could they find it?

Ask anyone this question and they'll say: "It's probably impossible".

On the other hand, if they looked within and found their own source of information, they may get 'inspired' like you have been and are, therefore they will gain inner information which will help them understand where they've gone wrong and where they could get more correct; otherwise they'll keep banging a wall and look for another avenue which will in turn become a dead end. It is all a question of **learning by finding out the answer from within**.

BR- Could you compare Life Light in say a Spirit Being, me, a tree etc.? Secondly, any kind similar on different, far away planet?

That whole process of becoming a Being of any kind is very complicated, as you may guess; that has to do with following many 'rules' for it to succeed. Moreover there are Lights of Life in many other places, different from the Earth world, but that is not possible to give you evidence of it because you could not go there (nor your scientists now). So you won't have any evidence of it, which is a pity of course.

25

On the other hand we could tell you that the Life you've known and know is not very different but you won't notice it.

All it takes for something to 'live' or have Life is to be able to sustain itself in its environment. It does not matter what it is. So if you think a rock has no Life, you are wrong - any infra red or other modern technology instrument will show you the vibrations within that rock and the Energy which can emanate if it is triggered, or even not triggered.

What it won't tell or show you is **why** that particular 'object' has chosen to be there, to be created or rather create itself, as all Urges create if they are sustained.

You cannot know why others choose to be there, unless they can or choose to tell you! But it can be guessed at sometimes. That's why you have to be aware of all the possibilities of the Inner Urges.

If it is urged intently, it will achieve its goal. One cannot fail with the Inner Urge: the Inner Urge will get its own way, one way or the other.

It has to be screamed for, wanted so much that there is no other way you'll get it done. And it 'happens'. Happens or creates itself or lives depending on what you are talking / thinking about. It is the key, foundation rock and rule, of all creativity and creation and Life so to speak. It has to be wanted, urged from within the originator.

As it stands seen from here, it looks very simple, obvious and easy. As you see it, it may seem very hard, unreliable, even unfounded possibly. But **if you try hard enough for everything you wish for, you'll see there is always a result in the end.** It may not always quite be the actual result you planned if you were wishing for something 'against the grain' of your own Soul and Spirit... but if all is well, you'll see it happen somehow, in a direct or roundabout way.

SSS

CHAPTER 2

The old man with a beard, on a boat full of beasts *(Noah and his Ark)* was not a real man as you may have understood by now - he was a figment of the imagination of some people trying to teach and instil wisdom and knowledge in those who had gone off the right track *(See Spirit Teachers' explanations of the symbolism of Noah's Ark in T L&D)*. So we'll say, make sure, all of you, that you do not take word for word what has been taught to you from childhood, without really analysing what was said and thinking: "Is it possibly true or not? Could it be just symbolic?"

There is so much said which has nothing to do with reality, it is a shame to see the public alarmed by 'facts', which are not facts but made up stories to either frighten them into submission or scare them off the wrong track. It needs to be rectified.

So we shall start Chapter 2 now to explain more which needs to be known.

This world of Matter where you readers all live, is a little place compared to many other places. The Matter your world is made of has been made with great care and consistency, to make sure everything works together as should be. There is a lot of dedication and devotion to the task involved in this.

So you'll have to respect this Earth you all are on, not treat it as if it was yours to do what you want with or destroy. You would not bash your car about, crash it into walls or dig burrows into it just for the sake or fun of it! You would not use it as a heap of metal to cut pieces out of, when you want a bar of metal, just after you bought that car?

So why do this to the precious world you live in? Why do you let others do it? Why don't you **all** protest more than you do?

There is not enough outcry, just not enough! You should all be screaming at every politician, manufacturer, hole drilling company etc. to make them see what they are doing wrong. You should **all** be campaigning against the destruction going on, from the forest trees to the sea floor and waters being treated as dumps for filth and dangerous components. You cannot use the Earth as you have been doing: it is creaking under the strain, and you **will** have more earthquakes and destruction by various so-called natural disasters, if you do not prevent more damages.

That is up to you to see to it. We cannot do anything about it from our world and you cannot blame a 'god' in the sky for helping or not helping you. You cannot expect anyone to do the deed of resuscitating the poor dying world you have turned it into.

This is of paramount importance and yet few really pay attention to it, compared to the amount of populations there are in the world of the Earth.

HOW YOU CAN HELP

It is not on the Moon or Mars that you will find the solution; it is in this world of yours, in your mouth and your hands and your feet and your Mind, which you should be using more to make those responsible stop — and also for yourself to consider what exactly you could be or should be doing to prevent more damage, wherever you can.

Do not subscribe or back or buy from those who destroy the world for their own benefit. Do not help them by buying their goods. Do not consider them important or make them feel important: instead make sure the finger is pointed at them at every opportunity.

These are all the little things you could be doing, because you have no right to consider the Earth yours, as individuals. The Earth has been built, created, planned by millions of myriads of Beings in our 'World of Mind', Beings who have been here a long time, who have the experience of working with various Matters who have creativity and creation as their 'hobby' you could say.

It has also been built and improved by those first pioneers who came to see how things could be improved. You were not really or necessarily there though your Mind and Spirit may have been involved in the procedure, but that, you wouldn't even know of it now!

Therefore please do not feel you own it, none of you, because you do not! You do not own the air, you do not own the sky or Space, you do not own anything apart from your flesh body because you chose to create it as it is.

You'll have to blame yourself for anything you don't like about it now.

So do not create more harm for that world which is a wonder in itself, as the creation of every little part had and has been meticulously planned and organised. It is to be admired and respected and those who don't do not deserve being on it! They should be 'shot' one could say, but this is not a spiritual remark and must be taken as a sarcastic joke!

THINK AHEAD

There is also another point to consider: When the seas are full of debris and pollution, when the waters of the rivers are chock-a-block with harmful material and / or dried up silt, what will you do for cooling, washing etc. yourself? What will you water your plantations with? You will not have enough rain over the whole world for that. It will become a barren desert with no one living on it, if you don't watch what you are doing, as the long-term effect is looming over you and you do not even see it!

It may not be now, in your present personal life, as we write this book of warnings, but it will be in your family's lives to come and you will be crying out: "Oh 'god', make the rain come down!" But there won't be any water left on Earth to evaporate as clouds and make rain to come down. So you will be your own destructors and you will still blame or call upon some invisible and non-existent god as a personality who has all the powers you imagine it has!

That is one of your many problems, oh Mankind of little faith and understanding! You cannot 'pass the buck', hope for someone else to pick up the pieces, blame others and not yourselves, ask for others to do the work but not lift a finger yourself!

This is fundamental truths which so many choose to ignore — and those who do not believe in any god of any kind will still be to blame themselves for not doing anything to stop the ravages going on.

You cannot close your eyes to the constantly increasing general destruction of the world **we** have created, for the whole of Mankind to come as well, and not just for you, little individual person.

As we sound very harsh indeed, we must point out we are aware of those of you who do care, who do fight against the harm done, and who do make a point of being careful in their way of living, so that they respect what they are given.

Of course we do and of course we do not blame or accuse you. It is because there are some people like you who care, that there is a little hope to wake up the rest of the populations. But we have to shout at those who don't pull their weight and ignore the true facts!

You have all been warned many, many times. Do not complain when droughts set in, when floods kill everything, when earthquakes shake the life out of everything around. You are responsible, not us, not anyone else in the universe.

30

You, Mankind, as residents of what used to be a wonderful world of which you have no idea, in a way. That tendency to think material and technological achievements and constructions mean you are very clever, makes us laugh because even though you know how to go to the Moon and beyond, you cannot create more clean water to fill rivers and seas, you cannot build a new Earth free from pollution, you have no way of inventing pure and pristine air, like we gave you!

In fact you can do nothing that we (from our World of Love and Light) have done for you, residents of our Earth – that Earth which is our pride and joy as a creation for the unusual experiment of living in *physical* Matter, even though each inhabitant is a *Spiritual* Being, so has a Dual Personality! That's all we wanted to make you think about for the time being!

𝕾𝕾𝕾

CHAPTER 3

Before we elaborate on the existence of Worlds BEYOND the 'Spirit World', we need to remind you all of some key points we explained in our first book. As Mankind started planning its journeys on the new Earth, it had to devise many projects suitable with the environment and the abilities of a flesh body. So far no one had had a flesh body made of this particular type of Matter, so it was indeed a new experience, but as men (and women of course) went to Earth, tried their own designed body and came back to complain of the mistakes or misalignments, there was something else they had to take into consideration.

It was all very well to have a flesh you could do what you wanted with, but there was its limitations. So wanting to fly in a body of Earth size and shape was not practical, in fact impossible... But the birds could do it so why not Men?

It was a conundrum, as they wanted to will themselves into doing things but those things had to be done, or be possible, within the parameters of the specifications of that flesh, you see what we mean? So the rest had to be solved differently. That's when the **Mind Power had to be used** to create, invent, design, think of something different.

It could have been done more easily no doubt, but that's how Men decided in the end to solve their inaptitude for things they could not do as the body had limitations... They could only use their Mind Power to overcome them and that's what happened when they tried to invent new things, objects, plans of many various types — from constructions to artefacts to use to help themselves, to many other things such as travel on a boat or even later with objects on wheels, to carry them from one place to another etc.

So this is what we are trying to explain: The inventions that sprouted over centuries and millennia have come out of the need of Mankind for objects to help them, which they could not have otherwise.

The **inspiration has usually been given from our side** too, because they had to have some starting point, some direction towards which to find the necessary tools or systems. But the fine point of all this is that **Mankind had to use its own Mind Power, therefore its own Creative Power,** because a Mind, any Mind is a creative tool. A Mind without that creative side is not a normal Mind.

So, we have those new 'Men' on Earth, with tools of wood, or metal or whatever else they started creating, making new things for the sake of getting more comfort in their lives. They used their Minds to design. That means they looked at the needs and in their heads and thoughts, they produced the blueprint, the template of what could be a successful result — or possibly a wrong, inefficient result if it was badly designed, because of lack of logic or attention to details, like taking into account gravity or weather powers. But could they have done this without the need to think it out first? No. They **had** to think about it first; they had to visualise what could be useful and workable.

NEVER DONE BEFORE

This may be obvious to you nowadays, but at the time they never had to do such things before, remember, since they'd only been 'Spirits' —that is to say Beings of Light and Mind — who did not need to use their hands or any artefacts and tools to make things happen: they would just think it strongly and it would appear!

So, the transition was a bit sudden for them but it taught them to use their Minds even more to make the result appear in a different way. It had to be worked out gradually, it had to be planned piece-by-piece, calculations or combinations had to be thought out and 'felt right' before they could proceed to the next step.

This is how inventions came about: through the need to have more physical things to make life more comfortable, from the point of view of those there; but had it been thought out differently, they would have made things differently! They could have ignored the need for physical objects and worked at making their Mind Power over the flesh stronger. They could have worked at it so that the flesh obeyed the Mind as much and more than it already does now. It is intensely influenced by the Mind and the Mind has to be at rest, otherwise illnesses will start cropping up. So Mind Power is visibly, and well known to be, a creator of illness as well as good health in the flesh body.

Therefore why couldn't Mankind have worked more at increasing its power over the body of flesh, to make it levitate, fly, do without food or drink or even never die? That is, if they insisted on living forever, though that would be rather silly because the Earth Experiment is meant to be shorter-lived than eternity!

This is what we are coming to: **the power of overcoming the flesh was and is there.** Few Men have learnt how to use it or have forgotten the inner and innate ability, it is latent in them: they simply have just not utilized it at all and let it atrophy or even disappear! This is something sad in a way, as there was a gift and a skill they could all have taken advantage of!

Instead they went towards using their hands and brains to make objects of various sizes and goals.

AMAZING GIFTS

When the 'first Humans' came, they could indeed fly as such, that meant going from one place to the other without walking. They **transcended the body's weight**, they lifted it up with their powerful Mind and they were able to move about that way. Much less tiring physically! They could also stay for a long time without eating or drinking: they had this ability. They had not lost it even a few centuries ago: there were still some people who could do that. Now I am not so sure but they'll be few in numbers, if any…

So we want to point out that, if they could do it then, why couldn't Mankind do it now? All it takes is practice, that would reduce or cancel all fuel bills and worries; it would also allow crops to grow without being destroyed for food: there will never be enough food if you keep growing it for cattle and animals as well as for People.

You cannot keep eating Animals, as Mankind has to go back to its original and pure plan of "not hurting anyone". So how can you keep killing them or worse, eating them alive? This is nonsensical, and the result will be more diseases, more upsets mentally and physically, more unrests across the populations, because the Souls themselves will feel ill at ease, unhappy, 'out of sync' with their flesh body which they had originally designed to fit like a glove. Now the 'glove' wants to take over and go in a totally different direction from the original plan — the need for inner and outer balance. Make people understand and we'll begin to be on the right track.

BR- Any chance for Mankind to re-learn those skills?

The practice needed could take a whole lifetime. So we doubt many will take the time and trouble to get into it, with the dedication needed for its development, you see. It is of the utmost importance to be 'still within' for long periods of time, to be well balanced emotionally and spiritually as well as physically, so there will be no hope for most of Mankind at the rate it is going on nowadays! It may be possible for a few Beings who have worked at it from a young age somewhere but few would do it as things stand.

There is hope though to have more coming back to Earth to emulate and encourage those who may want to learn that. But it comes and must come from within - if one does not have that built-in inner desire, it would take more than a life time, so what's the point of not succeeding... Yet there is a halfway measure.

MIND POWER OVER MATTER

The half-way measure is to tell yourself, all right I would have liked to do that (absence of food and drink and levitation instead of walking or driving) but I can't as things are, so instead I'll **cut down on my excess attention to physical needs and pleasures and concentrate more on my inner needs:** the need for utter calm, utter peace of Mind, utter blending with the world of Mind and Light (or 'of Spirit', as you call it) and make the days more useful in a spiritual way than in a physical, materialistic way.

The material side of the worldly life can easily be taken care of, as long as you have enough decent and basic food to sustain the body healthily (and it does not need meat from dead Animals for that! You can have other means of feeding yourselves!).

So, the Mind side can be worked more and that should be easy enough as you relax more and more often. But what's the use of it, you will say? Well, it is obvious: the use of developing your Mind is for your own good as well as others.

You can ask some 'superior Being' to make things happen for you and others and hope it listens and that works eventually or not! Or you can definitely hone your own Mind Power to the extent of sending your powerful Energies towards that goal or goals you want so much, that success, that health recovery…

When you start having successes, then you will know you are on the right track and doing things correctly. So that's why it is always, **always useful to spend time quietly**, in silence or in Nature's silence full of its own energies.

When the silence breaks for you to hear an inner voice, or see a person you've never seen before or for a long time, then you'll know you have started using the power of your Mind to overcome limitations caused by the flesh body! From then on, you'll believe more perhaps in sending thoughts to heal others at distance and to make things happen for you and others if they allow it by not being of a negative nature! Isn't this worth doing?

𝒮𝒮𝒮

CHAPTER 4

This chapter will have a new angle, a new flavour to spice up the proceedings and the contents. So we'll start with the flesh made of Matter. Flesh is a big word to cover all the sensations produced by the Matter forming the body of the physical frame for the Spiritual Being wishing to live in this Earthly world.

The 'flesh' is a very delicate combination of all sorts of vibrations, minerals, vitamins, Earthly components - and also some spiritual ones of course since it was **created in the Mind of the owner**, as well as of those who helped the owner create it.

The body has to be seen as an enclosure, a wrapping of all sorts of components which, when put all together, have the capacity individually of doing some wonderfully amazing feats and things. You cannot imagine how wondrous it looks to us, seen from here, hence the excitement of each individual Being who wants to go on Earth, for that short-lived Experiment. The body wants to live as long as the Will is within it. **If the Will that created it withdraws, the body won't want or know how to keep going** and even less resuscitate itself!

It is of extreme importance for Mankind to understand the relationship between the body of flesh and the Mind of a Spiritual Being linked to it.

A Mind has no place as such; a Mind is everywhere and anywhere. A body of physical flesh has to be somewhere for it to function as meant to be doing. So it's very important to remember the body of a person is only the casing of its Soul, not the Soul itself. The Soul itself is the personality of the

Spiritual Being when s/he has decided to live that particular life on Earth. The Soul wants to be in a body of flesh to feel comfortable on Earth, instead of being an invisible Being. So we've got that sorted out, haven't we?

TUG OF WAR

But **if the body wants to do one thing and the Soul another, then problems may arise**. A Soul is not permitted to hurt another one, by the Law of Natural Spirituality. A Soul has to select what it wants to do of course, it can choose and decide! But if it chooses to do harm, then the price of those unnatural actions will be visible in the anguish ensuing, when the Soul comes back here in our world. It is beyond description: **no one can imagine the torments a Soul can endure and give itself, when realising what it has done wrong...** But let's get back to the subject of the flesh body.

A flesh body is the replica or representation of what the Soul for that life, or Spiritual Being as a whole, **wants to learn, experience, practise in that particular life on Earth**. It has to be so. It cannot be otherwise.

The life on Earth experienced is tailored by every individual experiencing it - everyone has its own life as s/he had planned at the beginning of its trip. But if it was planned one way, let's say, and the individual changes his mind as he goes along (because the flesh or other pleasures or attractions of the Earthly world make him do so), then he will deviate... and some deviate a lot!

NOT BORN NASTY

That is where all the criminals, murderers and other 'non-spiritual person' fit in, because they were **not** born to be nasty, but they have let their weaker side, their flesh counterpart and influence take over their Spiritual side.

Also, the influence of those around them can have a great effect. They might have been 'nicer' but the bad, wrong, un-spiritual influences of those near them - or even the bad experiences they have encountered themselves - may turn them away from what they intrinsically know to be right and good. That's when they'll let their own personal anger and frustrations come out and have an effect on those around who had no reason to be hurt. It often has a snowball effect and a snowball can become a mighty avalanche stopping at nothing and stopped by nothing.

This is what caused and causes the evil acts of cruelty and other heinous activities. We know it is not an excuse which can be accepted in the end, nor will the Soul / Spirit itself even accept it as an excuse, because **the Inner Self is always available within:** One can always turn to it to find the answer...

But those deep in nastiness and criminal activities will not want to listen within, because either the flesh body's needs will scream for its satisfaction to be fulfilled; or the Mind, the distorted Mind we could say, will interfere and even block the inner voice of reason and spiritual behaviour. That's all can be said there.

The way to protect oneself and anyone from such happenings is to make sure you have no one nasty, evil, thwarted around yourself. Do not engage or start engaging in the slightest activity which has no spiritual purpose, but instead wants to gratify bodily needs beyond normal behaviour — and most of all, in **no activity whatsoever which means or leads to hurting or harming other Beings.**

THE RIGHT TO LIVE

All the other Beings on Earth have every single right to be there, as their choice of experimental trip! They have the right to exist in their own flesh body and have every right to stay alive as long as they decide to be in it. **It is not Mankind choice or decision when they should leave it!** Definitely not. So why should people decide to kill Animals when they, the Animals, have every right to exist side by side on Earth?

It is what Mankind has not understood or at least many of them, sadly! It is important to **remind others of the sacredness of Life** as labelled. Why? Because in the long term the one who kills, actually kills something within himself, he hurts himself.

He may not know it until he has come back here, in our World of Light and Truth, i.e. the 'Spirit World', but he will, definitely will, suffer from it. **Not** because he'll be judged by some grand power of a god, but because he will **judge himself** as a higher Spirit: his own Higher Self looking down at the little flesh puppet he created who wanted to do its own thing in the end, and broke all links with its master, its creator i.e. its Higher Self.

Then the sadness and remorse eating up the Soul who went wrong will be infinite. It may take it a long, long time to come to terms with what it has done, and it will eventually want to find ways to redeem what harm he caused. It is not always easy or feasible. The Soul would have to find ways to make amends and forgive itself. Who can be a harsher judge than the Soul itself? No one. No one is more inflexible and ruthless than the one who judges himself in the plenitude of the knowledge provided by the eternal Law of Spiritual Life. No one can do it for him. It has to be done by himself. That is the hardest for everyone who has stepped down the 'wrong track' he chose wilfully.

BALANCE THE NEEDS

The final part of this chapter is to remind everyone of the **importance of listening within.** No one can ever deny this point, as the **link of the flesh body with its Higher Self, with the spiritual levels of existence, has the same importance as the link of the flesh body with air and water.** You have to have that link kept afresh constantly and that's what the flesh body desires and needs overshadow too often in those who give priority to what they can do on Earth.

The importance of a healthy body is not denied: eating, drinking is essential to feed it, of course—but should everyone concentrate on that solely? Should everyone ignore the calls and even screams of the Inner Self when the food is the wrong one, when the food has come from hurting others who lived happily until then? No, not at all.

There are more than food problems. There are the desires of the flesh with respect to sex life and needs, to pampering the little thrills (often so limited and short-lived) of parts of the body being excited temporarily and providing excitement and no doubt pleasures.

But should these kinds of pleasures mean others need to suffer? Of course not!! There is and was NEVER any such intention originally when the body was created by each individual, to provide pleasure at the expense of someone else's life or pain and misery. No one would have ever wanted to come to Earth to inflict those on others. No one would have been allowed to think of it that way before he set off on his trip.

So **why did it happen later on? Because the flesh needs grew stronger and were fed.** They were fed possibly from childhood or later, by bad parenting, bad companions, bad ideas promoted over the world, bad everything.

It is **not** to say enjoying sexual pleasure is bad, no. It is to say: there are limits within the Law of Spirituality: "Thou shall not hurt others".

If it harms others in ANY way, then it is wrong. **If it harms no one, then it is fine.** But if it starts harmless and is over fed; if the needs of the body become paramount and essential to everyday life; if the person becomes obsessed with every kind of possibility to gratify those senses of the body, then it has become a danger. It will lead gradually or swiftly to a degrading of the whole thing and possibly, to experiences which are unnatural, because they cause harm. Harm if in turn, they are causing pain, emotional or / and physical injury to other creatures and Beings who have every right to be left in peace and experience their own peaceful life on Earth.

You can turn a child into a 'monster' if you feed him on wrong ideas and let him think these are right. He may not be able to fight them off at first, but as he grows up he'll have an Inner Voice telling him otherwise; that is where the balance between the Spirit and the flesh comes into action, where the physical pulls one way and the Higher Self calls the other way. You cannot have balance when two forces pull in opposite direction. **Always look for balance within if you want to have peace of Mind, health mentally and physically**. Pull one or the other too hard and there'll be problems and instability.

Instability will result in eventual collapse whether physical or mental. Probably physical anyway in the end because once the mental, emotional and spiritual sides have great problems, then it will automatically reflect on the physical flesh — leading to its gradual or sudden destruction, called 'diseases' and death.

You see, all and everything are linked. All that you do has a reverberating effect on other parts of your own Self — the Self which should have been enjoying a happy, tranquil, peaceful life on an experimental trip in the world of Matter.

43

All is left to say is: there are, of course, some people who have come on Earth to experience certain traumas, certain lessons, but that is another discussion to be for another time.

Now we'll close this chapter with the hope people who read it will understand the importance of following the inner guidance from their Spiritual aspect.

It is not difficult to find the difference between Spiritual guidance and other parts of the Self's guidance: If what you feel you 'want' to do is against the Universal, Eternal Law of doing no harm whatsoever to anyone Being of flesh, be it Animal or People, then you are definitely on the wrong track, my friends. So, it is in **your** personal interest in the long run to get off it quickly, as the Person or Animal you have harmed or are harming will long be gone back to our world, feeling whole and happy again, while **you WILL still be suffering from the trauma, the remorse** and agony of what you did - and you did it just for the sake of playing with a temporary toy and yielding to its pathetic desires!!

SSS

CHAPTER 5

You have a question in your Mind about the Soul reaching out to you and you to it. This is a very tricky yet easy question. There is the fact you are all, we are all our Soul. **We have as many Souls as we have different personalities integrating in various lives.** Each life on Earth had a personality varying from a 'previous' or 'future' one, yet there is still the same thread holding them together and linking them. That thread is the Spirit Force, which they are made of fundamentally.

A Soul is an individual personality for that particular purpose in that particular life on Earth, therefore it could be male or female, but the Spirit within is not male or female - it has the Spiritual Energy everything and everybody is made of. So your Soul is your inmost personality as you chose to be on Earth; it will have the knowledge you wanted to have for that particular life. It is not always listened to by the Mind of the Being on Earth who may be influenced by the physical flesh desires and environment.

A Soul has chosen to be in a body for a particular purpose, and if that purpose is not adhered to and followed, then the Soul feels unhappy to have failed its journey. But if the Soul feels it can fulfil its desires, aims and lessons, then it will 'sing within' and will be happy.

So, you can reach your Soul within, if as a Human Being you pay attention within and you listen to the core of your Spiritual Being, the Spiritual Being you are in the first place anyway!

WHAT IS AN ENTITY?

An Entity is a Being made of Spirit Force, Spirit Energy. An Entity is a 'Being conscious of itself', who has or has not, been on Earth or elsewhere. It has knowledge of itself as a particularly sensitive personality.

WHERE IS THE SOUL?

The place of the Soul is nowhere. **The Soul is not an object, which can be in a particular place.** The Soul is everlasting as it has the Spiritual Energy as its main drive, hence it is eternal; but it **has a focus on one particular life** at a 'time', you would say, though the Soul would not see it as 'a time', because there is no Time as seen from our point of view.

All lives blend and overlap, helping each other or hindering, if a soul has some problems. So the sensation of being one or another personality is not as defined as it looks from where you are: **you have many Souls forming your one Spiritual Being which is made of Spiritual Energy**, is that clearer?

It is important to understand that to reach within oneself and to **listen to all the impressions, which your own Soul and Spirit give you**, is the most valuable exercise and practice you can have. It has the power of guidance on the right road that the Mind has not got as such, as it can be influenced by the bodily needs and desires.

So yes, do listen within, yes take stock of what is said from your Inner Self, as this is what is speaking to yourself — but we mean 'You' being the 'Real Whole You' as a Spirit Being, not the 'you' that you think you are, as a particular physical man or woman of a particular country or status.

A mountain of ice is just a mountain of ice protruding on the surface of the soil or water. A mountain of ice has started well below the surface and comes to the top and above. That's what an iceberg is - a mass of ice visibly floating on the water - but deep within the sea, you will have more ice rock than above.

This is the same with the depths of a Soul and even more its own Spirit. When a Soul or personality comes to Earth for a particular purpose, it has more depths within itself than the visible person you know or meet. The depths hide what is really the true Being – a true 'Spiritual Being' we need to say of course — as all Beings are spiritual since they come from what makes them exist: the Essence or Energy of Spirit.

Or, said otherwise, **the Spirit they are chose to be a Soul in a world or another,** one being the Earth world that you know at the moment. If one does not look within and under the surface, one does not see the real person in all its splendour, because the Soul you see is only one facet of the 'true Whole'.

KALEIDOSCOPE OF EXPERIENCES

The 'true Whole' Being: the Spirit who tries to learn various lessons by going on trips to various places to hopefully make 'his' knowledge grow at each trip. But the trip could be either a failure or an enchantment: this means 'he' may want to go back for 'his' own reasons. As the trips develop one after the other, the **Souls involved create a magnified Spiritual Being. They enhance 'his' knowledge** by being what they have been or are in those various activities and adventures. The whole point of each trip being **to learn something which is new to the original Spirit Being, so that the combination of the knowledge acquired makes the Soul itself shine.**

47

But the Higher Spirit shines too — assuming the knowledge has been positive — as knowledge acquired by doing harm, though it is knowledge, it is still a negative aspect which would have been better not to experience, since it goes against the Universal Spiritual Law.

A Soul is only one aspect, one facet of a higher knowledgeable Spiritual Being who, like everything and everyone in the 'Creation', wants to enlarge, improve and extend itself to find more purity, more interest, more adventures, more discoveries — but all should be within the Universal Law.

So, when one of the Souls of this Higher Being spoils it by doing something really wrong, there is a setback. That is because although there will be some knowledge acquired in the end as "One does not do such thing", the overall impression of it will be sadness and greyness in the Light which should have been shining after the trip…

The Light is the innate Light within a whole Soul, coming from its origin, the Higher Spiritual Being. The Light is what keeps it going, keeps it alive. If the Light is dimmed by actions which go against the Universal Law, then, as said before, the individual on Earth and the Being in the Spirit World will feel it one way or the other. One way being the fact the Soul won't feel as connected as it should be to its origins. The Soul should feel happy to be, to exist, to have joy in its inner heart. So, if the Soul, i.e. the Being on Earth, feels miserable, it is because there is not as good a connection with its origin.

AWFUL LIVES

BR- What about people whose circumstances are terrible?

The life they lead has often a cause brought on by Humans themselves. They might have caused their own problems, their illness and their surroundings - all this could possibly have been of their own making by not behaving or thinking the right way. The 'right way' being the way the inner person would have wanted it done. It is always difficult to discuss each case in particular and not to apply a general rule blanketing everybody, as each one is a special case.

But overall, you'll have to look for the disentanglement, the break of the link at various degrees, the break of what should have been **one** Being in his flesh disguise, obeying the one Universal Law. **If there is something wrong, it has to be looked for within this Soul,** this person. That's where the cause resides, always. The cause has its prime origin in a Soul which has not the right link with its own Higher Self.

BR- But what about horrendous cases such as (in 2008) that Austrian father imprisoning his own daughter and fathering her several babies!

The case you mention is horrific indeed but we cannot judge everyone by that measure. The father has lost his inner link, totally lost it, and his appetite for flesh pleasure was horrid and unnatural obviously. But...the girl had the choice - **she had the inner choice to 'die'.** She could have and even 'should have' died: all it takes is to leave the body as **the Will is what keeps it alive.** So **why didn't she leave her body of flesh**, to leave him and his abnormal lust behind?

But the worse you say is: the children. Why indeed did they go to Earth to be born in such a case and situation as this? You'll say it is madness. It is indeed, seen from your point of view; but we could say there is more to it than that. **The Soul choosing to be born there sacrificed itself to make the man see his wrongdoing; yet he did not see it.**

49

BRAVE VICTIMS' SOULS

BR- Seven children, imprisoned in a flat too! Why want to suffer that way?

That man was hideously out of sync with his own Higher Self. The children were only 'children' because they were born on Earth and that's how one grows up. But **the Souls in them were Spirits wanting to help things be rectified.** He had to be shown 'in big' the error of his ways. He did not! Time and again he repeated the same abnormal behaviour and that would have carried on had he not been arrested - but **the Souls of these 'children' knew what would happen!**

They knew there would be a discovery, so they made sure there was a shock and a scandal at what was discovered. It was their life plan to go 'down' to Earth and rescue their mother. She did not have the heart to leave. She could have left but did not. She could have let herself 'die' but did not.

BR- Why not?

Because her Soul may have wanted to experience this in a (strange to you!) twisted way of thinking? It may have been her way of punishing herself for something she felt she'd done wrong? It could have been for many reasons!

The fact is if she had not wanted at all to stay, she **could have flown out of her body** and 'died'. She did not. And the 'children' as said, **were Souls who came to make an impact to change the situation.**

BR- Weren't they therefore 'interfering' with his or her life plan or Free Will?

The father **had NOT chosen this as a life plan,** we can tell you that now! He had **let** his twisted bodily desires win

50

over the moral way to behave in any situation - but he had known it was wrong at one time. Unfortunately he told himself he was doing well to protect her from other men or something similar, to brainwash himself to believe he was "doing good, not bad"! He is very twisted in his Mind, he will have a lot to do on himself when he comes here and faces the reality of his actions.

BR- Yet some would say he did not kill nor starve them...

He did something no other person would want to do who has a link with their Higher Self or Spirit. It is **not normal for a Human to do this because there are usually consequences in the health of the children** and this is why it is not 'normal' as you'd call it.

BR- Have you actually tuned in to this case I am speaking of?

We have picked what you told us and looked at the situation seen from here, from our spiritual point of view, as this is what we teach when we try to explain things to you on Earth.

ANALYZING ONE'S LIFE

We can now resume the discussion we had earlier then. So, we were saying the Souls who want to stay away from their own inner directives are not going to stay happy within, they will suffer - not only when they are on Earth because the 'sun' will not shine within themselves, but they will also feel terrible and awful when they come here and eventually face the facts of that particular life;

That life will hopefully have been 'useful' in a way to teach them what one does not do when one wants to follow the Universal Law — but it will have tarnished the glow, the Light,

51

the Beauty of their Inner Self trying to build its own light brighter than before.

Our explanations on the Soul versus the Spirit are part of it too. They are all teachings for Mankind to learn and grasp. It is always important to let Mankind learn from what you are given: if you are pleased to learn it, so should they be pleased to get it. Whether they understand or not is not the point. It is important to provide the seed of knowledge for them to work on and think about, water it, nurture it.

That is your job nowadays *(This is a comment to me, BR)*. You have done your work teaching all sorts of things before in your Earthly life. You have one new, 'final' one now to the end of your days…which is not here yet, don't worry, to let Mankind have access to what we teach you, for them to make their Mind up. If they reject it, it will not be your fault, or ours. It will be their Mind impinging on the Spirit trying to grasp old knowledge forgotten, which needs reviving, that's all. You will have done your job, we'll have done ours and that's what it is all about.

$$\mathcal{SSS}$$

CHAPTER 6

The help given to Mankind as it set off on to its trips to Earth was magnificent and gigantic! Yet you may not realise, any of you, that we had to make sure some of us here, stayed by your side from a 'distance' - as you'd see it- yet not far but close enough to your Mind to inspire everyone towards the right path, if there was any hesitation or wandering. It is not fair to let someone go away for a long time into a jungle of some kind, without giving them some guidance if they require it. Always *if* they ask, **if their Soul asks for it.** It is therefore the duty of those in charge of you all to see to helping you, but without infringing on your Free Will or your personality.

It can be hard at times for us here, because we see ahead the errors which are going to be made out of either stupidity or ill-advice from others around you — or simply letting the physical body and world take over the cries and needs of the Soul, your own Soul. That's where we have dilemmas to cope with because we don't want to interfere, yet we want to help you as much as we can.

ROLE OF YOUR 'SPIRIT GUIDE'

This is just to explain why you all have guidance from here and how it works - or 'does not work' if you think it does not, when you make mistakes and **no one is stopping you from making them**... We all know about Free Will, we've been there ourselves in our days on Earth. It is hard indeed to have to make the right decision if temptations and problems push you around. It is therefore vital to understand the role of your 'Spirit Guide', your friend in this world, **expected to look**

after you yet without infringing on your own will. You may all have a little more respect and understanding for the personality doing that job because, at times, it is not an easy job!

You cannot expect to be able to say: "Please make that happen. I want that etc." It is impossible for a 'guardian' to magic out a solution for all your self-created problems. You have to **learn to work that out yourself**. But having said that, there will be help given in the form of **thoughts towards the right way of thinking,** of behaving, accepting or not wanting more than what you really need, for example.

So, it is not as if you were abandoned on a desert island without anyone helping you at all. You are not alone, you are loved from here, all of you. Even the 'criminals' are possibly even more loved in a way – don't be shocked. That's simply because they have failed themselves so tremendously! So we know how much suffering they will endure within themselves when they arrive here and they eventually become aware of what they've done and why they've done it... It is so, so sad to see, we suffer for them and therefore 'love' is a word we should use, because we know we want the best for all of you and those who fail themselves have blinded themselves to their own inner guidance.

What can be done from the Earth point of view is:
• Seek out knowledge constantly.
• Seek out why things go wrong.
• Seek out what make things happen whether good or bad, as you call it.
• Understand why you can't have a happier life than another person: was it because of a life plan aiming to know that kind of life? Or was it because you have messed up things by not listening within?

ANSWER IS WITHIN

All this needs to be sorted out, worked out and understood. That is when **the turning to one's own Inner Knowledge comes in useful.** It cannot be done overnight, it can only be started with the best intention at heart. Then and only then, can the guides come in close and help the seeker open his Mind to what he rejected or did not look at before.

It is *so* important to have that knowledge: the awareness that **you will find the answer to your problems by going deeply within yourself**, beyond the confines, limitations and ruling of your brain and Earthly linked Mind. You need to reach the Soul part of you, the Spiritual part of you, where the Truth resides as part of your life plan, your 'destiny' for that particular life.

There is a great need for Mankind to be aware of its origins because, as we explained before, the Souls are not linking enough with their material bodies. It has been left to chance instead of being a regular occurrence. The Souls are getting lost, confused, misled, all this means men (and women of course) are not on the path they should be on, which should be a normal, ordinary path of following inner directives for their everyday life. Not directives in the sense of being told what to do by a 'superior power', but directives to be looked at, considered within the Free Will frame — to see whether the inner suggestions wouldn't be better than ideas instigated by the material world and way of thinking.

WONDER AT MARVELS

The main point here is that we have to try to help Mankind look at itself again to understand itself and prize what it has — as this is precious and far beyond little inventions, games, toys and superficial pleasures of the material world. When you look at the beautiful Earth and see what it offers you

— as wonders of the mastering of Matter by Souls made from Spirit Power — you should be marvelling at everything you see, yet very few do! They take it for granted and damage it if they can, to make way for their material life pleasures or comforts.

This is so wrong, because **Mankind cannot replace what it destroys: it cannot make a new tree or forest by itself, it has to rely on 'Spirit Energies' willing to come back to grow as trees again otherwise there will be none left!** It is to be appreciated, realised and grasped; it really is to be thought about. You would not have anything left on the Earth if no more 'Spirit' Beings wished to go back to fill it again and grace it with their presence, such as trees, plants, flowers and seas and mountains as well as other things such as air, water, sunshine etc.   It is to be pondered on.

When you have a wonderful tree in front of you do you just think "There is a tree; it is green, blooming"? Or do you think: "This is one of the wonders of Nature and of the 'Spirit World', as this is a Being who has especially **chosen** to come to Earth to experience it as a beautiful tree of stature and majesty no one could match by building a brick building!"

So, those are the thoughts which should run through people's Minds. **What you have got in front of you has to be pondered about,** so that you can learn to appreciate their beauty, their 'magic' in that it is **not** man-made, it cannot be man-made! It has within it a 'mysterious' (to you) Power, which has given it Life.

That Power is not simply given to it by 'someone else', some 'superior' deity, it has the Power because it **is** the Power, in as much as it has that Power within itself. That way you will see that the tree, or whatever wonder of Nature, built itself, chose itself to be as it is, because that is what it wanted to be, to go on to Earth, for that experiment which all are experiencing.

56

EXPERIMENT KICK OFF

The start of the tale should be: "Once upon a time" (which does not exist as such) there was an enormous, gigantic, **eternal** WAVE OF LIGHT. A Light that had special powers. Not just to light up the world around itself but to create it first of all!

As it created that world, it made itself into different shapes, shapes which have a Will to live, an Urge to be in existence. That way **the Urge grew as the forms took shape**. The Light had a 'place' for itself: it is within them all, within all these shapes which decided to be solid for a change instead of being an intangible Light. That's what it should be like, what should be said.

The tale is longer and more substantial than this of course, but the basis is the same: **one intense creative Light filled with the Urge to re-create itself in various forms. Why? As a challenge to see what it would be like to feel the physical world itself,** rather than 'floating' around or above it.

It's all to do with the Inner Urge, the intense desire to have a shape for the fun of experimenting that experience, that's all. Anything else can be done elsewhere in various other ways. This particular experiment is the one relating to Earth Matter. **Earth Matter is not like other Matter**, so its experience or rather the experience of it, is varied and special to those who come to it - **it has to be lived to be believed, known and appreciated**. The very fact of being alive in that particular environment makes it special for itself.

FOCUS ON FLESH

But it has been spoilt: spoilt by those who, over the ages, chose to change the outlook and the goal of those experiences. The changes relate to the fact that the flesh had been given more importance than it was due to have. Flesh is only a covering to protect the solid inner structure, which allows one to stand and walk etc. That's all the flesh was for, to be visible to others, relate and do things with your arms, legs etc. But the fact so many Humans have decided it is so important — that 'looks' matter more than the inner Soul, and the pleasures demanded by the senses 'have to' be quenched — means all this has changed the goal posts and made life on Earth a totally different experience from what was planned before, at the beginning as you'd say.

The beginning was a beginning in a way because it had to be built upon to make the right structure and right shapes for those planning to live there for a while; but as said before it was not understood. When the first inhabitants saw what was happening, they 'panicked' in a way because they realised the pleasure of living with one's Mind leading the body had become the Mind wanting to enjoy the body of flesh, instead of being its mentor and guardian. It was gradually becoming a disgraceful state of affairs, which meant the Soul was not in charge totally as should have been all along.

MOVING THE GOAL POST

The Soul should always be in charge of the Earth personality because it is **its** body of flesh. The Soul has in each physical creature, its own representation on Earth: its own flesh body as a tool for experiencing the Experiment in Matter. **The Soul should be in charge, in total charge**. So why have so many people let the Soul's advice or screams be ignored? That's the biggest mystery for us.

The Soul cannot be ignored in the long run, sooner or later it will get its own back because it suffers dissatisfaction and disillusion; **it will reflect itself automatically in the flesh** that it has fashioned for itself. An angry Soul will be a very angry, inflamed, 'tortured even', body. The Soul cannot do with 'no outlet'. It has all its outlets in its body of flesh, which it has made to its own specifications. So any changes brought to the body by the Human ill treating it, will not be well received by the Soul personality itself. What will ensue will be death at best— or worse: all kinds of diseases and miseries.

It is so simple to understand, yet no one or hardly anyone seems to grasp it. It has been said time and again, yet it has been and still is ignored by those who obviously think they know better... Well, they'll pay the price with their health - physically, mentally, emotionally, and even the health of the frustrated Soul which will need lots of healing when it comes back here, once out of the physical focusing it had when linked to the flesh body.

An experience to be had properly is one where you follow the rules as set up originally. Then you will enjoy it to its full. Change it, make it different in a way that is clashing with the original intentions and goals, and you will see the whole set up will start to crumble, creak at the joints and finally be a heap of rubble which will be a shame to its own living Soul. A Soul would not want to be ashamed of its physical representation, it would want to be proud of it. We are not talking of beauty in the eyes of the beholder as **looks are of no importance** whatsoever, all the more since the flesh ages and dies finally! No, **the shame will come from what the Mind has done with that body,** in as much as it has not attended to other Beings in need, or done harm to others who had not asked for it, or did not deserve to be hurt, whether Animals or People, of course.

So this is the end of our chapter to make you think of what you have in front of you in Nature, admire it, respect its own skilful creation. That's what you are here for. Admire what other creatures, other Beings coming from the so-called Spirit World, have done to express themselves in the world of Matter. Then you should want your own expression in Matter to be worth being proud of, so that the Soul driving it (which is your own Soul, your own inner personality) can reflect itself proudly from beginning to end, during its stay on Earth and its games with Matter. This could be or should be food for thought!

§§§

CHAPTER 7

There is **within you a spark of Light, Love and Creativity which will never, ever be extinguished**; so why not use it over and over again so that you can change and **improve your life** for the better, all the time, as long it is not detrimental to others. It is essential to understand this, yet so many ignore it or are incapable of grasping this concept, which is normal to us here but seems to be foreign to those on Earth nowadays.

We have been here a long time ourselves but we know what it is like to be on Earth, cut off from one's origins. Yet we had faith in our link with the World of Mind, which we had not forgotten, as deeply within, there was always the place to catch up with the link, as said before.

So we ask all of you reading this book, and all those who have not read it yet but could be told about it, to have the intelligence to look within to find what there is to find, if one looks carefully enough. It is essential to be aware, that's it. Aware of everything around you, aware of what is in your world— and what is in our world when you need to link back to your origins. As we said before, those who close their eyes and their inner eye to what exists have created a hole for themselves to live in. What a wasted experience! Coming to Earth to live in a hole has no aim, no goal!

So we suggest you look within, for the Truth you need to go by and for the guidance which will help you sort out any problem you are not sure of.

As you know, we cannot tell you what to do for sure, as this has to come from yourself. But your own Inner Self,

Higher self, that Being which is you, the Real You, can and will guide you as you step forward on your Earthly path, whether you've step on the 'wrong ' path for the time being, or just missed out something which should or could be important to your development. So, listen and look within; we've said this so many times!

But now we wish to add another point for this new chapter. It is **the Intensity you need to put into anything you do**. You cannot just wish for something, without putting that heartfelt desire all the time, in what you wish for. **A passing thought is not a creative thought**! A passing thought is only one of many millions going through your brain every day. So you need to make the difference between:

• A passing (even though repeated) thought.
• A really beseeching, desperate, thirsty appeal for that situation, that something you wish to have happening, in a desperate attempt to make a change for the better, for yourself or others.

You'll have to build up this momentum, it cannot be created overnight; you'll have to have it coming from deeply within yourself to make it happen. We need to repeat this often, because repeating makes it sink in gradually - in the same way as wishing for something desperately and constantly coming back to that inner wish, **will help it happen as you create the right waves and vibrations to make that change towards you** and not in the opposite direction!

DETERMINATION AND GOAL

Have the courage of your convictions, have the conviction you will succeed, have success as a goal, have the determination to see it through for your own sake and for the sake of those you seek to help. Have an AIM in your daily life. Do not go round aimlessly towards trivial material pursuits which will not fulfil you and your Soul in the end.

You'll have to **find what your own Soul and Spirit wish to achieve** as a Human Being on Earth. We cannot tell you individually. But when you have found it, make it your goal, ultimate goal. Because when you come back here, you'll be looking at what you had planned to achieve for that particular trip... And you'll definitely be disappointed to find out you had ignored every road sign, every hint and nudge, every word of advice given one way or the other to try to put you back on the "right track"; the right track being what **you** had chosen for yourself, not for us. So we can only say: Look, Listen, Learn, Live in the right way you would have wanted to live, if you had listened all the time from day one of your trip on Earth.

What is there for us in this piece of advice, you may say? 'Nothing' could be the answer, in as much as there is no material gain or even spiritual ones. But the joy of helping someone towards the Light and happiness, instead of letting them fall in the black, dismal dungeon or hole of ignorance and misery, is enough for us as a 'reward'. Though we do not need or seek rewards, as we enjoy doing what we would be pleased to have others doing for us if we needed help too.

That's all can be said on that Friends. Look, listen, learn, lighten your life and live it to the full of your Soul's expectations: that way and that is the only way, you will definitely feel fulfilled. An unfulfilled Being is an incomplete Being and that is not what the plan of the Experiment was about. Have faith in yourself and your own inner abilities, which are latent in all of you, whatever and whoever you are.

NO ONE PASSES 'BEFORE THEIR TIME'

BR -Could you please remind readers of what you said before, about some departed thinking they have "gone 'before their time".

The Soul of someone who has just passed over is not always aware of why and even how, at times, it has come over back home. It is always a shock to leave one place to go to another. So it is not surprising some say they've passed "before their time" - but what do they know as their right time? It is impossible for them to know at that stage.

Yet when the Soul has had time to study itself and its aims, goals and desires for that particular life plan, then you'll see it will come round to **understanding why it had gone** from where it was, to come back **then**, at that particular time, that period of its life.

That's all we can say for that; because, as you well know, indeed NO ONE, whether People or Animals (yes, Animals too!) no one goes out of its or his own chosen body, to leave for the World of Light as we call it, **unless the Spirit of that Soul was ready** - even though the personality on Earth may not feel ready and would deny strongly and even vehemently it/ she/ he wanted to leave others behind! That is usually impossible for an Earthly Being to admit they were ready to leave their family and loved ones behind: but on the greater scale of things, when a Soul sees on the horizon of its plan that it has achieved what it had chosen to do, or it has had enough of that place for whatever reasons, it has no choice but wanting to come back to where it/ he/ came from.

A Soul has no knowledge of its time or day of passing, but the degree of the inner desire, the pull from within - by its Spirit wanting to leave the flesh instrument (that Earthly vehicle) - that pull will indeed be very strong... That's why the person on Earth will find himself going to a certain place, do a certain thing or whatever, which will lead him to leave the flesh...

BR- So, if 100 people are killed in a plane crash all their 'Oversouls' wanted to leave their bodies?

All wanted to leave their flesh body for their Spirit to be released to come back, fully aware of its goals. All came back because their own individual **Higher Self/Spirit had a goal,** many goals no doubt, and **had finished its journey there**: it wanted to get back to where it had come from...

So you may also have 1,000 or 1,000,000, it will be the same: all have or had a reason for going out of their body for good. There may be many reasons to choose one or another particular way of going. If the person wanted to make an impact in people's Minds - for example to say: "You see, I have gone as I believed things should be done/ helping others/ or protesting against such and such/ or just disappearing from your sight so that you do not have me as a burden".

There may be so many different reasons why someone 'dies' in any particular way, but you have to remember the bottom line of it all is: " YOU cannot die at all!" No one dies! That's because he is still alive the split thousandth of a second after he's left his flesh body. **He has NOT died: he has changed consistency and appearance** to your Earthly eyes, but he is NOT 'dead', nor is your cat or dog or donkey or snail...

You have had many Animals in your life and you feel for them, but they have not really left you! They are still near you, yet you do not feel them, because you have not focused properly on to them. You can try to do so; if you do, you'll no doubt have results, but you cannot create something out of nothing yourself. You would not 'invent' one of them even if you wanted to! It would have to be the 'real thing' if you saw one: you should not tell yourself that you've 'imagined' seeing your cat or dog or donkey. You should know that if you see it, it's because you will **have** seen it!

That's all we need to say on that subject. You do really know the answers at the back of your Mind or the bottom of your heart. You've let doubt come over but you are right to ask and check. You can never be too sure.

PREHISTORIC PEOPLE

BR- I was asked by a reader: "Why don't we seem to receive 'spirit communicators' from olden days, say from a 'caveman' 200,000 years or more ago?"

If you were a 'caveman' or before, would you want to worry about communicating with people who have technically not been born yet? And if you were in a state of understanding one can communicate, for what reasons would you be interested in doing so?

BR- Do they still 'exist', since all is 'now' as there is no time the way Humans think of it?

That's because you think in a linear way. The mark or imprint of Energy left after the man has left the Earth is still there in the Universal Energy Field, but the creature as such is not necessarily there.

What you see as fossils shows they've left, but what you don't see is the Soul of each one changing when they've come here and absorbed more knowledge — or more specifically (if you are talking of the 'first' pioneers of the Earth Experiment), they've remembered they were Beings of Energy and have discarded their flesh bodies to recover their personality as a Being of Energy, understanding their own

66

individual plans, needs and wishes. If the line of creation was still and fixed, it would be clearer, but because it is not so, it makes it much more difficult for you to understand.

The Soul of a 'caveman' (who was not really the first one there anyway) has as much 'Spirit' Energy as anyone. If they chose to go when the Earth was first designed, they would have most likely been rather 'advanced' Beings who probably took part in the Earth design! So they went to test their workmanship and work.

If it had been a Soulless Being it may have been different but no Being is Soulless: its Consciousness may vary in intensity and level but it is still a Being who has life at his core.

BR- So I could not ask for a 'caveman' to communicate and tell me what Animals he sees around him?

If the knowledge came across, it would be from those Beings who know about that era; it would not be from a particular 'caveman' pioneer because the era has evolved forward into a more productive period. It means the original 'men' and 'women' who came to Earth have taken their leave from that physical place and **not taken with them, in their Minds, what they were doing then.**

We'll add that the essential point to focus on is not 'who' can communicate or not, but the fact that they existed at all! It was such an extraordinary accomplishment that it should be revered, admired and praised! Who would have thought one could create such as physical flesh with all those senses, and other creations, simply with one's Mind Power? THAT is what needs focusing on and being in awe about!

The fact that there are often only communications from fairly 'recent times' (for you) does not mean there were not communications before. In your 'ancient times' like Roman or

Egyptian, there were communications from their own departed. But the aim is not to communicate for the sake of it - the aim is to impart information about either world to the other one. So if you had an 'ancient Egyptian' talking to you now, would you really know he is an 'ancient Egyptian'? Or could it be someone who either pretends to be one in order to please you, or be a descendant of those people and recalling what he had learnt from hearsay in his family or in books?

BR- Does Tutankhamen still 'exist' as a pharaoh somehow, 'somewhere? I recall Mum 'saw' (in your world) French King Louis XVI and his emotions...

My dear, the question is not sensible. If the historical period still existed as such, you would not have descendants: it would have frozen still with no 'future' as you see it. **The period exists as a memory of 'energetic event',** or events of Energy, emotions, traumas and joys. THAT is what is imprinted as forever existing. It can be looked at, if one has learnt to focus on that particular level of frequencies, if you want to use such words — we do not label things, we feel and experience them. So if you could focus on that particular time of when Tutankhamen existed on Earth, you would relive the period and see it happening as if it was 'real' and 'now' to you. But it would not be you (modern person) living the pains and joys of those who did experience them. It is 'past' in your words but **it is still in existence now as an imprint in the Eternal Consciousness and Field of Energy**. It has its place as 'now' for any moment. We mean: anybody looking at it from any of your centuries would 'look at it' and experience it as 'now' for them.

Therefore, if you wanted to talk to Tutankhamen, you would be looking at the man who had been in the 'frozen time frame' of Energies filled with events and memories... But the real Being (whose disguise of flesh was that pharaoh) **has not remained** in that state of Mind. He hopefully has progressed towards more exciting discoveries whether in your physical world or *perhaps elsewhere*! It all depends on what he, the Being, chose to do and experience.

So those who have contact with the Earth from 'more recent' (as you call them) periods are people who have still some work to do on themselves: they have not moved on to very much higher levels of Mind and understanding. If people talk they are still within reach and have not moved away, even if they have reached some higher understanding. By 'moved away' we mean: left the concept of having been a Human and wanting to be one.

On the other hand, you could have some very advanced and knowledgeable Beings who have chosen to learn more and more to progress far beyond those Earthly experiences — then to come to impart that knowledge to those willing to receive it! This is in order to help Mankind realise and grasp that it has more to look forward to or aim for, than the material world Mankind has seemingly ensconced itself **into, nowadays!**

The aim of teaching from our world and beyond our world, is to pass on what we (or those who do it too) know, because you Humans, have limited your own Minds by thinking what your instruments can measure is all there is to understand. Moreover, your theories may not be right if you close your Minds to the existence of all that there is beyond that realm; the realm of physical worlds is far inferior and terribly limited as you can guess.

It can be 'high knowledge' which is provided **but** that is only given by those who have gone beyond the Earth experiment (like we have done), and who now see it as what it is and was – then they kindly wish to help those struggling on that planet. So, is it clearer now? You would not actually talk to a 'caveman' because he would not be there to talk to you. If he had been one, he would no doubt have progressed to far superior levels!

So, if Tutankhamen does not come and speak to you or show himself, it's because either: He is still stuck in his Mind and thinks he can't communicate with the Earth; Or else he has progressed and moved far from that area of his Earthly life: He has either gone onto being many other Humans, possibly forgetting he had been Tutankhamen, or gone away from the cycle of reincarnation on Earth, because the Being wanted to do something else, somewhere else.

Is that clearer? Those who do move on usually have now different interests and occupations. Those famous mathematicians, astronomers and other scientists will hopefully now realise that what they were so bent on, when on Earth, was paltry compared to what they can grasp now at Energy levels! What they used to say or think will not be of such importance or interest (to them) now! So it is **unlikely they'll come and tell you what to do**: their Minds have flown to more refined states and stages, also far from the Earth environment, vibration wise.

SSS

CHAPTER 8

Following the announcement of 'Big Bang Test' in Geneva (September 2008), I asked my communicators for their opinion on the experiment.

We have a gentleman here who wants to talk to you... *(Change of communicator)* Last time we spoke you were asking about the phenomena of trance and closeness to Spirit World, which you wanted to understand better. Now you want to know about the non-existent (as such, physically) 'big bang' as they call it. We know there'll be experiments on that subject, but it is important to know that no one will ever manage to reproduce such a nonexistent event, because we ourselves have not produced it in the first place — i.e. when **we, of this World of Mind Power, had to work on the creation of many a 'Universe'**, or more precisely many a place of physical appearance, but all of different appearances!

ETERNAL LIFE-GIVING ENERGY

Energy has to come from somewhere. That somewhere existed already before, anyway, and the creation of those 'balls' or whatever exploding in 'mid-air' in a lab is not going to give either evidence or proof of the so-called 'Original Creation'!

The Matter you are made of on Earth is a very selected array of vibrations, which all have their place, so that the results as correct and well-balanced to produce bodies of various sorts. But the **Life-giving Energy comes from the Source: the Spark of Life** which we all have in us and which is in this World of Light which bathes everything else, everywhere, it must be remembered.

For anything to be 'alive', the Spark of Life has to be of an intensity that no one could possibly imagine. It is of such a degree of concentration that no one could possibly grasp what it is and how it functions, because it is not functioning with terrestrial or man-made means. It is not a visible way of giving Life, it is a 'self-combustion' way of giving Life!

BR- Do you mean by 'burning itself'?

Self-combustion implies Power within oneself, to produce enough Energy and force to ignite the inner fire, to create the Energy necessary for the next step.

So, we are saying no one could understand that, as you do not have that on your Earth! But if we could say this: Imagine a non-existing candle suddenly appearing in all its splendour: you would think it is a 'miracle', wouldn't you? Yet if that candle turned out be the reflection of another candle which itself was more real, because it was solid to the touch, you'd wonder how it happened. Well, this is what we are trying to explain:

There is a current of (let us say, to simplify things to the extreme) mighty 'electric power' constantly underlying everything. That Power is there, everywhere, at the core of every little thing, all over the 'Universal Web of Nothing' at the 'origin'. We have therefore a gigantic, infinite web of 'electric' power, not visible, not used yet, but extremely and tremendously potent, which could ignite anything touching it, because it would explode at the slightest vibration.

If that Power was made to react to another such electric vibration of possibly a slightly different kind, then the reaction between the two would be gigantic (or even ginormous as you like to say), and the results unpredictable or possibly predictable in some direction, depending on what is known.

72

That's what the problem is about - a Creation of an 'intensity-impossible-to-fathom out', producing even greater intensity! When these waves of intensity gather at a pace no one can keep up with to measure them, they will create waves of Energy 'all over the place'; these waves will bounce against others and each other and create even more waves of similar or newly-formed Energy. That is what we are trying to make you understand!

Those Energy bands and fractions and particles, as they bash each other and create little ones becoming big, have been imagined as one single Big Bang! But the truth is: those **Energies already existed before**, so who or what created them?

They came from the unified Thought Power of those wanting to create Physical Matter! (Listen to the words: Wanting to create! 'Wanting' on Earth should create too, but do you always see it as such, is another question?)

So, to come back to your question: The 'big bang' talked about by so many scientists, has nothing to do with the real Creation of this physical world you are in! You are **not** the residue of 'big banged' particles, osmosing with others, or exploding into others, to create the minerals forming Matter from an amoeba to a donkey! No! You are not that.

You are the results of thought-out processes, which were first worked out 'mentally' here! Then they were put to the test by creating them both in our world and in the physical world, which — it had been decided — was to be created as a very interesting and intriguing experiment. But **the source of those Thoughts came from Beings already in existence BEFORE** the particular creation of these waves of Energy, which will result in sparks of Life, being breathed in **any** living Being, from a tiny microscopic alga or moss, to an amoeba, to any other Beings!

Those Beings have always existed indeed, as there is no death in the World of Light and Energy! All changes but it may not change as you may expect it!

So why worry about so far back in so-called 'Time', since you cannot — and not one of you can — grasp the enormity of the process! To have Beings who have always existed as Light and Thoughts of a magnitude no one can grasp in this puny world of material activities, is beyond any Human comprehension!

DEFINITION OF THOUGHT

BR- So there was ONE already existing Thought Power at the 'origin'?

That idea had already been discussed many a time. One underlying Energy FIELD and vibrations of unimaginable magnitude is the only answer to Reality!

If some people want to call it a 'god', or a 'giant' or a 'dwarf' or any other name, that is their prerogative and own idea... But there has NOT been **one** Being as such, as you would call or think of 'a Being', whether powerful or not! It has to be comprehended that **the only One Mighty Force is the Universal** (i.e. all over) **Power. That Power has Life within itself**— that means: **as it intensifies itself, it will shoot out thoughts.**

BR- You talk of Energy Field and of Thought - could you please define a Thought?

A Thought is a 'piece' of Energy made by a thinking Mind. A thinking Mind is a self-creating Energy Force; self-creating means creating by itself, without anyone else's help. But Self-creating may also mean: creating itself.

74

So, there is this 'double edge sword' of creating itself more and more every time. It has an Urge expanding outwards and also creating outwards expansions and variations (like waves bashing each other and creating other little or big waves, some half-broken, other long rolls of water).

Therefore we have this simplified picture of two pointers —< which means: a same thing can do two things at the same time. That is what that 'Sea of Mind', that eternally lasting and existing major Force does: it exists, has always existed and is at the same time, **a source of Energy, constantly changing and multiplying itself.**

That means the build-up is phenomenal and not describable. As Thoughts produced themselves, reproduced and 'fathered' more variations, commutations and permutations, the tremendous range widened, broadened, spread, intensified: the 'original' (if ever there was one!) Thought had long lost its 'original' shape or pattern (if we could use such meaningless human words, in such a complex and complicated, but weak in a way, explanation!)

We cannot easily find words in your language, which **you** would have in your head, to be able to explain the nearly unexplainable to a Human Being! As it cannot be seen or touched, it is not within the senses of an Earthly person, and even mathematicians or other scientists would find it difficult to convey what is in fact an inexplicable subject, unless you have experienced it from this end: ours!

BR- Some people assume thoughts come from the brain.

You well know it does not come from the human or animal brain. What is primordial in all this is to take into consideration the fact that Eternity exists and always had existed! That's point one.

75

Secondly: Eternity is not a jumble of words to make feelings last or seem to. It is a background to the fact that nothing 'needs to have a beginning'. Some things will have one no doubt but lots do not need to.

So, what is 'Thought'? Firstly, try and grasp that the background in all Universes 'levels' is Thought Power also known as Mind Power – i.e. it is the ability to be, to exist and to constantly create whatever impressions and urges or desires one has. Therefore that eternal Thought Power is a ginormous and mighty Force, beyond all understanding, which can and does constantly **feel the Inner Urge to not only exist but extend its existence into different forms**. It wants to 'be' more, to 'be better' to experience more than 'now'.

It is a constant need to actualize whatever urge and impression occur. It is indeed a kind of **limitless boundless 'Mass of Energy' throbbing with that desire to extend itself.** By doing so it produces 'shoots' of similar Energy which in turn are throbbing too, full of that urge and desire.

So well that the **key to actualization is the inner desire and its intensity**. The more intense the desire, the more likely and quicker the realisation and actualization or formation of that desire will be – in various forms of existence. It could be an innumerable amount of possibilities.

What you know of is the current physical Matter which you are all made of and surrounded with, but there are numerous other planes and dimensions, which do not have that kind of Matter and exist **differently.**

So, what is Thought?

The moment an idea, an impression comes strongly to the surface of that sea of Mind Power, a 'thought' is born, promptly giving birth itself to some more thoughts! A thought is not created by a brain of course; a brain is only Matter out of this particular type of Matter. But the brain can conduct and channel or block the flow of thoughts received from the Mind of individual Beings.

Therefore, a thought is a 'piece' of Energy emitted by the potent impressions and desires of an individual Mind, which itself is a powerful tool of every Being in existence.

When each individual Being starts its journey into existence out of the 'mother board' of the Mass of pulsating Energy-raring-to-go-and-'BE', its first impression will be that Urge to grow into being something different from the original Mass of throbbing Energy! The moment it feels the inkling that it has succeeded and it 'exists' as an individual spare 'shoot of Energy', will be the **fundamental step to CONSCIOUSNESS** - it will grasp that it 'is real' as itself! That potential of Consciousness was latent and only needed a little trigger to become a bud.

What is done with it depends on the individual 'shoot'. It may be slow at realizing it exists; it may be much quicker and it is grasping its own individuality and starting to be aware of other 'shoots' around itself and comparing: "I am me, they are 'them".

This will make Consciousness blossom even more. As every strongly felt thought and impression automatically CREATES what had been 'thought', the resulting fireworks display of creation is soon astounding, whether on a small scale or a gigantic one!

SSS

CHAPTER 9

The learning you are given here is not acquired through old, 'learnt in advance', parroted knowledge. This learning is through the dictation of learned people who have suffered a lot in their previous lives to put across the same kind of knowledge, yet had to stop at death point of that life, before it could be repeated again, to more modern ears, in order to have a long line of teachers who will not let go of the Truth! The Truth being that **all are One.** All are the same yet all are different...All Beings have the same Source within themselves and outside themselves in a way, since they emanate the Energy born in this world of ours.

You have your own world in a way, yet that very world which you think is so 'solid' somehow, can appear thus only because it has been imagined, made up, thought out and visualised as 'solid'. To do all this it had to be seen in someone's and many Minds' eyes. This is where imagination and visualization come into play.

The players are those who designed this world of yours by 'playing' at deciding what they wanted to put into it. One of the players in it would be **you,** of course, as you designed your own part, your own role. This is valid for all who have gone to live on Earth at any time.

So the point we wish to make is that the 'starting point' is not, as thought by some, in one big personified deity, but in *any* one entity who will be going there as a living Being.

What is a living Being? A small replica in the flesh Matter of what the thoughts, wishes and desires of that Being are. If the desires match the body of flesh well, it will be a well-balanced body. If the desires do not match what the body looks like, there will have been some discrepancies.

BR- I am not sure what you mean exactly…

A Being of Flesh should be representing its own thoughts and ways of thinking. The moment the way of thinking changes compared to the 'original' way of thinking, then the physical reflection will be confused, blurred, not exact… and the diseases begin! It is essential to be reflecting what you want to be and express yourself through that body.

As you cannot do too much to change your shape, as the body has grown, you can constantly make sure the shape does not deteriorate and stays healthy. How is that to happen? By constantly selecting correct foods and drinks of course, but most of all by choosing to be on a better pathway, **on a more peaceful pathway of thinking**: i.e. by changing your Mindset whenever you see yourself causing trouble around you or receiving trouble!

A person whose emotional and mental state are calm and even, has a smooth outlook to life, an unruffled pattern of thoughts and usually quite a smooth life, or at least inner life. This is what you should all aim for. As the even and balanced path shapes itself in front of you, while you go along, you'll know you are doing what was meant to be: you will feel better for it and you'll know you are right in your thinking because your bodily health will feel well-balanced.

HOW YOU THINK

BR- When you suggest that I 'tell my Mind to be quieter', doesn't 'me' asking my Mind is like my Mind asking itself?

All of you on Earth have got a Mind. All of us here have got a Mind. The Mind is the produce of the spiritual Being thinking one way or the other. If the spiritual Being says to itself: "I want a quiet Mind", it will create for itself a quiet Mind. If that Being says to itself "I'll have an active Mind" it will have one. The Mind does not govern the spiritual Being— You as Eternal Spiritual Beings, all have a tool and many at your disposal.

BR - Doesn't thinking/saying to oneself uses one's Mind?

You have a car, you drive it at your own pace and speed. You need not let the car go fast if you don't want it to do that. You need to understand you all have a 'Mind **Power**' rather than 'a Mind' as a separate aspect or object. You have a Power within you, which is a **tool,** more than being a part of you, the Eternal Spiritual Being. **You control that Power yourself** by wishing, feeling, sensing what needs to be done or you want to be done. It is not you. **The Power is the Energy within you, which creates what is being thought**.

Let's explain differently if it helps: **A Mind as such does not exist! A Mind is a 'piece of Energy'** in a way, **a way of thinking** (We have to use words you grasp, as we don't use words here). A Mind is not an object as tangible as a flesh (or other) body.

The Power spurring the Mind is the 'Mind Power'. The Mind Power is what drives people one way or the other. They can 'live fast' or 'live slowly' mentally (this is put simply of course). If you think of something, you have to use the Power of your Mind to make that thought exist, to create that thought. **That Power of your Mind is the 'electricity'**, the current **which lights the thoughts into being in existence,** into being 'thoughts'.

80

So, you think one thought at a time, as you trigger your Mind Power to send impulses and 'electrify' your vague thought into a more acceptable, conceived thought. As you think lots of thoughts, they bombard your head but what you really do is fill your whole Being (as a spiritual Being) with ways you are thinking. You **fill your thoughts with Energy** every time you bring that thought to your attention, **every time you dwell on that thought.**

Let's have a single thought as a subject to make it easier. So, you have 'A thought'... You keep it in your focus every so often, maybe many times within a short period. As you do that, it gives it impetus, you fill it with inner 'electrifying Energy', which comes from the Mind Power that you have. Not from a separate Mind, as an object which does something at a distance or from a distance, separate from you — but as **a Power within yourself,** the spiritual Being, which triggers more thoughts if **you**, the Being, activates that Power. Therefore that is how you create more thoughts, more actions.

But to come back to the beginning of our explanations: that Mind Power is what you have as **a tool, to create whatever you want to think about,** whether to tell yourself you want to think calmly or not think at all, but rest mentally, being in a receptive state. Or else to be active mentally and gather all your fast thinking capabilities to be able to do lots of things and actions (as well as thoughts of course), so that you can act quickly in some situation or other.

You need to see the Power within you as an Energy, a light, a current, a flow that can be held back gently or pushed forward furiously hard, if need be. It is the 'you', the Being you are who makes the decision by willing one way or the other.

BR- So to recap: Everybody is a Being of creative Mind Power, a Being made of creative Mind Power, which can in a way control itself. Fundamentally we are a Being of Energy, of Light which is self-creating and also creates outwards constantly by sending 'bits of Energy' i.e. 'thoughts'— which in turn can or could create and extend itself more if intensified.

*So, we **are A self-regulating Mind Power, a self-regulating Creative Energy**. Is that right?*

The answer to your question is yes! You've got it, grasped it. You now have to grasp the aspect of **Intensity.** The Intensity is what makes a difference to all this. If the Intensity is not there, the Creativity will either be nil or weak. So all rests on the **In-ten-si-ty** of the thoughts sent out by that 'all-creative-Being-of-creative-mental-Energy'.

The creations it creates, the happenings have to do with the way the thoughts are directed and respond, bounce back or blend with the Beings and Energies around. If others have the same Energy Intensity, you'll find there might be clashes, or else a tremendous bond of friendship, love or just creative links which blend. If there is no link but repulsion, it is because the Energies are not on the same wavelength. **That's why some people hate each other or love each other.** But the results always come from the Intensity of the firing out of the 'all doing-all-sensing-Energy'. If the Intensity is not there, there will be no results.

Look at it this way. You have a Power within you which **burns constantly like a pilot light on stand-by and can do anything in any direction. You, the 'Spirit' Being can decide which way** it burns, it lights itself, it sends its thoughts out and most of all with which Intensity! This is what it boils down to.

So, if you choose to have a strong fire burning all the time, at high speed and strength and flashing out big flares, you'll be soon burnt out. But if you decide to have a strong

82

powerful 'Mind fire' within you, which you can turn on full at will when needed, but you also can turn down to a very, very low level, as good as still, then you'll have control over that power.

That is what you wanted to learn to do in your present life. You have to **control that Intensity**. You have a lot of intensity within you at all levels. You wanted to learn to reduce it at will when needed. That's what you are doing when you learn to 'tune in' to us, or learn to control your anger and rage because the world around you does things wrong. You cannot burn yourself up because the world is filled with people doing things wrong! You'd have no life left and you would have to start all over again! Do not burn your body and your Mind Power by lashing out streams of Intensity in all you do. Learn to 'calm down all the knobs': turn down all the knobs of volume and Intensity, to have a more balanced or calmer level **when** you wish to have it.

It is good to have Intensity and fire and 'go' within you. But it is also very good to have calm, quiet, peace of Mind and most of all balance. That way you are a balanced Being, who can tilt one way or the other the moment it wishes or needs to do that — but also go back to the balanced level as the norm, rather than the sky high (or deep down, rare for you) levels.

I think you have understood now. You seem to have a more balanced feel within, i.e. I think you have grasped what we told you and that's very good. We are pleased with the result of our conversation.

BR- Thank you for explaining so well.

ᔕᔕᔕ

83

CHAPTER 10

I suddenly received an 'Automatic' psychic DRAWING (on writing pad) of 2 juxtaposed CIRCLES linked up by one in the middle – next, the first words are written in automatic writing. Then I hear the rest dictated at the same time as it 'writes itself', as usual.

Worlds within worlds, that is what everything is! Everything is worlds within worlds and again, within worlds, at infinitum! So goes the saying in our world: nowhere is limited, there are NO boundaries anywhere. Boundaries do not exist! Everything overlaps, blends with each other, merges. So to understand the mystery of Creation and Creativity brought by the so-called 'magic' of Thought Power, it is essential to understand and grasp **the total lack of any kind of boundaries.** What looks like boundaries to you all are simply figments of your imagination which has been tuned in from birth to the vibrations and frequencies of your **type** of Matter! Only then will you able to grasp what we are talking about or hinting at.

That utter merging of all that you can imagine, will always mean mysteries 'around the corner' to anyone who does not understand the simplicity of this statement**: no boundaries means no limits, therefore all blend within each other somehow. THAT is the beauty of the secret of Nature and of all the Universes that exist, will exist and could exist**!

Then our world is no mystery because no one can deny we exist here, since we are talking to you and also to many other Beings, not only in your world but also in any other dimensions - Beings who do not communicate in the same way as we do with you, but who can pick up our thoughts as vibrations of a certain frequency which match theirs...

You have a certain type of frequency on the Earth, which can be adapted, captured, picked more easily than you think, by many others who would or could want to link up with you. There is a great debate going on where you are, as to whether there are people or Beings living in other parts of this Universe of yours. (A Universe you *think* you know, yet that you do not know at all... since you cannot even see or reach an infinitesimal portion of it!)

Then the answer to that question is: yes, of course, there are Beings in other worlds! What does 'Beings' mean? It means 'bodies' of a kind, living independently of each other, able to cope with their surroundings and wanting to be independent and self-sufficient.

But this is not enough in some cases. It can also mean: **a Being is a self-creating entity, as it thinks**. So if a Being thinks itself 'too small' (let's say, to help you with an example you could relate to), then it can make itself grow bigger and taller, so that the 'problem' is overcome. The natural laws in places like that are simply **the law of Thought Power over Matter of that kind and type.**

If all 'Matters' (we need to use the word in plural!) were the same, there would be no fun in creating new places, would there! We need to have variety in Creation...

So, the law says: no one can go wrong, all can do what they want. But the creation of Animals on Earth has added an additional and interesting angle to the various possibilities of Creation, as Matter has to adapt to what the Thought thinks...

Make them all understand that the Matter they are made of, has nothing to do with any other 'Matter' constituting many or a single other world of a constitution unimaginable to any of you, no matter (ha ha!) what your level of thinking is...

BR- Could you explain what you mean by: "the creation of Animals being a new angle"?

The Creation of Animals was meant to be a new angle as the creatures from this (our) side wanted to express themselves that way.

BR- But they are 'Spirits', Energy Beings?

They are indeed what you call 'Spirits' but what is that? What 'Spirits' means is they are Beings (who have possibly lived before) but have no 'body' of flesh or Matter, as they are here if they have lived before.

BR- What about from what we'd call the 'beginning' of Creation of the Earth?

As the idea of creating the Earth (as now called by you) came gradually, all sorts of Beings 'passed by' so to speak, brought their ideas and input. All sorts of thoughts were offered and put together.

The idea (of Animal shapes) germinated as some 'Beings of Thought' wanted to express themselves in that flesh Matter *in a different way* from what Mankind was going to do and look like. They wanted **ideas of speed or smoothness, fluidity, acrobatics, all sorts of possibilities to be available and expressed** in a way which is different from what Humans can do. It was better that way, rather than making or trying to make 'Humans' do those things as well, or at least some of them doing it! So, 'Animals' are the **Thoughts of speed etc. expressed as Beings** who can do some of those things or feats mentioned before!

We can see you may be a little confused but all comes clear when you know and remember the Power of Thought is what drove all this Creation into action and actualization!

86

It was Thoughts which wanted to express themselves 'physically' as you would call it. That's why the shapes, forms, abilities are different and exciting, if you consider the whole range available. To be admired and respected too, because, at times, no one can do what another of these Beings can do. So it is indeed part of the wonder of Creation and Creativity of the Mind Power of all those Beings, or not even 'Beings' at times, expressing themselves!

BR- What do you mean by 'not even Beings'?

That was hinted at earlier and explained before. If those thoughts take a life of their own, they will create a result, as **the intensity of the Urge will move forward towards actualizing themselves into shape or form of some kind.**

BR- Where did the 'original thought' come from of being an 'Animal' and having those 'abilities'? Was it a side shoot of another one?

The Energy of Thought Power is everlasting, infinite, varied and impossible to describe. It has a variety of impossible descriptions on a scale unfeasible to label, of ways of shooting out new ideas, as you said.

The 'starting point' is never really one specific point as a thought: it's more likely to be an inner Urge to feel itself, see itself in this or that way, to explore the possibilities. **An Inner Urge is always at the source of anything created and creative.** The 'thought' so to speak is only an expression, may be a bit more specified or clearer, of an Inner Urge.

The Urge grew out of possibly seeing or realising there were other possibilities, other avenues. Creative ideas are excited and exciting Urges wanting to express themselves and attempting to do so as they 'go along'. It is always an infinite path with no stopping, lots of side tracks and avenues and many new doors opening themselves to the 'unthought-of before'... Does this answer your question?

BR- I think so, thank you. So if I understand correctly: Animals as we know them had not necessarily always been Animals. At what we'd call 'the start' it was more like 'ideas' of shapes/ speed/ flying etc. which took hold of the imagination of the 'Creative Urge', let's say — and they eventually took shape somehow?

Then over time some came to 'Earth', other Beings as Spirits decided it was a good idea and experiment, so carried on becoming 'Animals' and creating a way of thinking (I'd say) like an Animal, if that exists or makes sense. Please correct me if need be.

Let us say, you've got the gist of it anyway. Saying the 'way of thinking of an Animal' is not quite correct because that way of thinking may only be related to that particular species for so long. Then, when an Animal leaves the Earth, if it is a pet, the bond of love will first link him to his owner and they will be reunited- But as both progress, the Animal (like Humans do too) will **eventually** evolve to a much 'higher' level: you'll find they forget what they've been 'before' so to speak. Therefore they become High Energies with a great creative Force within themselves, a Power provided by their thoughts or Inner Urges, if you understand what we mean.

The Inner Urge is always there, suppressed at times possibly, but always there within the 'inner sanctum' of that Energy which the Being is, in fact. Do you follow?

The basic, **fundamental Energy of a Being** of any kind or shape **will not ever disappear**! So it will remain its basis and this basis being a Thought Power in itself, a Creative Energy, cannot and will not remain still or stagnant. It will

88

automatically want to fire away more of itself into Creativity, always abundant Creativity! This is an endless fireworks display to use words you may grasp and visualize better.

The 'lost' attitude as an 'Animal' say, is not really 'lost'. It has enhanced and enriched, improved, altered or added to the original Power. That Power now has more facets, skills, Inner Knowledge - and anything else it has absorbed and been through over its experiences on Earth or elsewhere. As there is no end to this Creativity, you see why Eternity exists! It has to be, to help fulfil all these myriads of myriads of never ending possibilities…

BR- Indeed! I do understand. Many thanks.

SSS

CHAPTER 11

We told you before there are numerous **Universes, which can be tapped into** if one wishes to go there. There are indeed hoards of possibilities, that is why the number is endless. But if one chose to be a Being fleeting from one to the other, that would not make sense because it would probably never adapt to one or the other.

On the other hand, if one chooses one particular place or level to go to, one can concentrate on that type of Matter or vibration range — to perfect its use and one's behaviour and handling of it. Therefore it is always advised to concentrate on one type, one area of 'work', of experiments and then develop those necessary skills there. If you are not sure what we mean, we could explain better with a couple of examples.

If the level of vibrations required was to do with the Earth, say (then you'll understand better no doubt), the Being could choose to be a Human or an Animal or a Plant or whatever else it may select, of course. But it is essential to prepare oneself for the trip, as you know since we told you before (*See T,L&D: Training course before birth*).

So, if we prepare a Being for a trip as a Human, he'll have to think as a Human in a flesh body. If he had felt he wanted to go as an Animal, he would have had to choose which kind of Animal he wanted to be, then he would have to **adapt his thinking and mental behaviour**, to that particular type of Animal. It is **not** just a question of 'jumping into a flesh body" and thinking he'll be able to cope with it, as we said before.

Therefore, the truth to consider behind all that, is that all Beings have to weigh the pros and cons of the trip they are going to make, understand why they want to go as 'that Being' and finally make the necessary adjustments for that expedition, in many different ways and levels! They may even be asked to practise a little in our world, before they make the big jump into the other one...

GUIDED, NOT ABANDONNED

Another point to be considered too is that the Soul choosing to be one 'thing' or the other, is not going on its own! S/he/it has its followers: those who will stay in our world and watch over 'him', while 'he' goes to grapple with a new life elsewhere. That too has to be organised ever so carefully. This cannot be imagined or understood unless one is here. We have so much to take into account, so much responsibility towards our 'protégés', we cannot risk jeopardizing their trip and their experiments. This is all very well if it is to do with the Earth, as we have been to the Earth too at some point, so we know what to expect more or less...

But if those Souls wish to go places or levels which have **not** been tested or lived by any of us *('guides')* who have lived on Earth, then the protégés have to be **guided by other Beings** who have the experience of those particular areas or levels of thoughts and behaviour. That calls for a totally different type of personalities from the ones you personally are used to, my dear.

This is where you reach what you could call 'science fiction' in your films. We have no films here, we only have Reality... This is where new ways of thinking and accepting new ideas come into. If you wish to try to understand, we can attempt to explain to you what you did not know before.

91

BR- Yes please!

The level of Thought or Thinking of **Beings who have NOT been on the Earth,** will be different from your own way of thinking. You'll see things in a different way once we have tried to explain as clearly as possible.

Another point will be: The **Intensity** of the Power of Thought, could be or would be very different. You don't seem to be aware how much Power you have, compared to other places where they use it far more! Power is the key word and tool. Power of Mind, Power of action, Power of creative Thought: all that is one. **As they think, they create,** like we do here. But there will be different ways of creating whatever they may want to create. The slow way is to think slowly, bits by bits. The fast way is to see something or some action all done, ready prepared for use.

So, the Being who goes there knows why he wants to go to that particular level of Thought Power. It would probably be why he chose it, instead of another level where the focus may be less intense in that direction — but more focused on the Inner Self and the levels within, which are and have worlds of their own. Beings of all kinds exist 'physically' or even in a 'mental way', if you can guess or envisage that!

Another way of putting this across would be to say: All possibilities are open to those wanting to try anything, as ANY thing is possible. **All possibilities exist as potential, powerful vortexes or centres of Energies, which are ready and willing to be put into action,** even before someone comes within their vicinity.

The mere thought of 'doing such and such' would start the ball rolling in that particular direction. The creature or creative Being which would be involved would have triggered it into action, by figuring out its own existence within that particular 'time frame' or exactly 'action frame'. That's where the Power starts exerting its influence and those who have not experienced it before, will be surprised at first, but delighted afterwards.

An example may be more fruitful to you: a little insect in your world does not know what it is capable of doing until it starts doing xyz. It has to learn its way through handling little objects or twigs or leaves etc. The bigger insect, which has already been a little one but grew up, has now more experience in what he is doing and he'll cope even better. But when he sees another little insect, it thinks it's silly not to be able to do things well... *(My deep concentration means I have been very relaxed and now I cannot keep my eyes open any longer... and fall asleep!)*

I tune in again 2 days later.

BR- I apologize for falling asleep earlier and interrupting my communicator. He is welcome to continue his talk if he wishes. (He does exactly that at once, as if there had been no interruption- It still amazes me! Earth 'Time' is meaningless to them)

Essentially it's a matter of convincing oneself one can do it before assuming one cannot. It is not impossible for a 'young one' (insect or other) to do things older or more experienced Beings can do. It is just a question of believing it can do it and not mistrust its own abilities. If trust in oneself was paramount in whatever one did, there would be far more achieved everywhere, in any world or dimension! It is the usual reaction of thinking: "I can't (yet)" which holds back any Being, whether Animal, Human or other form 'elsewhere'. They all have the faculty to think one way or the other.

93

BEINGS OF MIND

BR- Is thinking the same everywhere, whatever 'the place'?

As you 'think', the Power comes out of yourself, your own Thought Power - That in itself is such a Creative Force, which you really have no idea about! It's so intense, it can do anything...

Yet it is not used enough within your own world!

As to 'other places', as you call them: there are so many **diverse ways of expressing that Inner Power, which is a constant Urge to express itself into some kind of Reality**, whatever that may mean, wherever it happens!

It's an Inner Urge to have more, better, different, intense and yet calculating if need be. **It cannot create without Intelligence behind and within it. It has to be controlled too, to be successful in its Creativity**. You cannot create 'things', let's say, which would be destructive to the Self creating it. So it has to have within it, a built-in Intelligence which directs the construction, the creation, the gathering together of the necessary components to make it a viable success. That **Intelligence** is not added to it from somewhere else, it comes **part and parcel of that Inner Urge and self-creating Power**.

The Creative Power is a multifaceted action pack if need be. An action pack, a pack of actions that feel the need and **Urge to be created**, as the idea of 'them' is emerging or even just germinating in some corner of the 'Thinking Urge' to create - or the Urge to think, which is in itself an Urge to create!

Create: that is the key to creation, obviously! But that implies the deepest **Urge to 'BE!** Be whatever 'being' can or may mean, wherever... This is what is so difficult and nearly

94

impossible to put across to those who read these words. Because of the intensity of this inner desire to have an outlet as, or into, any kind of 'structure': it is an endless representation of itself or a succession of representations, as they develop into more developments...

This is indeed mind-boggling at times and even always! But that needs to be known, to understand the world you 'know' is nothing compared to what could be known, if one could overview all the universes, the dimensions that could ever exist! A totally impossible task, of course! But understanding, or at least accepting, they do exist will make a dent into the narrow-minded conception of what Creation or Creativity is and means...

Our job here is to try to put across the view from an angle above and beyond the ones that may be seen, or heard, or thought about by Earthly Beings. Humans have not even come out of their shells so far, yet they think they can judge and work out a cosmos, of tiny dimensions within their instruments, yet in reality far bigger and forever unfathomable to them!

One must accept that all over the multi-Universes of physical or non-physical Matter, **there are Beings of Minds that have nothing to do with your own Earthly way of thinking.** Beings of Thought Power expressed in so many inexpressible ways, because there are no words for it! So, when it is accepted or glimpsed at, that there are far, **far more ways to exist than having a flesh body and a little Mind reduced to only thinking of materialistic thoughts**...then the door to REAL understanding starts creaking open gingerly!

It is not a criticism of Mankind as such: we have been part of it (when we 'trained' in order to understand Humans). It is a mind-opening exercise to try to encourage some people at least, to think further than what they are used to do. If they think: "Oh! There must also be something beyond all this, there can be things we'll have to understand and experience", then they do open their inner door to Knowledge.

95

It can be poured a little at a time, like with a dropper, into their gradually more receptive Minds, which will hopefully soak up the new information, as it seeps into the cracks made in the old ways of thinking... That's a slow operation but one really worth working on to improve Humanity - and its general attitude to what it does not know or refuses to even consider. We have your interest at heart, all of you. So we'd only give what you can take in, as you go along...

SSS

CHAPTER 12

BR- Can you please give more precisions about the actual creation & birth of Humans - How was the process started? You said 'pioneers' came to test various body possibilities, so they won't have come from sperm/egg mixture & birth from a female?

There is a difference between being 'born' straight from our world and the birth you experience on Earth, of course! This is what you are asking, isn't it? You want to know why the pioneers were not born as is done now and why and how it started. Well, we know the bringing of pioneers in the Earth world was a momentous event so to speak, because they were the first ones who could tell us, the 'Spirit' scientists, how things really were and how it felt to be in a flesh body etc. But the system had to be different for them - to project themselves in a flesh body they created with their Minds, because it had not really been done before and it had to be tried out.

The projection of Mind into a body still occurs nowadays even as we speak, but people are not aware of it! They think the egg/ sperm have created all there is to see in their body and some even think it has created their Minds! As you know, this is not so! 'Birth' had to be done differently 'later on' because there was not enough Energy supplied each time to project the whole Self into a whole (adult) Human. If people started doing that, you'd have an over population within minutes with people popping in and popping out at will, with no continuation, no link.

BR- Please elaborate on this?

Once the first pioneers had helped the creation of a 'finalised' flesh body, 'Humans' decided to come to Earth. The Human race could be started as such, because there was a finalisation of a constantly reproducible flesh body, in as much as it would have two arms and legs etc. Once the flesh body 'blue print' was finalised, it was decided the rest of Humanity will have to be organised, so that they can be controlled by a system of reproduction which allowed them to have links with each other.

BR- Why? All travellers can make friends or business or activity links, without any need to be related!

If it had not been so, you would not be here today. You have to understand the label of 'Human race' did not come right at the beginning. That was forged later when there was a race to speak of. If there had not been the Will to go and live on the Earth for the pleasure of it and to help each other there, there would not be a Human 'race' — but 'bits' of travellers, here and there, sometimes.

It had to become a more organised structure. There had to be some more defined pointers as to how the new venture would run itself smoothly, even though they definitely all had the universal Free Will. It had to be thought out differently simply because a self-contained system has to have its working parts in good order and working according to a plan, so that the self-regulating system could work more efficiently.

If there had been another type of structure, you would have had a different Earth life style. It had been chosen and decided as it is, because that is what was selected, planned and settled upon, all those millions of 'years ago'.

SEED TO MATURITY

Since that is what was determined, then **the plan was** set to start **from a seed to grow into a more mature form** of whatever was on Earth, from Plants to all Animals or Humans. No one was self-producing. It had to be through this system of 'egg insemination', or germination etc. because that is how it was set by the many millions of Minds coming to this conclusion, for that particular Earth life. If it was not going to be like this, then it would be done elsewhere and called something else!

We know you find that irritating and not 'logical' or whatever, but **we** have no say in why that was decided so! We are recording for your knowledge what actually happened, in order that you can not only know yourself, but pass it on to others, so that they do not imagine a tree was made by a 'deity' who had nothing to do with you or the tree as such.

You have to understand that the **Will to live in a flesh or any physical body** is the primary reason for **any** Being to come to Earth. Why they individually want to do it is their own, personal reasons and aims. If they had wanted to do or be something else, they could have gone elsewhere, among the many myriads of facets of the Universe**s**!

So there is no need to argue why this had been decided upon! It is more logical to try to understand how it happened in reality, compared to how it's alleged to have happened by 'magic of the gods' or some other fanciful fairy tales!

We know you want details. All we can obtain is by 'foraging' with our joint Minds and Wills, into the 'Facts Box' which records what happens all over, everywhere. It may not be so easy to put into words, you would realise, but we are trying hard to place this in a context you could understand, do you see?

This is why Mankind has chosen to become Mankind: Because the idea of living in this 'newly' created Earth was and still is fascinating to many millions and zillions of Beings with Minds in our world...and elsewhere if you want to be precise!

All Minds are linked. **All Beings all over the Universes are linked by the process of thinking, of having Energy within themselves**, which can produce creative results. So if you wonder why you have not seen weird and wonderful creatures other than what you know on Earth, it's because the pattern of living on Earth has been set 'long ago' and there is no way of changing it at will. As we were saying: there always are possibilities of doing things differently, but why do a mixture even bigger than what is there already?

CHOICE - NOT SURVIVAL OF THE FITTEST

BR- What were the first 'finalised' Humans like, physically?

All can be said my dear, has already been said earlier. The ones we see as 'finalised' Humans are the ones who chose the best and most suitable physical body for their trip into Matter. That was a certain **group of 'People' who chose the shape of those you see around you all the time**. They were not hairy apes or monkeys, because that was not needed. They chose to be smooth skinned, smooth enough, because it was more convenient than having hairy, furry bodies, as far as they were concerned. We do not know why some hairy bodies survived in the Animal world, because we have not looked into it... yet. But if you wish to know that, we could also investigate it. If you wish to know about Mankind, what was given to you above is the answer.

You have fossils of many ape-like men but they were not the finalised man. They were not even 'tries' to be men.

100

They were tries to be Animals who wanted to copy men!
The fossils you may have found on Earth as 'erectus' man, or whatever, are pieces of either Animals trying to be upright or bits which had nothing to do with a 'slow evolution of Mankind'. (Those which were found are very few compared to all those who have lived and disappeared!) The reality is that 'men/humans' of all shapes have come to Earth to try out possibilities but did not stay. The changes or so-called 'evolution' were **not** done by trial and error and 'selection of the fittest', but by *selection* of those pioneers who had 'popped over' and tried the Matter of flesh and its feasibility - then popped out of it and **told us** so in the 'Mind World', **so that the scientists working on the case would adjust the shapes and details.**

So there may possibly have been some hairy human-like Beings for a while but they not have liked it since it was decided eventually that Mankind should be more smooth-skinned.

BR- So you are saying Mankind did not stem from apes and monkeys swinging in trees?

As we answered that question before, you can look it up!

BR- Anything else you wish to say before I stop? (NOTE: By now I was really ready to stop and get on with what I had to do! So the reply given below was very unexpected and to me even more 'proof'!)

All that has been given to you now and above and before is for the enlightenment of Mankind as to its origins and its understanding of how it came to exist on Earth.

It has always existed as Spiritual/Energy Beings and has only chosen this temporary dwelling and cover or 'vehicle', as a practical way to live in that world of air, water and soil etc.

101

So, if there are some little bits of information which cannot easily be accessed to, at least for the time being, you have to realise that the 'time scale' of your 'years' may *prevent your scientists* from ever finding out properly!

On the other hand, *from here* where **we have access to the Facts Box or Eternal Records of all happenings,** you do not realise what gigantically huge task it is to try and plough through it, to determine what is in the end a very, very minute 'moment' or aspect of not only a developing and evolving world but also an **idea!** Because **the Earth creation was an IDEA!** The idea of putting Thinking Creative Energy Beings, in cases of flesh Matter, to see how well they could use more of their creative Energy, to make what turned out to be a 'life' in that new world...

So if every detail is not answered to your complete satisfaction, it has many reasons for possibly being so. It is very difficult and at times, very likely beyond the scope of our own grasp as well as yours. We'll do our best to find out as much as we can and we will still search for more. But this is said to try and reassure you that what has been given to you so far, is very genuine and told honestly, with only one desire at heart: the desire to spread the Truth... That's all we wanted to make you think about. You have not interfered with the results. You have listened and written what we told you all in good faith.

BR- I understand. Thank you very much for your efforts.

SSS

CHAPTER 13

BR- Could you tell me (again?) more about how "there is no 'Time' as sensed by Humans"?

An example may help you understand this strange and inexplicable concept of 'TIME' as you Humans call it. As you know, this has to do with the Sun and the Earth passage around it. But there is another level that should be considered. It is the fact that people focus on various angles in their lives. If they constantly think of what you would call 'past', in our world they would actually live it again - and that makes their 'past', present! So the **focus** is what matters: **FOCUS is the relevant key to the understanding of what feels like 'passing time'** to you.

If you saw ALL your thoughts literally happen 'now at the same time' as you think them, they would not be one after the other- they would be instantaneously now. But the fact that you often tends to focus on one thing then another, makes that slipping from one to the other **'create a distance' in your Mind, which you construe as 'Time passing'**.

BR- But such as historical events centuries ago, surely they are 'back in time'?

The time lapse you feel is due to the fact you are focused on this 'now' you see as your life - But the reality is that they took place as a side shoot of an explosion of events.

BR- Surely inventions show it - e.g. we could not fly in an aeroplane, now we can?

The explosion of events of Creativity and Thought processes leading to it, such as creating an aeroplane or a car etc. is due to the creative Minds of both people in your world and some in ours, who put their Minds together to lead to such improvements.

Yes, it can be seen as 'time lapse' since it produces something new that did not exist before... But the overall feeling of 'Time' in creation of the Universe is different. The time lapse between summer and winter is obvious, as the Plants look different. But the inner time lapse within the Plants is not felt like that! It is constant 'nows'.

If you took any Being from our world to transport him to another part of our Energy World, then you would see that he would find his way and would not be troubled by differences, as it would be recognisable to him. This is because those levels and areas are levels of Mind Power and Creative Energy. So, if he felt he had experienced one 'event' there, he would still be experiencing at the same 'time' whatever situation he is in - You would see the same in a dream. In your 'Reality' you are in your bed (a sleeping body) but at the same 'time' you are in the dream galloping around, living a new life and different lives, having days of travels etc. Yet you are not really doing so. As you travel through and into your Mind, you can be aware of many happenings, which have possibly their own various lengths of 'time', but you are not actually experiencing various time events.

SEEN FROM THE HUB OF A WHEEL

So in the same way, you would see the creation of your history events in the passing time of 'improvements' etc. but we cannot see them like that, because **we see them as all arriving as the same batch, all radiating as spokes of a wheel and we are on the hub.** We can positively say we, in our world, know that you Humans exist by and feel 'Time' passing, but *we* see all happenings and all possibilities happening. So, when the need to look into your 'future' happens, as you well know, **the only 'solutions' can merely be seen in those 'more probable possibilities'** *(NOTE by BR- It is vital to grasp and recall this point when asking psychics / medium to foretell future events)*. But when scientists say 'Time has no meaning' in our world, they mean we have a different point of view because **we observe things in a different way, from a different angle.**

SSS

PART 2

REACHING BEYOND
'the Spirit World'....

****

"The distinction between Past, Present and Future is a stubbornly persistent *illusion*"

Albert EINSTEIN

"I shall not commit the fashionable stupidity of regarding everything I cannot explain as 'fraud"

Carl G. JUNG

PART 2 - PREFACE

NOTE from BR - To help my readers understand better the context and circumstances of the next chapters, I need to explain a few things before sharing more dictations and knowledge received as Part 2 of *'Worlds Beyond the Spirit World'*.

TRANCE & INDEPENDENT DIRECT VOICE

The importance of pure communication from the 'Other Side' is constantly demonstrated in séances of trance and direct voice mediumship. **Trance** is when the medium's own Mind is 'put aside' while the 'Spirit communicators' step in and blend their own Minds with the speaking mechanism of the medium. That way, if the trance state is really and properly 'deep' (since there are various degrees and levels of trance, from light to deep and totally 'out'), if the medium's Mind is not interfering (as could happen if he, or she, is not 'out of the way'), then communication may be absolutely fascinating and enlightening.

But of course, even better than trance is 'Independent Direct Voice' communication. There have been umpteen genuine **Independent Direct Voice** communications over the past couple of centuries that are world famous and well-documented in the world of Spiritualism - amongst many, such as Leslie Flint in UK. Those are easy to look up on the Internet or in books and other publications- Recordings are available too in most cases.

In such séances, the scientists in the world of 'Spirit' have learnt to juggle the right amount of vibrations and various Energies to recreate a human voice, WITHOUT using the vocal chords of a human medium. They create an amazing and complex kind of 'voice box' or 'spirit loud speaker', made of interwoven vibrations, no doubt. It is an extremely delicate operation and takes several years of experimentations for the Spirit scientists to polish up and refine the results – then of course, individual communicators have to learn to focus their Minds and send memories clearly and strongly, as well as doing whatever else is necessary to handle the juggling of vibrations!

The medium's voice and vocal chords are not used, yet his/her strong but refined Energies (as a Being of Energy) facilitate the phenomena. But once success is achieved, there is no better evidence of survival than having your own departed loved one speaking to you —even with his/ her own voice if they can manage it — using characteristics phrases, mentioning private memories and letting their typical personality come through in the dialogues. That is NO fraud. It is extremely evidential and has been witnessed and tested all over the world, in supervised experimental conditions with impartial eminent personalities in charge.

So, the above is to give a rough idea of only *some* of the many feats that can be achieved by scientists in the World of Mind and Light beyond the limited physical world, in séances run by sincere and honest mediums. Their only aim is to help provide evidence of survival to the world of Humans who have forgotten they are Beings of Energy themselves, though ensconced in a flesh body. (If readers wish to find out more about *genuine* séances, I am including some titles in my recommended reading list, at the end of this book)

I don't have space here to expand more on that.

APPEX GROUP

I now only wish to explain my part in the experiments conducted in my own home. What had started years ago as a simple 'Open Circle' of mediumship development practice, soon became more special. My friends and visitors had come regularly as 'students' for a few years to practise with me and unfold their mediumistic abilities to 'give messages' to each other—communications which they would receive clairvoyantly, clairaudiently and clairsentiently from departed loved ones of the recipients.

As months passed by, we noticed that on some days we were receiving some more profound communications (from some teachers or 'scientific' speakers), of a philosophical and educational nature, for the group in general—whether through my own inspired addresses or via a couple of the other 'students'. They also hinted that scientists in the 'Spirit World' would like to try doing some different work with us, as our blend of Energies was suitable. It intrigued us.

Then, apparently 'coincidentally', as the group seemed to reduce itself to a few very keen regulars, the tone of the communications reached higher levels of knowledge. As we sat regularly weekly, two members of what became our dedicated group of six, developed even greater abilities at going into really deep trance. Over time that was polished more and more and we had an amazing array of various people talking through those friends: some departed needing help, others wanting to share their teachings and of course our loved ones 'visiting' us.

In-between, we were also asked by our Spirit scientists – who had made themselves known -- to allow them to try and work at finding ways to eventually and hopefully producing Direct Voice communications and manipulations of objects, if feasible. This being done by controlling and manoeuvring the kaleidoscope of vibrations that *we* emanate as a small group, as well as Energies in the room and those of the Earth, which the scientists in the 'World of Mind and Light' blend skilfully in numerous experiments. They asked us not to bring any more outsiders to the group, so that we were a 'closed Experimental Energy group'—which I suggested we called **'APPEX'**

(Ancient Physical Phenomena Experiment), since the use of Energies to produce physical psychic phenomena was the norm in very ancient times, until Mankind lost its focus and psychic abilities. After that, scientists in the 'Spirit World' had to invent and create what is known as 'ectoplasm', to help give evidence of survival via physical materializations and creating ectoplasmic 'voice boxes' for direct voice communications. *(See more explanations in 'Witnessing the Impossible' by Robin Foy, leader of the 'Scole Experiment').*

Our Spirit Team needs to get used to, analyze and juggle our individual Energies to assess what could be achieved with them when blended. When an experimental group consists of sincere, genuine friends like ours is — in harmony with each other (as this a vital component in Energy manipulation), and with a common spiritual goal devoid of ego and selfishness— wonders can be achieved by 'scientific Beings' from Other Dimensions, who know more than Human scientists on Earth. As time passed, we were happy to let them try what they could if the Energies in our room were strong enough.

But that is a different topic, as what matters now in this book, is the fact (among many happenings!) that at times, we noticed we were getting a different type of communicators through our trance mediums. The Spirit organisers seemed to use the combined Energies of our two trance ladies to help channel new communicators... who turned out **NOT to have ever lived on Earth**!

They were gradually introduced by a go-between (departed Human) 'Matthew' whose task was to be an Energy link for them and facilitate their approach and explanations. He described the few who came over the weeks as 'gassy' Beings, which puzzled us at the time.

Eventually some of those Beings, who obviously came from a world of **Mind Vibrations higher than just the 'Spirit World',** started sharing some intriguing information as to what they could do, even though they do not need a 'solid' body and never had one. They not only gave us hints of future events on Earth but also tantalising details about themselves; adding that much more information will be given "to and through the writers of this group"— as apparently that way would be easier for them, than communicating in séances and them having to send their thoughts to be transmuted into words by the trance medium's mental mechanism.

As I am one of the two 'inspired writers' in our group, receiving teaching from the Spirit World, I could not wait to ask my own communicators. What my Masters told me stunned me as much as it might surprise some readers. But I promised them to share their knowledge to whoever has an open-mind and is seeking to understand the truth about Reality.

PART 2 of *'Worlds BEYOND the 'Spirit World'* will need to be read slowly — It may feel quite challenging to most readers. This is simply because it reveals to us concepts and aspects that we, Humans, are not used to thinking about and have probably never been told about before. My Masters from the World of Mind are very aware of this — but, as they say, if those facts are never pointed out to Humans, no matter how hard to grasp those concepts may feel, how will we ever know what is really going on behind the **illusion of 'solidity and physicality' which we con ourselves with**?

Microscopes and Quantum Physics show us that what you think is a solid object is in fact very hollow, with atoms spaced widely apart! That seems mysterious to many people! Yet it is how our senses interpret what we see and feel that gives us an impression of solidity.

In the same way, the notion that we all survive bodily death and CAN communicate with the Earth once 'dead', is hopefully now understood by you dear reader, yet this is sadly still a shock and totally incomprehensible to numerous other Humans!

111

So, please do not give up if you can't quite grasp or visualize some passages: I find them hard too! But simply get the general idea that this information is genuine, such facts DO exist, and please always remember that Mind Power is a wonderful and extraordinary Force. Then please keep reading... as not everything is difficult to grasp... and there is NO exam to test you at the end!

§§§

CHAPTER 14

BR- Could I have greater detailed info about the communicator who spoke last week in my APPEX (Ancient Physical Phenomena Experiment) mediumship group (via Ellie in trance): Where' does 'he/she' come from/ which world/ which Beings are there etc. Also what are the 5th/6th dimensions she mentions?

*(BR- NOTE: I purposefully did **not** look up any information on Internet or elsewhere, about any possible 5th etc. dimension – which I knew nothing about — so that my Mind did not contain any preconceived ideas).*

There is something you need to understand clearly: It is not possible to describe in human terms things which are not man-made. So we'll do what we can, but do not expect highly 'scientific' terms as you'd call them, to explain things which have nothing to do with your Earthly world. It is very important you and our readers grasp this, because if you don't, you'll feel we are not giving you what you hope for: you cannot go and tell your human scientists that we give you an equivalent of what they would say, because they could **not** give you such descriptions, since those facts have no existence in your World of Matter, compared to finer levels of existence.

We'll start with the fact that you've received contact from other worlds before i.e. during your own 'séances', but you did not always realise how detached from your own world they are! They came to give you all a taste of what could be done and said.

The communications can be difficult at times, when they have to contact you and need to use terminology you grasp, yet which is not 'familiar' to them, in as much as **they do not use words where they come from**. So, we'll say this is to state that you've already had other contacts before. But we'll specify this more now. There was a 'lady' who came to talk before, who said she was "from beyond your world" - she was sensed by you all in the room as being of a finer nature and higher mental level than others who have 'spoken' to you.

BR- Yes, I remember that.

It is most important that you realise we encourage such Beings to come to you all-because it elevates the nature of our communications and Energy links between you, us and the experiments we want to achieve in those 'spaces of time' you allot to us (*during our regular 'experimental sessions'*).

We can also say that the latest 'personality' who spoke to you all had already been to your group before and is of the highest level of integrity and spirituality. 'Her' Mind is pure, wanting to help others reach more clarity in their purpose and clarity in their own understanding of who they are as Beings of flesh with a 'core' of 'Spirit' or Energy Being.

This said, we'll let you know that you need not fear any 'wrong' interference from other parties who have not got this level of spirituality and purity. We can assure you the aims of this exercise in communication is to ensure better links with Energy Worlds of the highest nature, to provide us (as scientists working with you) the best possible links and Energies for successful results in what we are planning to do with your own Energies. You'll be surprised and delighted when we succeed in our endeavours.

(*NOTE- These scientists are aiming at producing, one day, Independent Direct Voice in our APPEX group*). These explanations were to set the scene for you all, so that you understand there is no need to be concerned as to the genuineness of the communicators you may be involved with.

A THOUGHT WORLD

As to who 'she' is, we'll come to that. First, the world mentioned is not a physical world (like you know yours is). It is a different type of 'Matter' - yet it feels like solid Matter to them, though they **know** it is dissimilar to yours. We all know what other worlds experience and can compare. So they can compare what they have with your own Matter and with others too.

The world they have is not limited by solid boundaries as you *feel* you have on your Earth: it is a much finer substance that is not comparable to your world, so you'll have difficulty with grasping the exact nature of that 'other' world.

Did she say 'it is dusty and reddish'? Well, this is how it feels to those 'living' there. But they are not confined to it. It is a kind of 'centre place' from which they can project themselves elsewhere.

You'll need to imagine a big ball of light or even 'fire', which does not burn - a huge glow of intense light which **creates itself at will**. When that light thinks itself 'solid', it appears so. When that light thinks itself 'watery', it will be so. When that light feels itself light or heavy, it will be either! So you see, how can you conjure up what kind of world that can be? It is impossible for your human Minds to feel what it is like, as nowhere on Earth could you do such things!

When you think of 'other worlds' you Humans tend to think of some far away planet with variations on the Matter you are used to. So that's how far you can get - But beyond that, it would be near impossible for you all to get the gist of it. It is essential to think differently, ok?

115

NO BIRTH NO DEATH

To start with, there is no 'death' or even 'birth' in that particular world, because they do not stop existing as such - they ARE, they know they 'are', they exist. But the modulation of existence, the changes within possible existences, stem from simple mutations of thoughts. If they think one way, it will happen that way- If one Being thinks 'he' is a light feather, say, (to use Humans' words), 'he ' will feel he is. If he wants to be as heavy as a rock, he will be.

BR- Isn't this like in the 'Spirit' World?

That is true but in our 'Spirit' World as you call it, we have many people who have been, and are going, to the Earth world for their own type of experiment in that particular type of Matter. So we know what they have been and think they 'are'- and **gradually they have to shed those memories as Beings of flesh to recover & find again their true selves as Beings of Light.**

Those other 'Beings of Light' (like the one who spoke to your group) have got other agendas. They **have NOT chosen to be on the Earth,** they have chosen far more freedom of Thought as Beings of Mind. They really are Beings of Mind only. But that Mind Power is used in more various ways than you are using on Earth.

You are supposed to be using your Mind Power to see how far you can manipulate your type of Matter with it, including the Matter of your flesh body.

Those in **that** particular OTHER WORLD you spoke of, are more interested in feeling and sensing their Mind Power. They feel their thoughts and see them create themselves but this has a much wider range of actualisation and sensations. It is so that the very fact of thinking becomes SO real to them

116

that it becomes absolutely instantaneous - yet still real in their own understanding.

It feels utterly valid, not as if they were 'dreaming' like you do in your world. In theirs, ALL thoughts have such Life Power that there is no doubt they ARE definitely factual as the Beings are 'made of Thought'/ are as a Thought - they just 'ARE', without labelling themselves with any kind of Matter as you would. They are aware of existing fully. They do not need to 'see' themselves or each other, as they 'know' they all exist. It's a **constant inner knowing**, so there is no question or doubt about it! They do not need to wonder whether they are 'real' or 'exist'. They know they ARE.

Their aims and purpose are for an even finer unfolding, development and **refinement of their inner Mind Power** - that power being a hugely potent creative force, with myriads of facets as to what it can do. ALL of you have it, but you Humans have focused it too much, or much more, on to the material and its relationship with the material world, which surround you and your own body of Matter!

Those we speak of have no worries as far as 'material goods' and 'world' are concerned. The description of a dusty reddish world was not the best thing that could have been said, of course, as that can only be one of many aspects. That was an aspect that could present itself, *depending on what the thoughts were* about and the emotions & sensations behind them.

NO GENDERS

We can also tell you that the personality talking to you, though 'she' may have felt feminine to you is **not** that - 'she' came over as such as you had a subtle light Energy coming forward and blending with the Energy of your medium (a lady). So the result may have felt 'female-like' but it is not technically true, because as **the world 'she' comes from has**

no solid bodies of flesh like the Earth has, the personality is neither male or female or Animal or Human!

It is a blend of Energies which created that feeling for those who 'felt' it. Those *(in our room)* who listened, heard a voice created by the voice chords of the lady medium on Earth *(Ellie)* who is a gentle person herself (yet can be powerful too!). So the 'real' personality who contacted you is a Being of fine Energy, pure Mind, who has a great interest in what goes on elsewhere and has done so for a 'long time', by your standards. 'She' chose to link up with your world because **she wanted to experience what that type of communication is like.**

'She' is also an expert amongst many, in improving things thanks to the use of Mind Power. 'Her' speciality is sensing the flux and influx of many waves of Energies and sensing where they are going and why.

'She' has knowledge of what takes place on Earth, because 'she' **has been part of what was planned and created as an Experiment.** 'She' certainly is NOT a 'god' of any kind, in case some people may imagine this! 'She', like many others in her world, has a great interest in beautifully balanced and enhanced Energies. And any imbalance creating havoc is soon spotted.

So, those in her world have taken interest in helping those whose Energies are out of sync, as you say. Imbalances are never a good result in anything. All balancing is done by Mind Force. Thinking Mind creates. Mind means thinking. Thinking is the core of what Mind is. Mind being a 'non-stop creative force, as said before.

Therefore, we have those 'Beings of Intelligent Thinking Light' (if you want to describe it like that) who are very **interested in what goes on in many other places** - but the Earth (being one of their 'pet subject') is fortunate to have their attention!

BR- Have they 'always' existed in that world?

That world is only a make-believe environment for those who wish to see an environment at any given 'time'. But it is not really one of solid construction as we said before.

BR- But she talked of a 'different Universe/ being in-between Space'...

What we mean by 'Space' here is not what you Humans mean by Space. When you talk of Space you mean the expanse between planets, stars, galaxies and what fills your universe. We talk of 'Space' in a very different way. We do not mean anything physical of course. **Our 'Space' blends with any other 'space' so it is only a level of degree of intensity of Thought,** because you'll all have to realise one day that absolutely everything is made of Thought Power, Thought Energy- or if you like, 'Energy That Thinks'! That Thinking **Intelligent Energy is pervading everything** you can think of and even what you do not think or know of.

Therefore, that will have to be a starting point for those who want to grasp what we are talking about, no matter what 'world' you imagine all Beings come from. You have to get into your own Minds the concept of constant and instantaneous creation of what is conceptualised, what is thought about, what is imagined and so on. **The moment a thought germinates, it is on its way to create with different degrees of intensity.**

119

5th DIMENSION

BR- 'She' also said: "Changes have to do with the 5th dimension"...

This is of the utmost importance for your Earth world. You Humans have been ignoring for too long all the warning signs you've been surrounded with, but what shall happen will be for the best in the long run. This is because no imbalance can be tolerated for too long, since such imbalance is against all that is made or conceived in any Universe. All have balance at their very core.

So here we are, trying to rectify things for the Earth which was created superbly balanced. Yet its whole system had been knocked off its precisely organised equilibrium by the very people and Beings who were supposed to enjoy it and look after it!

The 5th dimension 'she' spoke of is at the very core and is the essence of what is needed: to bring back the 5th dimension in your world, the dimension of pure Mind Power, **pure balanced Mind Energy which is the Source of all Creativity** and creations - all are one, wherever. The Minds of very advanced Beings are used to bringing their power close to those who need it or where it is needed. Those Minds have the necessary focus and intensity to bring back the balance needed.

This has been infiltrated into the layers of intensity which form your world. The layers of Energies have to be rectified. Some have gone askew, we can see them, but you probably cannot. This is why those who care for uniformity, balance and equilibrium everywhere have chosen the task to rectify what needs to be. **Those Minds or Energies are very powerful and can slip into those Energy levels which have gone out of sync and 'knock' them back** not so much into 'place' as into the right frequencies or intensity, depending on what is needed.

120

We know you'll have difficulty in grasping the 'technical' goings-on from that side, as it is not something that can be done on Earth. The main points being: you cannot allow intense Energies used to such fine degree of creativity to be destroyed by sheer wantonness and selfish focus of Energy.

Those on Earth who have created the problems have used their Minds and powers and abilities wrongly - and created a world of fear and of imbalance on every level, from flesh bodies to 'Earth body'. You have spoilt so much of your physical world that you are bound to suffer from the repercussions! Not only now but later even more, as it cannot be rectified in one sweep of a magic wand.

It has to be 're-created' therefore reshuffled into place. And **all reshuffling creates upheavals**; it cannot be done otherwise! Hence the earthquakes, tremors, sea levels changes and more 'bad weather' as you call it. It is also part of the new **changes**, or rather renewal and rectification: what took centuries and millennia to create will not be done overnight. So, we know you'll all suffer somehow. But it will only be for the better. **Those Humans who do not want to be there when those events happen, will simply leave the Earth!** Why stay and be hurt if they don't wish to live through it?

What you call **5th Dimension is the capacity to use those Energies surrounding you and your own world to rebalance what needs to be.** The five senses are not good enough. It's the Mind Energy that needs to resurface very powerfully and bulldoze the rubbish created in areas where the harm is done; this is done by affecting the wrong ways of thinking and acting. The more harm is done, the more will those Energies be needed.

They will be **reshaping the mental attitudes** of those who want to listen and stay to improve things. Others will have to leave, or pay the price of possible suffering if the reshaping of the Earth balance affects their own physical lives.

121

All we need to tell you is that **the 5th Dimension is not so much a 'number' than an INTENSITY OF FOCUS from High Levels of purity of Minds willing to improve what has been damaged, so that the rebalancing is achieved** at long last. But the purity has also to seep into human Minds, not just the Earth's Energy! So all in all, it is a huge task that takes quite some 'time' on your scale.

As to the 6th dimension: that will be the next step so to speak. Except that both go hand in hand- one lead to the other automatically. What Humans would call the **6th Dimension** will be a world of pure beauty where Minds meet Minds - people's Minds meet other people's but also Animals' Minds. So **when all Minds meet and merge and you understand each other**, there will be no need to talk or send electronic messages via machines! You'll all understand each other with one thought, so to speak. All that will be simplified and purified. No more nasty thoughts, as you would not want to receive any either! You would all (hopefully!) have understood by then that what is thought sends sheer Energy around the sender, as well as the recipient. And all those around are also aware of it all. So **telepathy will reign** openly once more. It reigns now but in a way which is 'hidden' and not understood.

When all know what everyone thinks, won't it be easier and simpler to communicate - and definitely more 'open'? No one can be devious because nothing can be hidden.

That's the next step, which we hope will take place! But... there is a lot of Energy work to do first to achieve THAT kind of level. No more physical domination. Mind can rule again in a good way!

All meant to make things go back to what it should have been long ago — And used to be but was spoilt by the over focusing on material aspects, to the detriment of the magnificent creative Power of the Mind, misused by so many as 'time' went by.

122

DISAPPEARANCES

BR- The communicator also said "Some people will just disappear, not die, just vanish- with their physical bodies!"

The fact some people can actually leave (including their body) is nothing too extraordinary. This kind of things happen in your materialization séances, doesn't it? So why not elsewhere? The problem is that people on Earth find it difficult to believe and accept.

The flesh bodies indeed need to survive where flesh bodies are the norm. So those 'special' people who choose to dematerialize themselves, have no option but go on to other worlds where physical Matter of one type or other is acceptable. What happens is not the norm, since **Earth people chose the 'removing the-Will-out-of-the-flesh' way of leaving that flesh** covering. But there have been and are people who KNOW how to 'dematerialize' their flesh by willing it to 'melt away', so to speak, instead of them simply leaving it by focussing on some other level of thinking.

The dematerialization is not extraordinary, if you have seen such feat at 'physical séances' events. It is just a focus of Matter turning into 'invisibility to Humans'- but others could still see it if they are tuned in to the right levels!

BR- Why do that instead of willing yourself out strongly? No pain is needed so why not do it that way?

Out of the majority there is always a minority. So there is a small number of people who have done that and some who can still do it too. 'Why' you ask? "Because it can be done"... and they enjoy the fun and the mystery surrounding their invisible departure, the intrigue and supposition. They have a mischievous nature and enjoy the trick they play on those looking for them.

BR- That's cruel of them. It can be very sad and worrying for families looking for them!

What we are trying to tell you is that there have been many cases of People and even Animals disappearing 'out of the blue'. This is not an invention or imaginative fiction, it is a well-known fact. We explained that if they wish to go to places where their 'physical bodies' are acceptable one way or the other, there will be such places within physical universes. If not, they simply dematerialize for good. Otherwise, they dematerialize the visible section and rematerialize it 'elsewhere' where a physical body is normal even if not exactly the same Matter as yours.

BR- 1° Can you explain dematerialization and re-materialization elsewhere?
2° Please say more about other 'physical worlds'? It is in our universe? Who would survive there?

We can tell you the dematerialization is very easy for our scientists who have the knowledge of this type of Matter, which is yours at present. It is only a question of affecting and 'playing with' the various parts of a structure and increasing the level of vibrations. The view from here is totally different from what your view of a body is!

Now, as to what can be done and go where: it is just a question of intense focus and the right type of Matter. Many 'planets' as you call them, or celestial bodies and other physical bodies in your cosmos, are simply made of similar Matter – but you have no way of seeing what's on them because it's impossible for Humans to reach them. You may say: why don't such 'vanished people' vanish to a known planet: Mars or the Moon etc? But is it where they want to go?

124

What is not seen does not mean it is non-existent! So when those bodies 'disappear' it does not mean they no longer exist. But *why* they have gone is more useful to know, than how. Because 'how' is self-evident to those who can do it. If you were in our world, you'd see Beings being apported from one place to another. Whereas *why* **they do it is to do with the mental attitude** of the owner of the flesh body! Such fun to vanish to the eyes of their 'pears' and fun for themselves! This is how they portray their reasons - also "because they can do it"! Not everyone would know how to do it. It takes quite a lot of Mind Power and know-how, but the actual 'dematerialization' is not such a problem? It is feasible.

But you wonder about 'afterwards', what does the body do to survive? The owner would go to another world of similar Matter. It is a problem for you to understand, not a problem for us to explain. What you need to grasp is that many other 'physical worlds' exist in your Universe - far beyond what you can see or reach and possibly even within a reachable distance if you had the right machines.

Yet, the existence of the flesh body is not so much what matters, since it has **always been the reflection of the mental attitude of its owner**. So if the owner wishes to change its attitude and way of thinking, he could make his body survive without all the pampering that he would give it on Earth. It is a body of Matter created by Minds, remember! It has been used to living off plants, water etc. but it could be trained to do without that, should it need to - so it should not be such a worry. Many people have lived for months onwards without eating. But your civilisation has forgotten about that! We do not see it as a problem: all can be done with Mind Will Power!

125

That's the best answer we can give you, as this is what happens everywhere: using one's Inner Creative Power! Make the world understand *that* - and you'll have won a great battle and achieved great results!

SSS

CHAPTER 15

BR- Could you please tell me more about the communicators who came from some 'other world' to speak to our APPEX group (Through Ellie's trance), and who said they'd "tell us more via the channelling writers of our experimental circle". Since I am one of the writers, I'd love to be able to get some information.

All of those who spoke to you at your home séances are **Beings who come with Love and Peace** in their Minds and 'hearts', because they want to help you all find those qualities in your own Selves and help you spread it in your world. We know this is true. We want to point this out, so that you realise they do not come 'just for a chat', but they **have a purpose to impart those qualities** from the use of their Energies poured into the Earth's atmospheric levels and the vibrations which sustain the Earthly world. **We** (as your 'go-betweens') have the task of disseminating their knowledge by helping you acquire it and pass it on to all people susceptible to be interested.

We have 3 points to make:

1*- You have to be very relaxed to acquire and receive the information which will be given to you with much love and interest in your well-being and your world.

2*- You have to be trustworthy - you must not squander or waste what is given to you. If received with the respect and recognition it deserves, the knowledge will be of much use not only to yourself but to all those you'll pass it on, for the good of Humanity.

3*- This is not a game, not a 'competition', not a challenge between writers or communicators. This is REAL knowledge, which is 'different' from what you have been told so far. We are opening a new chapter in your receiving what we wish to pass on. So we can start now.

BR- Who are 'WE'?

'WE' being the two main personalities you are used to, who have to '**CHANNEL' FOR YOU WHAT those 'superior external' Beings wish to pass on.** We need to not so much monitor than 'sieve it' into words that you can understand and accept in a format which makes sense to you.

That Knowledge cannot just been poured at you the way we receive it! It would not make sense to you, as it will be impressions, symbols and connotations unknown to you.

All that is needed from you is peace, quiet and a great focus in this simple task: receiving our words! (In case you wondered: We know what we are talking about, as we are simply passing on what is being explained to us all, most of which we already knew as we had to make sure we 'studied' the topic!)

Look at the sky. *See* what there is **not** to see visibly! Look at it in-between the stars and the planets. Look at what 'space' is *really* made of: not what you Humans imagine it consists of!

All those points are enough to make your mind boggle, aren't they? How can you see 'in-between' what you cannot see etc?

SPACE TEXTURE

Well, the simple texture of what exists in 'space' is not understood by Mankind! **The notion of 'space' having a texture** may sound very weird and incorrect to those who do not know what we know and experience- as the very word

128

'texture' makes you think of some kind of cloth, or wood, or other substance you could touch... We are talking of **texture that can be sensed with the inner senses -** that's why it makes it difficult for Humans to comprehend.

Life has a 'texture'; Life is not a sperm or a seed. **Life is the impulse** which keeps everything going on and on and on... So the Life impulse is not 'feelable' with fingers of flesh but with your inner senses when you are relaxed to the maximum. Then you can experience it superbly!

What we are talking about is more **to do with the inner side of 'Space'** than the outer part where you travel with your rockets etc. We can acknowledge the difficulty in grasping such a flimsy aspect that is not visible to you. But the **Energy side of it all has always existed...** and if that could be understood, it would help a lot!

What would you like to know about Space? This is what matters. **The link between Space's inner vibrations and Minds' inner vibrations is very important**! Minds can link into and with what you know as 'Space' but it not the summum of it all!

When Minds make the effort to be relaxed and focused, they can go through and pierce the superficial aspect of 'space' and **go deeper into Space's inner aspect**. Yes there is one!

THERE reside **many levels of concentrated Energies, which have never really been discovered or understood by Humans.**

Those levels of Energies are NOT physical in any way at all. They have resonance with lots of others - and **together they produce many more vibrational Energies which help worlds and Beings to be created at** (their) will... We are talking of Energies which make worlds and dimensions exist in a way none of you would understand, because you are not experiencing it on Earth.

So those levels will be extremely important because without them, nothing mentioned above would exist! You need to have a **tremendous amount of Energy to create worlds or Beings,** and that's what we are talking about.

BEINGS WITHOUT SURROUNDINGS

The Beings you have briefly encountered in your house *(during our APPEX group)* over the recent days are such Beings coming from worlds which have nothing to do with your Earthly world of this type of Matter. There are worlds which may seem to exist to whoever 'resides' there, but their world may not appear real, not 'solid' to another Being, you understand?

So, we are saying: **those Beings who came to talk to you have NOT been to your Earth in any Human or other shape. THAT was not the kind of Matter they wanted to experience. They are 'from-Beyond-what-you-think-of-as-the-Spirit-World',**

Theirs is the *imaginary* world of **their** particular existence. They invent where they are as they go along. They do not need a permanent 'solid' place like you Humans do: Humans need to have reference points — for example: "I am home. I am on holiday away from home etc".

We have here Beings who are not interested in that kind of 'décor' or not depending on their current 'surroundings'. Where those Beings come from one can invent what one likes, but one does not need to have 'a setting' round oneself.

This specific 'world' of those particular Beings has been 'created' by themselves in symbolic ways; so what looks 'red' to them or you, may not so much be a real colour as such, but **vibrations which represent the force they were exuding** at that time... If their 'sky' was blue, it was a blue of healing or a blue of peace- rather than a blue created by light rays like you have on Earth. Do you understand?

130

So this is the basic thing to understand: what you may see or sense clairvoyantly — when talking to them as they speak through the medium's trance — does not automatically correspond to what *you* Human would see or sense if this was happening on Earth.

If we tell you some Beings have a 'green appearance' it is not because they have a 'green' body of any kind...but because **their Energy** at that particular time of your focus or our focus, is the *vibration* of a green colour in *your* world, but **not necessarily a similar meaning** in theirs. It could be the correlation between two other Energies, which make them, look 'green' or they may think 'angrily', for example.

So, it is more difficult to explain to Humans things they do not experience with their physical senses or man-made instruments. If we could say: "We have a male entity with blue hair which is not really blue but implies he has a lot of healing Energy pouring out of his so-called 'head', you may be a bit confused! Yet that's the way we'd need to explain things!

So now we'll tackle the **main points** we wish to cover:

Point 1- is to deal with all that is *outside* your Earthy experience. That is only of some use to you all if and when it can be related to your world and your visible universe.

Point 2- is to do with what *is not at all visible* to you or your instruments, yet exists in an unordinary way: the substance of 'Space' is not something one talks about every day, yet it exists.

If Point 3 looks obscure, it is because it will deal with **Beings you had no knowledge of, and of worlds which have nothing to do with anything physical** in your Human sense. But their existence is nonetheless real and **they can be in several places at the same time**, without any particular or huge effort.

All that is mind-boggling but real. It's about time we showed you even in a very small way, what can exist which none of you may be aware of!

131

ESSENCE OF LIVING

It is the **Essence of Living** which matters, not how it shows itself in various forms or not!

The Essence of Living means: **the way pure Loving Energy can transform itself into so many events as well as Beings**! Yes, events. Because 'events' are thoughts made 'real' to those who experience them. So, events are 'Beings' of a kind since they are created by Thought, in the same way as thoughts are used to create various kinds of Beings: from thought-forms to Beings of Light, to Beings of many facets, yet as ONE ubiquitous 'ball of Light and Energy'.... which will mean nothing to you, probably, as this is very difficult to comprehend!

ATOMS 'BID FOR FREEDOM'

You Humans will need to open your Mind to accept such new and diverse information. We see things so differently from you all!

If you were in a huge balloon-like device where you could see Space all around you in one go, you'd notice there is no limit, no 'edge' to it of course, at least from your point of view. If one could probe deeper into it as Humans see it, it would seem endless and 'thick' with stars, planets and other bodies- but also with lots of 'space emptiness' in between.

That's where you start going wrong, because the **emptiness is not empty. It is packed with the densest concentration of Energies you could ever imagine! It is that very Energy which keeps everything else going**.

This is probably no news to your scientists, but it still is a mystery because they don't know what makes the suns, stars, planets go on their path! They think it is some kind of explosion which started it all and the momentum of it is carrying on... We could say: If it was true then the dissemination should be over by now, all scattered completely out of sight! But it is not.

132

We see things very differently because we know that the start of those particular stars etc. was meant to be: **it was planned,** it was not accidental. This is what **we** explained to you in our first book *(Truths, Lies & Distortions)*. Therefore, we will now have to help you 'look' deeper in between those 'places', those objects you see (or not) hurtling around and about.

This is where it becomes so much more complicated. We'll try and simplify things to explain to you that **the accumulation of Energy of each body of Matter in your particular Universe is not what your scientists may imagine: It is a 'bid for freedom' on the part of each component of each particle** which has been created: **Each particle of the new Matter 'wishes' to leave its 'enclosure' – enclosure of the whole body.**

So, we see lots of Energy escaping all over the place in a kind of whishing movement because the kinetics reaction is always the one winning. It has to be a reaction to other, similar (or even dissimilar) particles.

This is to try and explain that **we see the Inner Energy of every speck 'fighting' for its freedom and escaping from others' influence.** That creates friction and attraction and repulsion. And the end result is a mounting build up of **Energies which have an Urge to BE ELSEWHERE** all the time: they cannot stay where they are; they end up moving onwards and forwards. It is not because they are kicked into action, it is more because **their Inner Urge for independence and freedom** gives them the impetus to try and shake themselves off any restriction.

BR- I am very sorry but I'll soon have to stop as I have a mediumship group to go and teach.

We can stop at any time - we have no 'long or short' time here! We'll just say we'll cover more topics in greater detail as soon as you can come back to us. We are pleased to have started but it won't make any nefarious difference to us to stop now. We can resume when you are fit and ready.

SSS

CHAPTER 16

We have here someone who wants to talk to you to explain several things. As you listen well, you'll get more advanced information.

Those explanations are not easy to give because we have to reach the Minds of all those readers who will try to understand - not all can grasp very difficult concepts, so we try to minimize and simplify those facts – but perhaps you think they are *too* simplified and do not make much sense?

To sum up what we said so far: The Minds of all the Beings on Earth and elsewhere have one thing in common: they are made of the same 'substance'- i.e. not a physical substance of course, but the **Essence of Energy, the Original and Eternal Energy bathing all that exists**.

So, if you **think of an Energy as a kind of Light** (as that may have more meaning to you all) then you'll grasp better that **you can have light with different intensities -** because of the current given out through the bulbs, say. Therefore, any intensity that can be increased or reduced has its importance regarding the environment and area where the lamp or bulb is. This is why we want to use the example of light, because you have shadows and no light in places.

If you shine your light on an object, you'll blind it with brightness- but the area nearby will not be as bright if the light is very close to and very focused on one object - the areas nearby will not have received that focus and intensity and will be more 'shady' or less bright - i.e. more blurred, if you see what we mean. Why do we use this example?

Because **in any Mind there are areas and degrees of Intensity**. When you do not concentrate as intensely as you could do, you'll have less clear, less bright, more blurred parts, which will not pick information as well as, say, sometimes when you focus perfectly well. We use the idea of focus and intensity of light here, so that you get a better idea of our analogies.

But when you talk of Energies forming Universes and the 'Space' between physical objects there, you need to grasp and never forget that **MIND created those 'objects', those planets, those galaxies etc. The Minds of all those Beings planning those creations** for whatever reasons!

So **IF** there was less Mind Focus at times, or if the Energies became rather diminished or dissipated, there will be areas when the focus won't be as strong, where the blurring will occur, where the intensity won't be as fierce. That means **the probability of creations with a more 'shadowy' or 'blurred' side**—which is what we are coming to.

If you have less Intensity in certain parts, the Energies will be lessened - And if the Intensity of the Energies is lessened, **the power to drive them onward will have also been lessened.**

So, **the equilibrium or balance will NOT be as evenly produced and spread out as should be**.

This is all to do with the lessening of the Intensity of the creative Mind Force.

That could happen because all Minds have that weakness now and then. There cannot always be one steady, regular Intensity. **There will be phases or times when there is a weakening of its Focus**. And that's why we have to explain it so laboriously!

136

BOOSTED CREATIVITY

But when the Focus returns, **the BOOST given to rectify things will bring about a burst of Focus and Intensity and Force.** When that happens, the **power doubles** or triples or whatever- but the result will also be noticeable, because the Creativity caused by it all will increase!

So **the burst and boost will increase the Creativity**, yes? That's why **there are phases of 'on/off' happenings**. That's why the Earth (as well as other places in the Universe of the Matter you 'kind of know' of) has many times been up and down and round... It has had upheavals and that's well known. **When the boost intensifies, the burst of Energy rebuilds, re-establishes what had previously weakened.**

When it was weakened by human or other interferences, it will still be re-boosted.

When caused by the original creative Minds of those who backed the creation of the planet, the Intensity will be restarted and the improvement in the structure and environment of the planet will be reactivated. That's why there are so often upheavals and alterations and rebalancing etc.

When this has been done and **the equilibrium restored and the Intensity recovered, the overall feeling is or will be a vast improvement and a huge 'sigh' of relief within the planet.** You Humans won't see it of course. But as the creators of that combination, of that structure, of that 'invention', we know what goes on- and this is what needs to be understood. When there is a **'sigh'** (i.e. *rebalancing or levelling of all inequalities within the Energy field*), there is a lull, a kind of *peace and quiet within Energy movements*- and **that is where the Inner Spaces come into.**

IN-BETWEEN PAUSE

The blurring of Intensity had caused the necessity to readjust things, reactivate what had diminished. So the lull created by the rebalancing and the 'feeling' of renewed evenness made the gap between high Intensity and low blurs, a 'haze', an **Inner Space** *within the Intensity of the power* **of the Mind Energies**.

What you don't grasp, it seems, is that 'feeling'. It is NOT a feeling like you know feelings, because you equate them mostly with emotion or physical senses. It is not quite like that.

That' feeling' **is a state of perpetual motion brought to an 'hesitation' stage with slowing down and diminution of Energy-** Then the re-boost takes everything back to its original perpetual, regular motion. *It is an in-between state,* which can be equated to the movement of a pendulum with a hiccup caused in the middle of the swinging - then it has to recover, get back to its original regular swinging. **That LULL is the Inner Space within 'space'** you know.

'SPACE': POWER STORE!

The **'Space'** you know is sheer Intensity - sheer **Intensity of Energies of all kinds,** some your scientists on Earth don't even know of.

That 'Space' has been created to be where it is, so that **out of it one can produce various OTHER Energies and Matter if need be.**

As **Matter gets produced by Thinking Minds with elaborate projects**, the Space you have there is not a solid projection nor is it a hollow empty one; **It is layers of various Energies where Power is stored for more activities —** whether 'now' at the time of any happening, or 'later' for more development.

*(BR- Note- They added their aside **to** me: "When this (chapter & book) is completed you'll see it makes sense! As a human world would not grasp how to do it, we need to make sure the simplification is meaningful. What you have and need to do, my dear, is simply to listen and we'll do our best to come up with convincing clarification if we can manage to do so!"*

CONTROLLED PROGRESSION

What needs to be understood is that to have Inner Spaces is essential, because **the Inner Spaces within the Energies of the Universes are of great importance.** If there were not those ***Inner Spaces of reduced Intensity followed by a recovery*** (a second breath and a re-equalisation or rebalancing), you'd have chaos and alteration, but not good alteration - you'd have anarchy rather than equilibrium for progression.

Progression within balance, THAT is some feat to keep going and achieve! We have to have progress in as much as what grows can grow, yet you don't want what grows to develop out of proportion, so that the lot makes nonsense of it all!

So, **progression, but equalized and controlled,** without being altogether squashed. This is where the *lessening of Intensity* of the Creative Mind comes into. It had to be so. It was planned. It was not a fault in the system. **It is part of the system!**

When you have twice as much Energy coming out every second, say, YOU'LL EXPLODE! If you have a regulator you don't explode, even though you got to the near limit - the release valve helps. That's what the inner blur comes into, the Inner Spaces. **Within the whole Universe of this world of Matter that you know, there is an Intensity reduction on and off as a release mechanism**- and that's what many people do not understand.

This release system has been **provided from the beginning of the creation of THAT Universe.** It was NOT

139

one big bang explosion of one kind of Matter that spread out with scattered bits all over, willy-nilly. It was **a well-planned eruption of various types of Energies, of different nature, so that the whole was well balanced.** Each part had and has its part to play. Each 'object' was *placed* there to keep the equilibrium going. The juggling of those levels of Energies and Intensities was, and still is, tremendously delicate as it had to be ever **so precise** for the whole system to work!

What started it was the Will and Desire to create a new kind of Matter. There had been Matter created before, for other purposes. But THIS type you know of is a different kind, which allowed the manipulation of it by the MIND **as well as** using physical senses! The results have been excellent in some cases as Mankind and Animal-kind and Plant-kind learnt to practise those new skills; but the overall aim (as you've already been told) was and still is**, to make attempts at creating within one's own physical world.**

The Mind is used to thinking of new ways of producing physical situations and objects and ways of elevating one's condition there. **But never was it considered to use it to hurt other inhabitants!** That was never planned or wanted or attempted!

INGREDIENTS OF CREATION

So the 'Inner Spaces' we started our explanation with, are simply to explain that the outbursts of Energies produced to materialize what you wanted to see as 'physical' on your Earth, had to be produced in certain ways to keep the Earth world where and as it is - but with the prospect of improvement if need be!

What we planned on our side (away from the physical Matter arena) was finalised and projected from our Mind Energies, to the forefront of what would become your Universe. **A thought projected becomes 'real' as it is**

WILLED into the physical Matter matrix or template, do you understand?

What was to be the mould has been thought out, planned with our Minds... and projected with Intensity, Desire and an Urge for it (whatever 'it' is) to exist as a 'physical' (to you!) thing, or place, or body.

It's all to do with **Mind Power, Will Power, Intensity and Desire.** All those are the ingredients for the creation of anything!

When the Mind Beings in charge made the 'place' to be the arena of your lives, they had the foresight to make sure it could survive and stay balanced within a programme of restrained and controlled progression, yet allowed to expand at will so to speak. So the successful results mean there have been many worlds of Matter created within the same Universe.

BR- Is it the same or a different type of Matter?

Within your Universe you have only one type of Matter- what you Humans know of. But there will be other things you do not know of and cannot be aware of, as it is beyond your knowledge and most of all your familiarity. You Humans cannot recognise something you have never seen.

So you have a certain type of Matter, that's all you need to know. It is of no great importance to discuss it since you are aware of it anyway- but what we need to draw your attention upon is the kind of **invisible or unknown goings on** which maintain the whole structure steady (in the sense of 'not vanishing'), yet progressing at its own pace for its own reasons.

When the Earth itself was created it had to be so, it had to be as was done. It could not be done otherwise- or else it could have failed to become what it became. It was shaped as should be and consisted of what was needed to flourish as should be. As this is obvious we won't give details! But the inner 'destruction' as you may see it, is in fact a **construction**!

141

DISASTERS = RECONSTRUCTION

Each time you have an earthquake or a volcano, it builds or rebuilds, even though it may be seen as destroying. What is not clear in Mankind's Mind is the **purpose of the existence of the Earth**. It was certainly not an 'accident'; it was not a mass of jelly or a sea of magma or ambers. It was planned as one plans carefully a **very elaborate construction**. So the final result makes is all worth it!

If there have been upheavals within the construction, it was meant to be to 'warm up the engine', to 'fire up its pistons' as you say - and to **create outward an equilibrium of various substances which had to keep all on it surviving happily, in a balanced environment. And most of all, a renewable environment.**

You could not create Plants which lasted forever and ever. So they had to be renewable. Hence **the 'magic' of Plants growing and disappearing and reproducing** themselves! Mankind could not reproduce itself that way but could do the same thing in a different way... Mankind has come back many, many times - each time with renewed and sustained vigour! *(Reincarnation!)*

What is needed now is for the balance to be maintained and renovated when the Earth requires and says it needs **to renew it** – not when Mankind decides to destroy everything there is, without thinking what it is doing, simply because its ignorance of Reality is enormous!

What you have to ask is: why are you all (or nearly) bent on damaging what you have got- instead of maintaining it on its perfectly constructed path — conducted by the invisible, not physical Minds of the Creative Powers engendering all those creations of worlds of various Matter or dimensions?

142

Everything is to do with Mind Creative Power. All is to do with THAT Energy. That and only THAT! This is what creates from the simple spark, to the mightiest explosion, to the most wondrous creations of the myriads of ideas and their actualization and materialization... What else is there to say?

MORE THAN ONE 'SPACE'

We speak a lot about Inner Spaces and Space in general, as we are very interested in this topic. That's because there is a lot to say to dispel errors and misconceptions Mankind had or may have, since they usually only see the surface of the material world—as the inner aspects will never be available to them until after they come here, to see it from a new point of view and with our knowledge. So if we bring the topic up again, it will be to continue with a few extra points, which will be of benefit to you and any of your readers.

There is not 'one Space' as you see it. There are scores and scores and more of 'other Space' or Spaces since there are more than one. It is rather awkward to try and explain something you will never see from the Earth; but it can be done if you and the readers open your Minds as you read this.

As you see Space from your world of the Earth, you all realise you only have an extremely limited angle and point of view- and none of your clever telescopes will ever reach the 'end' of Space, for a very good reason: there is no 'end'. So the drama of falling over its edges is now gone (If you worry of such things you really need to think of something more worth worrying about!).

SSS

143

CHAPTER 17

We know all this sounds weird or even a childish way of explaining; but we have to come down to bottom level of simplicity to try and make the general idea clear! So, what you see has many other things going on under the surface. **In between those particles of Matter forming a planet or an asteroid etc. there will also be lots of other forces pulling one way or the other. This is what we are reaching: the under layers of the 'Inner Space'.**

Inner space' is not a 'solid' place of course - It is the dimension where Thought Power is felt more than on the physical creation.

BR- How can it be Thought Power?

Because Thought Power has always been the first and foremost Force which has driven anything created into being activated in a particular realm. So, **Thought Power or Mind Power is the background Force to anything existing.** If you were to deactivate anything existing (assuming you could!), you'd have a huge release of the Thought Power Energy that created it!

BR- How would it show itself?

That massive release could or would be felt as a powerful sweep of 'a release' feeling but thousands and millions of times stronger than you could imagine! We want you to try and understand 'Inner Space' as that is the clue to Other Worlds' entrance.

What we call **'Other Worlds' are not other physical worlds** (which do exist at times) but **entrance to the Inner Thought Worlds**. Those Thought Worlds take no space 'solidly'. So, they do not intrude on each other physically. They do not pile up in a corner as a pile of bricks. **They are overlapping and mingling**. If they blend with each other, it is without interfering with one another. Within those realms there will always be a smooth set of invisible rules: they can live with each other.

FORMATION OF ENERGIES

Why do we need to talk about those spaces and **Inner Spaces?** Because this is **where the formation of beautiful Energies take place and where Beings can be created out of them**, without causing an uproar or upheaval. It is done smoothly and simply, because **thoughts get implemented and applied to the creation** of whoever or whatever.

Those Inner Spaces are the key to what you call UFOs. They are the basis from where all expand... *(Deep relaxation and concentration make me doze off for a short while. When I resurface my dear Communicators are still there...)*

BR- While I dozed off, did you by any chance 'upload' any sentences in my Mind and Soul that you could 'pour out' easily now?

This is an example of Energies pouring out of its structure. A Mind can escape at any time, whereas a body cannot. Your falling asleep is the result of your Mind 'shooting out' or more exactly focusing elsewhere, not giving its full attention to the flesh vehicle.

So, if your Mind can do that, think what happens when the creative Energy, the Thought Energy focuses elsewhere!

145

That lack of focus disintegrates the physical because **the physical particles are actually kept together, cemented, by the Energy of the Minds which created them.** The moment the focus is altered, the physical will not be doing the same as before...

BR- (protesting) But my body did not disintegrate!

Your body resisted the disintegration because each of its particles had a Will and Urge to stay together where they were! But if they had the Urge to give up this coagulation, they would have fallen apart into a heap of particles soon degenerating and collapsing: that's what 'death' is about!

BR- Ok. Please carry on with your explanations about Inner Spaces etc.

We are telling you of the importance of all **Inner Spaces.** If all Inner Spaces were joined together, you'd never have room for them in your own physical Universe because (if they took space!) they would fill it all and more**!**

FOCUS & INTENSITY

It is an intense level of focus from the Minds which reach it. You need to understand that **levels of Minds, i.e. levels of focus, are of the UTMOST importance** when it comes to grasping the difference between simple passing thoughts (as usual for Humans) and **deeper, more profound concentration on deeper and faster vibrations.**

As the Mind focuses on higher and faster vibrations, it expands more and more and more and reaches very fast vibrations itself. As it reaches such higher levels, it swings to turning its own vibrations to faster 'speed' you could say, or frequencies. It is really all to do with **the Intensity of the Focus as it expands -** So the vital point here is: **the FOCUS of any Energy (which Mind is) is essential and paramount.** Even small atoms and sub-atoms have got their own focus, would you believe!

Therefore, we repeat, **it's all to do with Intensity, Direction, Inner Urge and Focus**. We know all this may sound strange, but we need to spell it out from the basic level. Basic level = everything and all are made of Energy, therefore they all have a focus to exist one way or the other. When that **Focus is accentuated because the Inner Urge has increased or is increasing, then the Focus speeds up and the intensity increases**. And when that's happened, there is no stopping!

If the Intensity decreased, the momentum would be slowed down, any actualisation would be interfered with one way or the other. So we are saying: **all increases of activity stems from the increases and the MAINTAINING of that fundamental FOCUS.** Point one.

BEDROCK

When that happens, the **inner levels get created**. That means: When the vibrations levels have increased (and are maintained) they have an 'aura' of Energy around them, or so it would seem to you. All **those vibrations emanate even more sub-levels of vibrations. They resonate and form a kind of glow or cocoon of some light, some Energy around themselves. THAT is then the bedrock for what is to come next,** if it is followed.

As the 'cocoon'/ the aura glow/ expands, its own Energy level increases and that becomes even stronger when the intensity of all the others add to it. This is why **all Energies must have a 'bedrock', a stemming point from which the results can be built upon**. Make that your Point 2.

If you took a bandwidth of your light and pushed is against a wall of rock, it would expand, spread sprawl out. It would not disappear into the rock, would it? So, as we spread out those Energies we spoke of, we see the results.

If you want to take *another example*, think of the sea. If you have a large wave coming onto a soft sandy beach, it will spread out and even ripple further and further, until the momentum slows down and runs out.

So we can say in the same way: if you have more light than usual you could make it spread out very far and let it spread widely to 'thinning' level at the edge of its display.

Why we explain this is because to comprehend the system and process of inner levels and spaces, you need to **grasp how Intensity and Momentum and Focus are so important**. You need to understand that **the more Focus and Intensity** there is, **the more there will be a spreading and expansion of the vibrations** which came and composed it.

URGE

So, while Intensity and Focus are vital, there is also Inner Urge. **Intense Inner Urge: Urge to do, or BE, Urge to go, Urge to... anything!**

That is why it is impossible to explain very simply such complicated (for a Human) intricacies within the system of our vibrations- invisible to you but visible to us! Not 'our' in the sense of our 'Spirit World' but 'our' in the sense of You on Earth versus 'the Rest'. We are only the mouthpiece, to explain what is explained to us in far greater details, which would drown you even more if we tried to give them.

So that's why as **Focus permits an increase of Intensity, and Intensity permits an improved Focus,** the combination of both allows wonders beyond the Earth world's wonders!

148

If it was well understood by your scientists, there'd be no problem, but would they understand? If you want to grasp what we mean by Inner Spaces you'll have to put up with elaborate explanations.

That was the hardest bit, so to speak. If only we could make it simpler it would be good!

Those Inner Spaces we talk about are not physical places stuck or slipped in between layers of your so-called 'space' in your (limited to you) Universe. It is not like that. **They are sections (or levels,** to be clearer?) **within the Minds, or more exactly within the Creative Focus energising the whole existence of everything. Within the Mind of each of its components is the actual Creative Energy which had the Urge to exist.** Is that clear?

So, **within that Creative Energy resides and resided the utter Urge to BE**: to be whatever it was going to be. But the moment 'it becomes' what it was going to be, there resides and springs up 'another' Urge of wanting to be more than that! You see?

Therefore, it means a constant increase, **an eternal expansion and crescendo in Urges to expand, side track, divert** etc! **It is always going 'to BE' but each 'time' with another aim or improved aim or renewed aim or a new 'vision'**...

So this **whole Universe** of yours and all the others, are **filled to the brim and utterly composed of those constant and constantly increasing Urges, wanting to be more and better!** This is why it makes things complicated when we try to explain in simple words for you and others to grasp it.

As **other worlds of Mind exist,** and you do not know it, we need to explain why and how they can exist - even if nobody realises and understand. So there is the result - a Mind has no boundary, no limit, no end of duration. It **IS** forever! And its power is so enormous that nothing and no one on Earth or in your comprehension could grasp it!

Therefore Mind and Matter are very different since both are the opposite of each other: Matter is finite has its limits and is not eternal. As we straddle both worlds to explain, we need to use examples to try and help you figure out what we are talking about.

§§§

CHAPTER 18

The knowledge we can give you will have to be listened to and not ignored. You'll have to pass it on to others to open their Minds, even if only a little... It is so important that Mankind opens its eyes to superior information as it has been digging its heels far too long into limited 'facts' or totally wrong ones!

We have here many superior **Beings with knowledge they wish to share. We obtain it from higher levels** purposefully. So, it is **not limited to one Mind** who may be influenced by its previous teachers and worse, by Earthly thinking which has such limited – at times obtuse - views that you need to start a chain reaction, or add to any already started.

We have here the summary of what we would like to cover for the part of the new book you will be asked to spread amongst your world's Minds that are ready to listen!

PLANETS' ENERGY TEXTURE

The surface of *any planet* is not always what you think it is ... It may have sand, soil, grit or other textures. But even the gases you may feel or see, or the temperatures you measure, will hardly mean anything, because what matters is **what the Energy texture is,** what vibration it is at and how it can be transformed or improved. Their Energies are what they are really made of. Not what you just see with your telescopes!

If the sensations could also be felt, you'd see **there are Mind Thoughts imprinted in the essence of the 'being' of the planet;** not so much that the planet is a Being but **the essence is a mixture of the thoughts of those who created it**

151

and the result of their thoughts, multiplying into other Thought Energies!

When one has such things to take into account, you realise why it makes it so difficult to explain. If we started with simple things it may make it easier? So we'll say this: When the Universe of this type of Matter was thought out, designed and put into place, it took many 'billions' of your years to plan and put into execution. It had to be so carefully worked out, tested and readjusted until it fell into place, for each part to play its role and each role to be suitable and successful.

What looks like a 'bunch' of gases or a rock flying across your space is far more than that. It had been designed to play a significant (even if minor) part in the unfoldment of the whole thing. It was not just to construct the Earth that it was created. The whole 'batch' of the rest of Matter had its own purpose, so that the Earth you see as the 'centre' of so much (and that you know now is only a tiny, minuscule speck in the rest of this Universe of that kind of Matter) has dwindled to a lesser level. Yet it was important because it was amongst the 'world's planned to be theatre' and the experimental ground of what Humans wanted to try and experiment with.

We can tell you that **other worlds** which have *similar Matter* to yours, but not quite the same Beings, were created but they did not go down the same path as you. **They felt Mind had more importance** and they used it more and better, thus giving them some superiority over you Humans - because they could overcome many a problem by simply 'thinking it out of the way' as easily as you flick a speck of dust off your coat.

They would prepare themselves properly by **readjusting their vibrations before attempting to do anything**, and they'd listen to the inner reactions and feelings. That way **they'd always tune in to what they were due to be doing** and matched their thoughts with their environment.

152

INTENSITY: KEY TO CREATION

The whole global concept of 'One Earth One World' is on the same par. It is to be seen as every part to match and fit in with the rest - whether on a small level or a superior one. **It is INTENSITY that matters - whatever is being built, whether a single thought or a Universe, the Intensity put into its achievement and its design has to be of the highest quality** — and the frequency of its vibrations is of great importance.

So when intense thoughts of a certain design meet other thoughts about that same design, the conjunction point where they meet increases the Intensity, which will be used to activate the 'creation', thought about. All creations have the same 'problem' so to speak... *(As I am very relaxed to receive the dictation, I am now struggling to keep my eyes open... and I fall asleep for hours! Such a shame. But I tuned in again a few days later)*

The knowledge given above is of the utmost importance, so we would appreciate if you could concentrate on what we wish to tell you and take it down as accurately as you can, so that the book following from this will be a great asset to the world.

(Note from BR- This may appear like ego's wishful thinking...whereas in fact my reaction was more a groan at the thought of tackling another 'profound' book, once more, taking my daily life over with all the extra time-consuming hassle of neatly typing hundreds of pages and preparing them for publishers!)

We need to carry on explaining about the **Intensity needed for *any* creation to take place, so that its actualization fits in with the pattern of its design**. It has to be so precisely focused that the slightest alteration or deviation would prevent its current actualization.

If we were to give you an example: Think of a star, a sun like star: it is **the sum of all thoughts of a 'Being of Energy'** but not a Human-like Being. It means a Force of Thought, a creative self-realising Thought Force which **knows** it creates with its Mind and potent Creative Power. That 'star' will have been thought out to be in a certain 'place' at a particular velocity, to fit in with what it is meant to do or help stay on a course. If there was a slight deviation in its creation, the course it is supposed to be on would deviate and the whole lot around it would be affected! This stands to reason, doesn't it!

So, the degree of Intensity of any Thought Power relies on the concentrated Focus and the maintenance of that Focus for as long as it is needed. Then we'll add: the Focus could have **various levels** in itself: because as a thought progresses, it has many off shoots which are automatically produced! So you see it is indeed **difficult to maintain an intense Focus** or a focused Intensity. It's all in the making of any Being, which has to be constantly worked on.

When stars and planets are made, they have been well planned and as such follow 'rules' to be obeyed in a way, since the idea has already been born and the blueprint of what it is to be done has already been created.

If the world that you know had not been planned the way it had, you would never have had it as it was done originally. **The fact you Humans have all had a part in its changes and upsets, means the Focus has been deflected.**

So we'll go back to the original idea of telling you that **when you have many Minds pulling together towards a goal, it is of great importance to keep them all focusing in that direction.** Now we have made that point clear, we hope, the next point is to consider what the ultimate aim is to be!

AIM OF STARS

The aim of all the stars and planets that you Humans think you know, was and has always been to **keep everything in balance**. It is not enough to have astral bodies not colliding, they have to help each other, or else make sure they do not interfere with each other!

The whole range of physical worlds that can be created demonstrates that there is no limit to what can be thought out and the exhilaration is still strong, so is the excitement of seeing or thinking of what can be done!

When a sun with its planets shines and creates an environment which is suitable for the kind of life **you** know on Earth, you then realise 'someone' at least has thought it out. It could not really come out of nothing to become what it has become with every part balancing one another, **with every Being on it playing its part, not only to survive but to help the survival of others** — or so it was planned!

The next step is to explain what happened when those stages were constructed in the creation of the Universe you know (No point talking of those you don't know yet, as you would not have a reference point).

The main aim was the creation of a mighty environment that provided a receptacle for Life and living Beings of Matter—Matter being made of the kind that you know: the Matter of this 'current' (to you) physical world. As we told you before, it was a new experiment as other worlds had been created but they were different from what you know.

So this is where we are in our explanations: the creation of this, your Universe, and world of Matter. As we have already explained in our first book (*'Truths, Lies & Distortions'*) their creation was very carefully planned as **an exciting EXPERIMENT WITH MANY OPEN ENDS**, as we could not always decide on outcomes which were **to be decided by those who would live them.**

Therefore the first time some Beings went to your Earth was indeed a great experience, as the first timers in a new world. We know we've explained *(in TL&D)* there were stages for this to happen as the prototypes had to be designed in our World of Mind- but once they'd experienced it there, then they had to go and try it on the Earth itself or else other worlds.

NOT DESIGNED BY THE 'SPIRIT WORLD"

BR- Was it designed from the 'Spirit World' or from 'beyond that level'?

The line of Thought is not the same. We mean: the idea of creating a world of this, your type of Matter, had long been thought out and was only put into practice once all the ideas had been pulled together and solutions sorted out.

The thought was *not* for the Earth to be "a haven from which others would take off and come back". The idea was for those to go and try and come back and respond to the experience and share it. But as it grew into importance, the whole concept, (which at the beginning was only an experiment) became something more ambitious and 'solid' i.e. more aimed for. This is where things changed considerably.

We know the idea was for a 'new world' to deal with a new type of experience, but the idea was sent from myriads of thoughts all over the World of Mind... That **World of Mind of course, was NOT what you consider as the 'Spirit World'**, because this latter is areas which are now 'inhabited' by those who are due to go to Earth and come back from the Earth.

The long and short of it is that the suggestions for a new 'construction' had stemmed from many millions of Minds - of Minds enjoying the challenge of creating more and more and differently. So when the idea of THIS type of Matter took shape, then the Focus became immense and intense - and THAT is what helped the creation of that new world of matter!

This is what we are trying to put across: **it became feasible and activated and actualized BECAUSE the Thought Intensity was so tremendously powerful, focused and fired up by excitement, hopes, enjoyment and anticipation and more ideas buzzing in Minds who love creating all the time!**

Therefore the stage was set with and on a basis of excited anticipation and intense Focus. This is why that **concentration needs to be kept and to remain in that direction**.

The moment the Focus got diverted and lost its intensity, **loopholes** started creating themselves **where the lack of Thought Power left a blank' in the actualization** — which meant there were weaknesses creating themselves, or being involuntarily created.

This is visible in areas where the Universe has places without enough Energy to respond to other Energies bombarding that 'spot'. There should be **a constant exchange!** The lack of response from one 'area' makes the bombarding **Energies fluctuate and lose their way, instead of 'bouncing back'**, if you see what we mean. This is an important point that many people may not grasp or be aware of.

So, the weaknesses are created by lack of, or reduced focus. That means, you **Humans have lost your original focus:** you had come to Earth to maintain its level of Energy but you've switched the concentration away from what it was meant for!

We had a terrain for practising Mind Power over Matter. Yet over time you **Humans made it a world of Matter empowering people to do more material things, but not exerting their Mind Power - It became unbalanced** as far as we can see from our 'outside' position. This is why the focus has got to be brought back into its existence.

157

HOW CAN HUMANS HELP?

When one looks at a wave on the sea, one should sense and feel its inner power, admire the way it moves forwards and builds its strength and force all the way to the end result... If it lands on a beach, it will spread but it still has enough power to reach high up on a long or wide beach. It is very potent, unstoppable.

That is what Humans should be doing with their Minds! They should build up the enthusiasm, the excitement, the anticipation, the intense desire to have a perfect result. And that result should be that the world around them functions properly, with no interference (The physical world of course, not the world of material activities!)

BR- How can we do that?

What is needed is for the whole of Humanity **to make way for the force of Mind Power from elsewhere, to come and reactivate the Earth world the way it was meant to work** right from the beginning. It had been a 'heaven of pleasure' in the sense that the beauty of Nature was felt deeply by those residing there. It was enjoyed thoroughly as a very new experience, because it was not just admired with the sense of sight, but also by all the other senses. It had to be enjoyed in a different way from what would be felt if one did not have a flesh body. So that was fine.

But the Focus changed and things went wrong. Therefore the Focus is needed and must be returned! As we said earlier: the material world cannot provide the focus of Mind needed to rebalance the creation of the physical World of Matter as you know it.

What we need is for **Mankind to 'step out' of its material world** and make space for Mind Beings (or 'Mind people' if you wish) to fill all the gaps and refill the Earth with

158

the Mind Energy that has been dissipated wildly, crazily, for aeons now, or so it seems!

This is happening gradually. You may not realise it but it is happening. Those who don't want to stay in that new environment will leave it of their own will. **They'll go of their own accord because their Souls will know what is needed.** Things cannot go on the way they are, so a big stop is being pulled out and the backtracking has been started, a while back now in your terms, but still not visible or understood enough. What we means is this: From **higher levels of Mind Power far BEYOND the 'world of Spirit'**, as you call it (which is reserved for the arrival and departures of Humans to and from the Earth World), from those high levels of Mind are powerful Beings who have been **involved in the original creation** of this Earth of yours. They know what is needed and they are doing their best and utmost to rebalance the damages - but the point has come (quite a while ago!) to having a great need to **cleanse and recharge** the lot anew! And **that** is happening!

STAYING OR LEAVING?

So, those who wish to leave will do so: no one 'is obliged' to stay! (*This is what Humans call 'dying'*) But we must point this out:
• If those who stay do not understand why they are there.
• If they do not participate in the cleansing, renewing and revival of the planet Earth itself by **using their Mind Power to help it** - then they will probably 'suffer' from the inconveniences and problems that will arise **when the big shake-ups take place.**

They could choose to listen within and trust the messages their Souls tell them - but so often such Humans do not wish to listen to it because it does no suit their mindless Earthly materialistic activities.

If they are in tune with the Earth physical world of Matter (not the materialistic activities of Humans), then they will know it is of utmost **importance to take part in the mental rebalancing of the population and in the Energy rebalancing of every area of the world -** starting with the area where everyone who cares is living or tunes to with their Mind. It can be done without actually travelling physically to various places.

Of course, the main power will be and is provided by OUR superior 'external' Mind Power. These Minds will keep exerting a meaningful influence all around and over the globe, inside out. This is **where the points of coordination meet** and make a difference when the Power is applied there: **it speeds things up.** It spreads the re-energising Power throughout the grid and helps the repercussions to level out properly. Power is coming in and coming out so that there is a balancing act going on constantly. So we'll sum up by saying:

We are telling you that the Earth is now changing more and more, as you may have guessed and already been told. This is for the better. The 'better' being that *great* need for a total cleansing operation and recharging of used up 'battery points'. When the Power has died out somewhere, it needs to be brought back into that area, or else the area will collapse one way or the other.

Therefore, **the Power is sent from external sources,** not only from where there are points of Power in the Universe you have (such as certain areas of accumulated stars, or 'strings' of stars, or planets: whole **galaxies are a Focus Power point** (a whirl of Power from which we or Beings working at it, can extract Power). But also from the various levels of Mind we have all over the Oneness that **'is'.** It will probably be hard to grasp so we may have to try and explain this a bit more.

160

The Power needed has to be ever so colossal of course, therefore it will come from gigantic areas of Power which are not always physical, since **the physical cannot exist without having been created by the Minds' Creative Force which have started it in the first place!**

There is a renewal of nearly or totally depleted forces, which could not survive unless one gave them a hand and a mighty boost. That's what we are explaining to you. It is what the Beings who came a few times to your group *(During our APPEX experimental sessions)* are trying to elucidate for you all in the group.

Those Beings belong to the ones who care for the Earth as part of their 'inventions'. Those particular expressive Beings **have been involved in the creation of many worlds,** as the Earth was one of their ideas (mixed with many myriads of Minds). Those have expressed the desire to try and explain a little what is to be expected. They opened the door to all your Minds so that you wonder and want to know more.

We are explaining a little more too, so that the whole has more consistency and hopefully makes more sense in the long run. It's a lot to take in for Humans who had no idea that all this is going on.

We have good reasons for letting you *(me, BR)* know: You have chosen, as well as your like-minded friends, to stay and be of help to those who are part of the experience and experiment in recharging and rebalancing the Earth... It is a long and elaborate tale, we know...but if we can shorten and summarize it: it means that you and others will be involved in the reconstruction of the edifice of Mind Power.

This is not all on your shoulders, don't worry! But it means **people will have to participate in sending their Energies and their living and constructive thoughts to the Earth world** they live on. This has to be restarted as it used to be the norm very 'long ago'!

If you can start doing it yourself, it will save you time to learn to do it. But you and others will also be involved in understanding WHY they are here and WHY things happen. Therefore we'll pull together those who have links and need to work or learn together and that will create a chain reaction all over the globe.

That is part of what is worked on. So **the Energies of Beings from external sources are not to worry about, they are only providing what the Earth needs badly. They'll come to your world in various manners.**

We'll say 'yes' before you ask the question - there will be some who will come as 'Humans' the normal way via babyhood. But there will be **some who will appear as Beings of light or shapes then will disappear**, as that's all they need doing, when they bring the Power to the ground in a more physical way, so its reactions are felt swiftly.

There will be strange happenings: lights or shadows or shapes of various sizes. All those will be signs that there are Beings of powerful Minds who send their Energies there and you'll feel the results in meaningful ways: Not to hurt anyone but to recharge and rebalance what needed to be set right.

We have a great interest in you *(me BR)* because we want you to fulfil your 'life plan' to teach the world. We know you'll manage it so don't despair.

SSS

CHAPTER 19

The distance between the Earth and the nearest stars mean nothing to you as such, but they have great importance in reality, because they've been worked out exactly, so that each one fulfilled its role superbly and thus maintained life as was planned. If it had been any different it would not have worked out as it did. So you need to admire and respect every bit of your cosmos and Universe. That is one point we were making.

Now we'll add that the very fact that the stars exist proves that we and those who planned the whole experiment knew exactly what we wanted to do and had worked out elaborate solutions to each angle and each 'corner' sticking out where there could have been problems. Hence the result where everything is working like clockwork.

JUPITER RISE & DOWNFALL

If you want a different topic we'll add that the stars that created the moons of Jupiter were old ones which disintegrated a long, long time ago in your scale of things - the moons were nearer than they are now.

Jupiter had been 'alive' in the sense of **having some life forms and Energies on it**. It was not the kind of 'people' you have on your planet; it was more little elements, **little miniature shapes of Matter which could think for themselves and decide.**

They did **not** exist in the same way as Humans - they wanted to experience the feel of a physical shape compared to being a Being of Mind and Thought. The shapes were not the same as your flesh but they felt more 'solid' than a Being of Mind would feel. It was not that important.

They felt their planet was not producing enough Energy to spin faster. It wanted to stay as was. All around was a grid of Energy which maintained its speed and momentum. When that grid slowed down over time, the reactions of the planet were different from when it was spinning at its usual speed. And that caused its demise in as much as it was not able to produce enough automated, self- produced Energy. It had to come from outside to maintain it on its pathway. It could not do it itself and that's what happened.

The ulterior and outside Energies brought in were to **keep it going on its path as it had its role r**egarding the Earth and the rest of the Cosmos. But it had been **disused as a place of experience and discovery** because the height of its temperature changed and the need for constant rehauling made it unsuitable for more 'shapes' to come and live there. No one was bothering about it.

PULSATING THOUGHT POWER

What we now need to tell you about is the importance of thinking 'beyond the small square'. You have all locked yourself in a 'square' because it looks as if you Humans put everything in a box or boxes—whereas the whole thing is gigantically linked as One! All things are all One, because the Energies of one link and mingle with all other Energies. If your scientists have understood that they are on the right path. If some have not, they are not.

It is important to think of consequences due to a lack of **throbbing Energies.** If they don't throb at the right rhythm and speed, there will be some disharmony and hiccups - whereas the whole as 'a balanced whole' is totally in harmony with every one of its parts inside out. So the parts that you do not see have as much, if not more, importance as the parts you may see

164

We want to stress the need for **understanding the power of pulsating Thoughts which constantly bathe your whole Universe** - and the others which exist too but we'll concentrate on the one you know so you do not get lost in the explanations. That Universe of yours being only a very, very small part of what exists and could exist and will exist and has existed! That area you look at with your telescopes is even hardly noticeable to us in a way: just to say how infinitesimally small it is... You have those **areas in between the vibrations** which you don't notice because you Humans don't know they are there: those are the areas of planes or realities with a different feel.

OTHER AREAS OF EXISTENCE

BR- Could you please explain that?

The areas of existence (or 'non-existence' as far as your physical world considers things) which is in a different format from what you all know, i.e. not a physical world, but **a world of Mind and Thought which constantly produces creations of non-physical Reality**, yet **are** 'physical' — or rather they come across as 'real' to those who experience them.

If we were to say none of the objects you touch around your room is real, you'll know it has been at last understood by most of your Human scientists, but not so long ago people did not realise there was 'space' in between the atoms and molecules forming Matter of any objects... So it does not mean if you cannot see then it does not exist!

This is why we are saying: the spaces *between the vibrations of Matter* of the physical world, contain **other areas of existence which are areas of pure, sheer Energy: Energy of Mind Creative Power**. It is 'in there' that reside the **hoards of Beings** who have no need for a physical home and world!

165

They feel at ease in a 'world of Energy' of no physical feel. Yet you Humans would think there is nothing!

So, we need to stress that the world of Matter that you know is *not only* made of Energy itself, but also *because* the Energy comes from those who have sent it into existence with their thoughts of creation. **They thought it to be in existence** because THAT was one more way of creating things around and beyond them.

What could be considered as blank and empty 'spaces' is nothing of the kind! And **that's where the highest Energy is usually, because it had to be there to sustain the rest.**

When the rest weakens, when there is a flux and reflux of Intensity of Thought, Matter created would disintegrate if there was not at hand a way to pump it up swiftly and promptly! So the 'gaps' are there for a reason.

When the Energy has waned, it is only because the thoughts had not been sustained, as explained before. So its renewal can be done on a kind of automatic basis: if it weakens in one place, it will be pumped up at once by the surrounding space (though invisible to you) in between the vibrations which create 'it' in the first place (whatever 'it' is).

We'll go further now: As you now know, the 'modus operandi' *(method of operating or functioning)* of all Beings and places is based on Energy. That Energy came from nowhere new: not a sudden existence of Energy - **It had always been there** in the background whether feelable, tangible or not. It just **IS**. Which means it **makes it easier for a pumping up and re-boosting to take place since it is always 'dormant' nearby.**

As it changes shapes or tempo according to the thoughts sent, it means a wonderfully wide range of creations can be produced at will. And that is the key word: AT WILL! It is **done at Will,** i.e. following and as a result of Thought: Thoughts - Thinking - Willing it into existence. 'It' being whatever and whoever wishes to 'exist' in whatever way!

We know it is hard to take all this in, but it has to be said somehow, even if it is in plain layman terms, because this is what we are trying to put across: simple, plain explanations to reach the Minds of 'ordinary people'— i.e. not scientifically-minded people — who would like to know where they come from and why.

This being stated we now need to explain more to help you all grasp the necessity of using your own Mind Power and Thought Power. You've all lost it practically; none of you is really using what you have built into you. It's as if you have closed the door to a magic box which could help you obtain what you wish at the flick of sustained balanced thoughts.

In the same way, it is important to understand that we and **those beyond the 'world of Spirit' are made of Thought Power** and we use it with all our might and intense desire - so that our thoughts 'produce', as the result of our concentrated desire and wish: we know how to use it, we know you could use it too! It's sad that we cannot convince you all to do so more.

It may seem to you that it does not really work in your world of Matter, but it does! That's why you all constantly see the results (without always understanding them) in your own health - this is why you all get 'diseases': you all thought or felt 'wrongly'. This is all it takes to be unwell or seriously ill. Multiply that by millions and zillions of thoughts every day and night and you'll see the impact it must have on **your body, which is made as a reflection of creative thoughts** wanting to design it!

$$SSS$$

CHAPTER 20

All we said so far is of great importance and interest. Therefore we shall carry on with the theme because it has to be told to the world of Humans. We know what we can see or learnt about, we are in the thick of it. You Humans are not and that's why you don't realise the wonders going on around you as you are 'stuck' on your planet, looking down at your feet, so to speak, instead of grasping the infinity of levels of Mind you could find, if ever you were able to dive into them!

This is not a treaty on astronomy. It is more an 'essay' on what can be done with Mind Power and some of the results that can be obtained. Therefore we'll carry on to say:

If you had not asked us about those Beings coming to talk to your own group, about the world they are in and why they are coming, we would still have told you about them, as it is part of what you would all have had to learn about! It is no good thinking you are a 'race' of your own and be blasé about it.

It is to do with the fact that **Mind** is at the crux, **IS the Essence** of absolutely **everything** that exists! It is so frustrating to realise Mankind is still not aware of it.

We are trying to inspire some scientists with it but they are slow and reluctant to accept it. So, we have to reach the rest of the world via the 'ordinary population', so that the crowds know even before the pundits do! Isn't that a strange state of affairs? The learners (supposedly!) are to know more and perhaps then teach the 'learned'!

VITAL THOUGHT INTENSITY

We have to add this now: When the formation and creation of your own world the Earth was planned, there was a multitude of **possibilities** for its situation and its 'looks'. So all this had to be calculated very carefully, as you know since we told you before. Not so much calculations in inches and kilometres but in **levels of Intensity of the Energies** that were used for every little part of it to be created at the right place, or at the concentrated level of intensity of Mind Power.

It has and **had to have a continuous supply of Inner Energy to keep it on its course,** as the path had to be carefully designed so warmth and cold were equally balanced. But there were far more reasons and calculations to make, which is why so many scientists in our and other worlds were deeply involved.

BR- Sorry to interrupt your flow - But this needs to be clarified: When you say "Our world" you mean what we call 'the Spirit World'? In that case, I thought it was only for Humans to go and come back during their trips to the Earth - and for kind 'Spirit guides' to be there to help them. So how could those in 'the Spirit World' be involved in the creation of the new Earth (and its Humans and Animals)?

What you need to consider is the Intensity of Mind levels and the aims: The aims of those BEYOND your current Universe of physical Matter (as you know it), were to find new ways to **have fun constructing some other techniques to express one's thoughts and creative Power**. So those whom you know as being beyond your own world had all those 'ideas' in Mind, and they created many wonderful levels of Intensity, teeming with ideas in the making. But **the level of Mind you call 'Spirit World' is even itself in 'layers' or**

169

rather in levels of Intensity, of Focus and of Determination.

So we know of it, ours, because we are in it by choice. **We chose to eventually be at that level** *(the 'Spirit World')* **to facilitate the actualization of the toing and froing to the 'new' place i.e. the Earth.** We had been to Earth ourselves eventually and we stayed mentally of course closer to the whole scenario of activities.

But **WE ARE ALSO Beings who have been and 'existed' elsewhere BEFORE the Earth.** We have all existed before choosing to help settle the Earth in its place. We were and still are part of a Whole, remember?

The nature of Reality is a far wider topic than you or anyone can imagine or grasp. This is why other Teachers in our world have already been to try and put a few seeds in Minds on that subject. In answer to your question: if you can make the effort to think of a huge, endless, concave surface with multi-layers of colours (This is just for you to picture it in your Mind), you can then see that all the layers are practically blending with each other yet are their own colours.

SPIKES OF POSSIBILITIES

When you talk of having existed forever, yes, because no one has any beginning in a 'world' of continuous, eternal Mind Power. **Mind creative Power is an eternal Energy spiking out into infinite numbers of possibilities.** The 'new' possibilities of actualization will have a 'start' in that new shape or actualization, but the **Essence of it/them/ will have always existed**, you see.

So you have always existed as being part of the eternal **Mind Power 'ocean'** but the ocean **never had a 'start'.** You were and are a droplet in it but that 'water' will always have existed. (The word 'ocean' of course is only an analogy, an image!) It is just the formation of a 'drop' into one form or the other or no form, which would make a difference to your eyes, as you see it from a Human point of view at the moment—which is bound to be limited by time and dimension.

*BR- I need to ask for those who still wonder: So, the Spirit World did not exist as such until after the Earth was formed? ALSO: Do 'other type of physical' Beings go there if they have 'death' or for other reasons? OR: Is there some 'departures/ arrivals' levels like the 'Spirit World' for some **other** but similar 'physical' worlds?*

That question covers many points at a time! We are here to teach one point at a time. *(Note- BR- Naughty me!)* The law of creation of anything works because the Minds focus on their aim and produce the result, actualize it as we call it. If your Mind has many ideas and aims and questions, you create a fantastically complicated jumble of thoughts trying to actualize themselves. *(Note from BR- That's me told off nicely for bombarding them!!)*

BR- Sorry. I keep forgetting. One at a time then.

My dear, we have worked out what you asked, but you must be aware of the importance of simplifying your way of thinking, especially if and when you ask us questions! *(Note- BR- To work it out, they told me they have to utilize their built-in "pattern-receiver-thought-processing-method"! — See "I'm NOT DEAD etc"... p521)*

The level of Intensity of any 'place' as you'd call them, is the all-important point. If Intensity is constant and streams non-stop, the level and speed of actualization of any creative act will be sublime and near perfect! **But Intensity does fluctuate** as explained earlier. So, the level being more or less intense in creative Power activity and sustainability **means**

171

that there are various levels in as much as **they are not 'places' but inner activities, inner states.**

This is to say: we, who talk to you, have been here (i.e. the level where we receive and help those who have chosen to experience the Earth physical life which you call 'Spirit World') for quite a 'long time' - because **we existed before the creation of the Earth as an experiment, but** we existed **as a Mind Power potential**, like everything else.

This state is not 'memorable': one does not recall being a Mind Power Energy, but obviously as things went on, we did transform into active Beings of one kind or another. It is practically impossible to recall such things and put it into words.

You just need to know that the 'Spirit World' is only one type, one level of intensity of Thought aiming at helping those who come and go to the Earth world. It was a normal by-product yet created for that, out of the necessity for Souls to focus onto the Earth and out of it, otherwise they would find it harder to realise where they are. This is simply because the Mind needs to focus constantly on to something - so, not having 'landmarks' mentally makes it more confusing and leads to disarray of thoughts.

Therefore, yes, the 'Spirit World' came into existence as a level of Intensity of Mind Power linked to those who have chosen that experience of the Earth life for a certain time. But they all knew that the Earth experience is **not** for Eternity. This is said in relation to the much larger scale of thinking.

In other words, please readers, do not worry about not seeing your loved ones again when you pass over: you will, if the bond and interest is there between you all. It is not to be 'worried' about. We are just answering wide questions for those who wonder what is going on, on the BIG scale of Eternity!

SSS

172

CHAPTER 21

BR- Could you tell us more about other Beings possibly on other physical planes?

My dear, the Earth is certainly not the sole place with inhabitants. It has been known for a long time that there are other places with Beings living on them. It's all a question of what you call 'physical'. If you are looking for planets with exactly the same composition as yours, it won't be the same, because the one you are on is and was an experiment, as you well know by now.

The composition of other planets has been studied by Mankind, though no one has ever found Beings on them yet - this is because what they look for is not Beings but what they call 'signs of Life' or 'source of Life'. Considering that **Life is coming from our world**, it will be difficult for them to find that on a physical planet - but the Life Force is not just what we provide from our world. **A Life Force is an Energy which has Intelligence built in itself.** It is not like a computer pressing keys, **it is an innate Urge to exist, to be** - And that comes from an 'Energy-providing side' or world.

If you found water on a planet it would NOT necessarily mean you have Life forms. There could be some but it is only of interest if these life forms wish to drink water or be in it.

If you had a planet with Beings similar to Humans, would it be an interest to you all? It could or should be worrying, because you won't know whether they'll be friends or foes until you test them! And would it be advantageous to reveal to them you exist, in case they wanted to invade you and take you over? So it may not be a good thing after all... And if you found one with Beings different from you Humans, would it be good too? The same concerns may arise.

So you need to understand that what is more vital is to grasp that your Earth was created from **Minds who are not and have not been solid, yet can create 'solidity' (to your eyes)** by projecting very strong Energies and manipulating the very essence of 'atoms' as you call them, and Energies in particular. That is what helps them create this Matter you know. That is not easy of course and requires a lot of know-how, which is shared amongst those who specialize in this type of analysis and work.

When the world you know was created - as explained to you before - it was a gigantic experiment; but no one was in any rush because everything had to be done correctly and precisely. Yet 'Time' (as Humans sense it) did not exist as such, because so much can be done at the same 'time' within different levels of thoughts, Mind states, vibrations or even frequencies! All those Human words do not really mean much to us, because we don't think or evaluate things or states that way, but you need to know the results are what matters and how they got there.

So this is what we can say: If this Earth had not been created, something else would have been! It was of no consequence. So many things and worlds and ideas have been put into actualization that is impossible to define each one separately. We can only say: you have worlds within worlds. This means your world of Earth and 'Matter' as you know it, is only one of many worlds that are in existence. Lots of other worlds of *different Matter* exist! This is of no interest to you, because you would not know what they are since you cannot see them!

If you must know, where there are 'solid' (to your eyes) Beings who do **not** have the same consistency as your body,

174

yet exist in a world seemingly *'solid' to them*, **it would be within a level/'sphere' of vibrations which would be either faster or slower than yours.** Because if it was the same, you would be facing a world similar to yours; and there is no other Earth as yours is.

NO BEINGS ON PLANETS

There are **lots of other Beings in all the other Universes.** But if you want to know where the **other Beings are in** *your* **Universe,** you will **not find them** on your nearby planets. Those planets are there only to help the balancing of the whole!

So the Beings who may have wanted to exist in this type of Matter would only want to be on your Earth. If they leave their bodies (like yours) they'd all be leaving the Earth. Then they are free to go and materialize themselves in whatever form they choose, even eventually to project in possibly a different type of Matter.

*(BR- NOTE to the reader - Though this may be correct on the scale of Eternity, do not worry about your departed loved ones doing so: they will be there to **welcome you when you pass over** to the Other Side of the 'veil', thanks to the bond of love and friendship. They will not have 'disappeared elsewhere' as demonstrated in my diary of years of communications from my family: "I'm Not Dead: I'm Alive without a Body".)*

Of course that would require a lot of precise work and help for that Re-Creation- but it is of little interest or use to you all, to look for Beings who have not got your capacities of communication, as you would both be strangers to each other! Once met, what can you do with a 'weird looking' Being who cannot understand you and you him? Unless they can use Mind to Mind exchanges- but is your Mind telepathic power in good enough shape to reach theirs, without the use of words in your own language?

It is only essential to know that the worlds of your Universe - of the stars, planets, asteroids and other creations of gases and light -are only there as a balancing act.

If the current Universe you know of had been created just to balance your Earth, it would certainly not have needed to be so wide and large! It was to include other planetary systems, suns or stars so that the **Essence of each one was used to get the right vibrations** all around yours — but also **around others** who were created in order to be the palette of frequencies and Energies needed to offer a wide range.

That way, **Beings in between those frequencies** could enjoy upping theirs to be able to **travel up and down the scale.** That would mean variations of focus and excitement at each discovery and experience!

TRAVELS ON MIND VIBRATIONS SCALE

When the scale of vibrations has been understood (if ever!) it will be realised that in between each 'note', each sound, **there are levels that can be reached with Mind sounds and vibrations. Mind vibrations are pitches one can reach by thinking in certain ways.** No need for Human physical bodies to do that. So the frequencies offered or just present, to those who wish to experience them, means **there is 'travel' in between those levels.** Not travel with rockets but **with Mind projection**—and that's what we are talking about!

The whole concept of your Universe (of this type of Matter) was and is to be able to project various vibrations into the 'cosmos' as you see it, but, as well, **in between** what your eyes or instruments can see! So the projection can be created into **sounds** or **lights** or **feelings**, or simply '**being**' there. And those **projections are sometimes picked by your**

instruments as flashes of lights and colours...but the bottom line is that they are of use to those who project them or 'ARE' them.

A useful experiment would be (if Humans had the necessary equipment) to **feel** what is in between the lights of a star, say, and another. It is not 'Matter' as you see it; it is not imaginary rays of unknown Energy which you cannot measure. **It is impressions and thoughts of a very Living Force that is projected for a reason, with a purpose**—and the purpose can be different, of course.

That purpose is what makes it 'live' because **nothing exists without being there for a goal,** since Mind is what creates. And it always creates for a purpose.

So, the Minds creating themselves into fast projections of thoughts (which are activated in different ways, according to where they 'land' or what Energies they use) will be **very fast thinking Minds,** i.e. powerful energetic Thought producers. But again it is **not a 'Being'** as such, as you would imagine with a body of some kind. It has no need for a body with limited dimensions when its own dimensions are **Eternity and Infinity! THAT's the dimensions of Mind states**. So who wants to be 'contained' in a body of some kind?

When those Minds project themselves to be on a trip of self-realisation and actualization, they become the Energy they project. Those Energies have varied effects on the surroundings. So well that they have a balancing effect where needed — or a restorative one i.e. they shake off old imbalances and replaces them with new, even equilibrium. This is why we talk of **Universal equilibrium caused by and created by Minds in constant flux and reflux of actions and actualization and reassessment.**

If there was not that effect going on, nothing could survive in a world of ideas projected in exuberant bursts for the whole to survive and be sustained.

This action is what your scientists will never realise is going on, unless they accept the invisible creation and 'creators' who, from behind and within the scenery, act as shepherds of the flock of myriads of creations.

$$\mathcal{SSS}$$

CHAPTER 22

We'll tackle now the next section in our dictation about the happenings beyond your Earth environment.

MAGIC OF THE AIR

The sky is only one small, very thin layer around your Earth, as you know. This is of no real importance in a way and yet it has a great importance, because it provides your world with the AIR you need to live as a Human and for Animals and Plants too, of course. If there was no Air there, there would be no Life as you know it. That's obvious, for all of you who breathe and die if you can't! This is what we are going to talk about, because **the Air has a very special consistency** that has been measured and calculated with extremely great care when the world of the Earth was constructed. **It took many a try to fix the right amount of each gas, so that Life survives in your world**. If you think it came 'by chance', you would be wrong. **There is nothing happening 'by chance' in your world!**

We (all those who have worked at that immense project) have planned every possible thing. The AIR was particularly interesting, because if you could not keep the correct amount balanced, there would be an excess or a lack obviously, and that was not in anyone's interest.

The way to maintain it was to have **constant Thought patterns sent** to that area. That's done by **maintaining it with one's Mind**. This is why some Beings *chose* to be the ones it was delegated to: those Beings — from the 'outer worlds' of

Thought and Mind — then took it on themselves to focus their Thought Energies to the type of 'gases' which were to be created. It is **not a 'gas 'to us; it is a band of vibrations of thoughts, which** provide the right balance for the purpose and the correct action on what is worked on. If it has an effect on to anything it has to be the correct one, of course!

So the 'work' was entrusted to those Beings of the 'Air department' as you could call it in your way of thinking! Those did and still do a great job naturally, as that is what you all must have.

Nonetheless, it looks as if the Air you are surrounded with is now being damaged seriously by all the inventions of mechanisation you all have produced and by serious lack of forward thinking on the part of your leaders! Nowadays, you Humans have created too many things which cause the Air you breathe to be unhealthy and polluted, spoilt and dirtied by that smoke you pour into it.

If you see to it in time, you may be able to clean it up but if you don't, **there won't be any clean Air left** as you go along...because **the reproduction of that marvellous state or element is not feasible by Mankind!** You can only destroy it gradually and that means those working hard on this side will find it very difficult to maintain the state you need to have. We can create but we cannot constantly be fighting more opposition and baneful activities!

You can tell your countrymen but will it make a difference? They won't believe that the Air they breathe had been and is created by Beings far beyond the Earth environment! Those are **Beings who have never been on Earth and are outside that level of vibrations.** It is essential to be from 'outside' to create 'inside'. So, understand they are from BEYOND your own Universe of that kind of Matter, since they are part of those who created it! You can't really create from within, can you!

180

This is why most people will not believe it, if you tell them the Air is produced and maintained by Beings of Mind and Thought, who do not exist in your physical Universe! But that is a FACT which we tell *you,* because you know we only tell you the truth, as there is no other way of passing it on to Humans: just tell those who can trust and understand and who will try to put seeds in people's Minds for future reference - when Mankind eventually opens its eyes to the revelations made – and then act accordingly, hopefully!

So, we were saying: the Air is being supervised by those Beings who have no other link to the Earth than trying to create and maintain it, revive it, save it and its environment - i.e. the Air is a kind of mantle for all to survive within it - That's the idea anyway.

Of course, it's extremely hard to grasp and accept, but it *will* be recognised and understood *eventually.* We need to start now, as things are gradually getting worse. All of you have to pay attention to the Air. No Air= no Life. No Life= death. Simple! Death is not a malediction, but it won't allow the survival of anyone on the Earth if no one can breathe, from Plants to Animals to Humans, will it?

So this is the message today. Many people are of course aware of this pollution. But few want to hear of the danger signals. It is much more 'important' for them to keep their machines going by using products which cause foul Air! This needs to be stopped. This needs to be addressed as soon as possible...

BR- Can you see a way out, a replacement for polluting fuels?

There is no way out. There is only stopping what is being done now. We can only see destruction getting worse for the time being. If there was **a replacement fuel, it will be found IF people WORK at it and for it. They need to**

181

WANT to replace the pollution with something which does not attack the precious Air you are surrounded with.

BR- Could you give me more information about the Universe: what are other 'places' made of?

It has not been long known to Man that there is a Universe beyond his notions- so don't despair we'll give you even more - The last centuries have been quite momentous for Mankind as it has discovered many angles that it had not thought possible before and had even fought against at some point! So we'll point out that the Earth is indeed not the only place to be focusing on, as there are 'zillions' of other inhabitable places within your own Universe of this type of Matter. But you need to realise you'll have no way of seeing what they are like yet. You may one day but it may not be for a long while!

If you thought the Earth is the only place to visit and experiment with, it would be an error! We said a lot about the Earth Experiment *(In their dictated book 'Truths, Lies & Distortions')* because that's the place you live in and it would make more sense to you to have details about your own world. On the other hand, you need to know **there are other places in your own Universe where Beings have some similarities but not all the same,** as it would be silly to create two or more of the same place. So instead, there are variations and those will depend on who and what was intended to exist there, if at all.

When the surge of Creativity focused on the creation of this Earth of yours, it included all the *other celestial bodies which help it reside where it is,* within the correct distance from its main star the Sun. The idea was to try that kind of Matter with those specific bodies of People, Animals and Plants you know of — and the **interaction with the substances** of the Earth physical world was made of. That interaction allows the growth and well being of those on the planet. **This was new as other places were not built and designed with the same purpose**.

So, when other Beings wanted to try something different it was organised in a different manner, of course! Their purpose was not what you know as yours. **Those Beings preferred a place of a more 'ethereal', flimsy nature, yet still within the same Universe**. That means **their 'bodies' of GASES** as you'd say, or similar to gases, were not solid to the touch, because they had no interest in that. **It was still the Mind guiding the 'bodies', but those structures' aims were to find ease of movement, adaptation and moulding to what they encountered**. They do not need to 'talk' or 'touch': they envelop, blend with what and who they encounter, and **perceive** them that way—as well as exchange information, appraisal and valuation of what they sense and perceive and pass it on that way - A blending and osmosis with whoever or whatever one meets.

When the final results came over as successful, the throng of those preferring that kind of adventure was as active as the one wanting to go and try the Earth Experiment. It was a choice at first, but there is no reason why one cannot 'eventually' take up the other experience at some point, when the first experience has been absorbed, analyzed, enjoyed and understood. There is no test, there is no 'competition'. There are only opportunities to experience things which are forever increasing and developing. So this is one other type which could be known about!

When the results came in from either or both worlds (this is just to reduce things to a smaller scale to ease comprehension), the scientists involved in both those experiments could compare notes and see what works well, where and how. But this was to see what could derive from an idea and how it could be manipulated to the best advantage. So, the Matter of the Earth being more 'solid' to the touch of those residing there, made them realise how subtle and ethereal the other 'place' must feel and why it is so. Because, after all, both places were created simply by Mind Power, remember! **Nothing is created which has not got Mind Power and visualization at its roots!**

Thus, the actualization of all those thoughts succeeded in two (in this simplified case) totally different creations, and that was the cause of much joy, merriment and relief, as well as excitement at the subtle difference in the 'feel' of what was created by various Beings, whose moods had affected the results in subtle and clever ways.

We know this is a simple explanation, but we have to use only simple words - we cannot give descriptions of gigantically complex juggling of Energies and synergies to create and balance! So this is only to make you comprehend the results one can get with Mind Power put to the test, for the simple reason that one wants to create something different; then one works at it thoroughly with 'all the time in the world' to achieve it.

This is just one small example to offer you. Now multiply that by thousands and millions and you'll see the experiments are still going on by your scale of 'time' since you have no other option to comprehend it, because you are not out of your world of Matter. So, those other worlds of Matter similar to yours but very unlike it, are **not within reach of your instruments** or machines so far. It is not just a question of 'going further' and seeing them, it would be too easy if it was possible.

It is also the fact that you **Humans do not know what to look for and at which level of vibrations to find them!** You cannot look for something that does not resonate at the same level as yours, since you would not find it! It would be unreachable for you. You would think it is a shadow or a sound ... but you may not realise it is a whole WORLD there!

MIRACLE OF WATER

What needs to be explained to the mass of the ignorant or ill-informed public is that the sea or the sky are not just 'things' which 'happened' because some rocks flew here or there, or some gases were 'simply emitted' by this or that... and so you'd have water and you'd have a sky! This is so untrue and incorrect that we are 'fuming' as you would say. We **need** to rectify the facts so that the new generations learn real facts instead of falsified information, which has never been the truth.

What you see in front of you in the sky has already been explained as AIR, which we told you about earlier. As to the sea, it is made of water as you well know! **The miracle of WATER** will never be totally understood by Mankind, because it thinks it can create a couple of drops with a mixture of this and that gas, but it is not so: not the real magnitude we created for the World of Matter and its inhabitants to live and survive all those millions of years. If we started from the beginning it may be easier.

There was the need for a complete blending of Energies: a smooth Energy bridge, a link between many atoms and molecules which had to circulate around bodies of Matter. The blending had to provide Air for those who required it and a liquefying substance for those who need to dilute other material. It is ever so complex and involved! So, the substance thus created had to be absorbent, but also be a carrier without losing the properties of what it carried! This was **the trick** to achieve: to dissolve without dissolving, carry without breaking - such a subtle difference according to the situation.

This is why it rested on those clever scientists, chemists and physicists of our world to solve the mysteries and make all that work properly. In many instances it had to be tried over and over again, for long periods of your 'time', to get the mixture right. You cannot expect to create overnight that new substance, 'Water', since it had to have so many wonderful properties - It needed to be right and it is now. You have to understand that what looks wet and fluid to you is more than that. It is an **accumulation of very refined vibrations, which must keep vibrating constantly to maintain the special texture and vibration of that 'new' substance.**

As Water was thought of and created, all the Minds involved in this new 'stuff' became increasingly more excited at the prospect and possibilities. If you wanted to store it, you could; if you wanted to let it go, it could spread; you could alter it with heat and cold and even blow on it to make it move as 'waves'. And so on... It had so many aspects - it fills the flesh body but it does not flood it; it fills the seabeds and lakes but does not prevent them from existing... It provides nutrition to anything living.

That texture has wonderful inner qualities; you cannot divide and dissect water unless you have a microscope - that will only show you things you estimate to be physical - We mean: What you see under your lens is not just what the actual Matter of Water is as a liquid. It shows the inner side of anything- but the electromagnetic aspects are probably hardly understood, because **what causes Water to be as it is, is the invisible and undetected reaction between all the atoms**.

If you took one drop of water and saw it as it really is, you would not put it back in the sea or the river or the tap - you would keep it and admire it and even put it in a frame to keep it alive... *(Those dictated last words were faintly 'automatically' handwritten as my body fell asleep due to my intense concentration!)*

The info we want to give you now is to do with the amazing substances that cover the Earth as most of them are taken for granted. If all of you paid attention to them a little more, you would see you are standing on **a marvel of**

186

engineering from BEYOND the world you live on. It could not have been created by anyone or anything within the Earth, yet it is often what your scientists seem to think! We want to keep reminding you that all that came to your world has been thought out very carefully, as **it was created by Beings of great knowledge and great powerful Minds, from beyond the little world and even the little Universe in which you are all 'swimming' about.**

WONDERS OF THE SOIL

Take the **SOIL** of the Earth and the mixture of various ingredients which form it. It had to be created from all the minerals and other substances that have been used to make the Earth. It was **not** something which just appeared over time as trees died or plants succumbed under cold, damp or heat! All **had been planned** so that Plants gained some ingredients, absorbed them. Then when eaten, Plants would give the flesh bodies eating them the right amount of components necessary for survival! This is not new information, but it is vital that it is recognised as being **a product of the vivid and practical imagination and mindfulness of those who designed the whole project of the Earth Experiment.**

When a new world has been planned and is being designed, it is obviously essential that every little aspect is thought about meticulously, before attempting to start putting together the components. So life for survival was meant to use Water's wonderful properties and Soil's marvellous composition to be reflected in and regenerate cells in flesh bodies — so that they keep going longer in **a temporary world where Intensity of Thought Power is the driving mechanism but also the engendering and creative Force.**

Consequently, the combined Soil and Water have permitted a greater range of activities as the bodies survived - and the Souls driving them could enjoy their Earthly experience for longer than just popping over for a short visit and testing. Therefore, thank that Soil and Water which have permitted all those possibilities! It is not thought about and recognised at all nowadays. Yet in the 'ancient times' of the Earth experiment, those Human dwellers had the Inner Knowledge- as natural Knowledge- that the Earth was so precious and was providing what they needed to survive during their trip. We wish it was done so too nowadays, because people could become even more conscious of the harm that is done to the world that gave them life - and is still trying to keep them alive, against all odds.

That is what those fighting pollution and desecration of the Earth scream against, rightly so. There is a wave of anti-pollution protesters but they look small seen from here, compared to the mass of people on your Earth trying and continuing to fight them by creating more damage instead of cutting it down and out completely.

That is why we come and plead on behalf of OUR creation: it is an amazing work of Art, a fabulous piece of engineering, a wonderful projection of Thought Power made real, actualized into a world tangible to those on it! Why take it for granted and ignore the astounding origin of this masterpiece? This is what needs to be put across.

CREATION BY BEINGS FROM BEYOND

We want to clarify even more precisely that **we, the Beings from BEYOND the Earth have done the work. Not a god on a throne, not a weird bunch of 'aliens'. We exist as Beings who have long been in existence, even before the Universe you live in was created by us all.**

This is so difficult for most Humans to grasp, as they will automatically associate this with some peculiar 'aliens' in some far away planet- or some magic deity of no consistence and with no evidence of its existence, apart from the result of having a wonderful World of Matter for you all to live in.

188

All this knowledge has been lost over the centuries and millennia. Why haven't we told you all before? We have! It has been said many more times throughout your history - but it was either discarded or distorted by leaders who maybe did not understand it themselves, or probably tried but the mass of the people could not grasp what was beyond their comprehension. So the knowledge was seized, warped and refitted to suit all kinds of religions, which too often were used for political use by rulers wanting to scare the population into submission: "If you don't obey us or our rules, the god who created this world we are on will be angry and punish you all. Look! An earthquake! An eclipse! A volcano! Those are signs you have to obey us... We have the power to please that god, obey us or else you'll get more of the same!" And so on...

So **WE** as 'Beings from Beyond' are here once more, having found another perceptive Mind— this lady *(me BR)* who writes down what we are saying—to try and instil more thoughts of respect and admiration for the world you are all treading and kicking most of the time. We have a job and want to achieve it by helping more people respect the world of the Earth. We have it in our charge, but we cannot help it if you are all doing the wrong things.

Make your youngsters aware of the beauty and the mystery of the creation of every little blade of grass, clumps of soil, water drops, the sky, the seas, the land, the mountains, the Life Force running through it: the Energy living in it and in you, the life Force which could only come from outside this Earthly world to produce all those on it. THAT is what youngsters should be taught!

But the notion of 'Outer Beings' will smack of 'religion' and scare off the religious authorities or even governments! So this is where *it has to be done gradually*, allowing the child to respect each little thing and creature he encounters. Then perhaps, as he grows up, he will be allowed to understand what the Reality of the world's creation is.

No 'Big Bang' would have given Life to the Beings on it. If only we could help scientists in your world open their Minds to this, instead of rehashing old sayings... Why don't they rehash that the Earth is flat or the Sun runs around the Earth? Because improved knowledge has at last overtaken the erroneous facts that used to be imposed back in time by the church leaders of those days – leaders who should be ashamed of enforcing their ignorance on the poor masses!

What is needed has been stated above. Now those are the facts that will need to be added: since 'Beings from Beyond' have created the Earth, they will need to explain who or what they are. How can that be explained or proved? It is our job to try and put across as much as we can, because **you cannot find us on a map of the sky or cosmos — because such places do not contain the 'worlds' we live in.**

We say the worlds since we can reach all sorts of worlds. You usually think of worlds in terms of solid places because that's all you know in your everyday life. The modern scientists of your present days will have a more profound view because they realize **there are far more levels to attain than the visible layers you are aware of** with your eyes and other physical senses. So, we appeal to those who understand there ARE extremely refined and fast levels or planes of vibrational Energy—which means those you cannot see or sense still exist and have amazing and mind-boggling properties as far as Humans are concerned.

There are various ways of feeling and sensing things that are beyond the Earthly physical senses which WE do not need, as we use our sense of Thought! Thought is a Creative Force that both creates but also receives. So **we sense and know by activating our Thought Power, our 'radar' of sensing via Thought Power.**

If you know of telepathy and Minds linking, you will understand a little better. This is what we use as a tool, constantly, forever. It does not run out of power! It can diminish or increase its Intensity, but it never runs out of 'fuel' or Energy! **This why we can exist forever** because we WANT to exist, to 'be', to intentionally exist. That means: as long as we want to think, we ARE Thought Force and Power.

Not all Beings can do that, only those who wish to exist and use their Thought Energy for good creative uses — and 'being' is a useful use. We can create ourselves and do; we want to 'BE' - We ARE and always have been.

Do not concern yourself for now as to "how could it have always existed from no beginning". This is not urgent for now. For the time being please be content to learn, to accept that there are Beings of Mind Power that exist and have existed for longer than Humans can ever imagine... Those bright Thought-powered existences are Thoughts in the making - they make themselves by the very fact they think. By thinking they enjoy existing and spreading their Energy as they do so – thus, it means they exist more- and can create what is being thought.

CREATIVE POOLS OF THINKING ENERGIES

So the gathering of such Energies into **'pools of Thinking Energies'** means we can have 'meetings of Minds'—Minds **who are very much alive,** as masses of powerful ideas, excited at the thought of being created... This is a never ending succession of **'bubbles of thoughts' exploding into Beings in existence,** themselves throbbing with the idea and the desire of existing and creating more new 'ideas', 'things', thoughts of something desirable and different. The bubbling Creativity within each is so exuberant that it constantly throbs as thoughts 'blossom' all over.

This is difficult to describe in Human words, with images which may mean something to you, to picture in a minor and modest way what is WONDERS of constant

Creation! What this leads to is to tell you we are indeed thinking Beings but **we are not made of flesh,** no arms and legs, no funny faces or weird skin. **We have no set abode. We have constant existence by the very fact that we 'ARE' and we think.** That is enough to exist. In the same way as you Humans will reside in your flesh body as long as your own Mind Being, or Soul and Spirit, wishes to be in that flesh vehicle. Then, when *you remove your Will* to be in that physical body (for whatever reason and purpose of yours) you will then return to what is in fact something similar to our state. But you may over time need to take some steps and different preparations to shed the idea of having been in a human body.

So back to what we are trying to explain: The state of a Thinking Creative Mind is a *wonderful* state which has no limitations and can allow all sorts of happenings. This is why when we, as a very gigantic (!) group of Thinking Minds — set on the mental path of wanting to create something in a different kind of Matter that had not been used before — we chose to design what eventually has become the little Earth Experiment. This to you is a colossal Universe and a great place to be, but to us it is one of many other ideas!

So if you think your Universe is wonderful, make use of the knowledge we are trying to pass over to you, to make you appreciate and understand it better. You will not discover little men on your nearby planets as you are trying to find. You will not find lizards and flies to populate others either! You only have a very narrow notion of what is involved to keep the Earth where it is as it revolves across your cosmos. It is huge but it is puny in comparison with what we know can and does exist.

FUTURE TECHNOLOGY

You Humans have achieved quite a lot in technology but that has not given you the answer yet; it will not, as long as you look for the wrong things! You should **look for Energies that can create, Energies that can be felt,** not by machines but by Humans — **because Humans are Beings of Energy** who have chosen to come to that Earth world. They are the ones who could solve it: by **sensing what it involves to be in a Universe made solely of Energies that act and react with each other**. When Humans can focus or 'tune in' to Energy given out - not only by the Earth and its surroundings but by THOSE BEYOND the Earth and 'Spirit World' - then those Humans with 'extra powers' will be the ones showing you how to sense the rest of the Universe and how to understand how it was created: by sheer Thought Power from 'zillions' of Minds - not by blocks of Matter exploding or even by 'burst of Energy', which may not be understood anyway!

This is where you should all turn your attention to, in order to **grasp what those underlying Energies are,** where they can be felt, why they have power, how they can be related to Thinking and Creating. **All this will be the new technology of the 'centuries' to come**- or before if you work at it!

Meanwhile WE shall carry on being who we are - **Beings from beyond your world of Matter with your well being at heart.** We want to keep our creation going for those who want to enjoy it and respect it and take part in what was actually called the Earth Experiment as we said before. So go on, "experiment!" But not so much with your machines, which you have now overdeveloped (at the expense of your own abilities), but by **developing your own sensing mechanism!**

What we are talking about is the re-polishing of the faculties you have always had 'before', because (as said earlier, but we want to drill it in!) you as Humans, are really Beings of

193

Thought and Mind — who have known of the Earth Experiment and actually CHOSEN to participate and actualize your life there, for some limited time in your new environment.

Your choice meant you would have to get to know the new world and realize what can be done with Thought Power. You would all know subconsciously, if not consciously, that you are a Being of Mind and you are there as an actor in the disguise of a flesh body- But **your Inner Self knows that is not the real aim of your trip.**

HUMANS 'AIMS

YOUR aim is to feel and sense the subtle Energies around you and compare them with your physical senses and your Earthly activities. You would feel the blue water on your body then realise the water is not really blue, but your senses tricked you into thinking it was. You'd feel the wetness but you would need to go back to thinking why and how it may feel wet. You would like the 'reality' of your physical senses with the subtle, more real reality of your Inner Knowledge...

This is just to give you a quick idea of what we are talking about. We'll explain in more detail later.

So if we can carry on with this as it was laid out, we'll say: **this aim is to revive nowadays what was the original purpose** of coming as a Being of Mind in a physical body - and experiment with the Dual Personality you were creating for yourself by doing so and being there on Earth. This seems totally lost in your modern world. You are going towards catastrophes if you do not revert to what you were meant to do, by your own choice, at the origin of you individual experiments.

This is to explain why we say it is necessary to do so. We are only passing on a reminder of what all of you Humans wanted to do when 'the Experiment' was so successfully created. This is the end of the sermon!

But the Reality is that **Beings of Mind do exist!** To find them, the use of telescopes and other magnifying instruments will be no good! The use of atom splitting machines will not lead to anywhere either because **Thought cannot be measured or weighed!** THOUGHT has the subtlety of nothing you can imagine as it is unimaginable- **yet it has Power you could only realise if you used it more often.** They say, "Faith can move mountains"- We'd even say: "Hope can do so"- as that is Thought in action. But your mountains on Earth will be nothing compared to what can be done and has been done with sheer Thought Power. An example: Your Universe! That's what we come back to.

We as Beings from beyond your narrow and limited field of viewing, have the Power of **using our constant thoughts for doing good.** No way could we want to do anything so-called harmful!

The Joy of Creativity is a very positive, caring Thought Power and Process. Nothing can be created of any lasting existence if it was thought out with negative attitudes. So this is just to reassure anyone worried we may do them some harm! Since we have created your world, don't you think we would want it to last and be a happy place? All the more since you have ALL chosen to have some time there with your own projects. All this is a 'drop in the ocean' of eternal existence. That stay and experiment on Earth is so minor, compared to what else can and will be done and experienced! So don't let it go to your head and **view the Reality of Existence from the correct point of view!**

Hence our talking to you all and dictating this book, as one of many ways we are trying to open Mankind's eyes. What is needed is to think: "What can I do to sense my world the 'right way', to enjoy it as was meant to be enjoyed and experienced? Also to be in awe of what is worth admiring - to spend time on fulfilling activities and discoveries which

195

make my Inner Being breathe in joy, wonder, admiration and satisfaction — so that **I realise I am a Being of Mind, experiencing the World of Matter from within the World of Matter instead of looking at it, observing it from beyond it"**.

That is a stage you may want to go back to. 'Go back' because you have been there before. Yes, you all have, when you Humans all chose to come and be pioneers in the Experiment, as said before. This is the thrilling feeling you need to recapture. Then you'll **know WHY you are on Earth** and HOW you can enjoy it more.

You all have, or nearly all, created yourself **a materialistic world, full of new rules, duties and chores, therefore trouble** - to keep up with what you imagine you 'have to do', 'have to see', have to endure. And **you all end up stressing yourself to the point of damaging your outer vehicle,** the flesh vehicle you are all ensconced into, to manipulate that material world.

That was NOT meant to be so, and deep down, you all know it. But you don't know anymore how to get out of it. You come back to this Earth world (= reincarnation) hoping to rectify your misunderstanding, yet most of you fall each time in the trap laid by your demanding physical senses and the silly 'societies' that Mankind has created, simply to satisfy the physical body and its needs to be satisfied, or else you are all even more unhappy.

The trouble is that the **physical senses needs can only be satisfied temporarily**, then they demand more and more! So where do you get off the vicious circle and crazy roundabout and turntable? By knowing what needs to be known - that we have come back so many times to talk to those who will listen.

We are NOT creating a 'new religion' or any religion at all. We are only opening or re-opening the Mind of Mankind to what it knew aeons ago. That's all. "Why should we believe

'Beings from Beyond' we cannot see or talk to directly?" you may say. Well, it is up to you!

Try and follow a different path from the one which lead you to impasses, dead ends or even more misery - or even simply sadness and feelings of dissatisfaction. **Want to know more!** Try and **open your Mind** to that 'new' facet and aspect! If you have been told to believe in a god and that does not satisfy you, try to find out for yourself by developing your own inner senses, your own latent abilities.

SENSE NATURE

Just try and sense everything in your Earthly world that is called' Nature'. THAT was not and will never be created by Mankind! So, **go into Nature** and learn to sense the wonder of the smallest spark or colour or blade or leaf or insect. Look at it **and FEEL the thinking behind the creation** of that wondrous creature—as everything has the Power of the Life Force leading it and filling it. Then see where that takes you.

That's a good start: Nature will teach you more than your religions or man-made 'scientific' books will really teach you.

You cannot feel and sense via religious rules or factual descriptions of the innards of an insect or a plant. You will not feel and sense the Life Force that created it and comes from Beyond that physical aspect. Nature for now. Then you'll understand much more and you will reopen the door to your inner, latent knowledge, as a Being of Mind and Light. Then you'll sense that since you are one, then WE can be too!

BR- No doubt I'll be asked: Where does the knowledge you provide come from exactly and how is it passed on?

If we told you 'it comes from the stars' you would not believe it, because you would imagine Beings in and on the stars talking to us! We have to be more specific beforehand to explain the background of what is going on beyond your sight and knowledge.

As we can all do that if we wish, the levels we reach depend on the desire we put in the search and the outlet it will have once we've got it. We need to pass the Knowledge on. It cannot be kept for oneself, as this is a world of sharing, loving and helping each other. So the levels reached will be relevant to the need to know certain facts.

What we look for will be reached by sheer **Intensity of Desire to know more. The level of Knowledge can usually be beyond words of the human world**. It typically is **sensations, apparitions and visions of 'knowing'**, of "that is how it is", of "that is what happened"—and **we have to translate all that in some kind of way for you to understand** and pass it on to others. So the level at the moment is what we know and have **acquired from BEYOND our** ('Spirit') **world** - and relevant to the fact that Beings from beyond this level of 'Spirit World' (as you call it) have been the triggers and the initiators of the creation of your physical world. *(NOTE- Please read more details on that creation in "Truths Lies & Distortions")*.

When that physical world was created, as has been explained to you many times, it was designed to be a happier place for those going there to 'find their wings' in playing two roles or facets of themselves at the same time. That means: knowing they are Beings of Light and Mind, yet feeling the amazing new experience of having bodies of flesh – i.e. physically oriented towards their physical senses and being governed by those senses, if one lets them do it.

Therefore the new experience had to be monitored as much as possible for those new to it—yet not to the extent of infringing on the Free Will of those who are happy to be in the material world and want the freedom to experience it. So, that is the side to do with your own world.

But **the Beings of Higher Realms seeing to the construction of the physical world,** had to be in charge of far more than that, in order to **maintain the existence of that amazing invention and creation!** That's what has been going on ever since, because the planet you know is only a tiny, puny part in an area of much more importance.

PHYSICALITY IN OTHER PLACES

BR- Out of the zillions of other galaxies and planets there must be other 'disguises' as physical manifestations, other 'travellers' who are Beings of Mind enjoying a trip in a different type of 'physical' world?

My dear, the world you know as your Earth is only one aspect of what can be created as 'physical'. We have already told you there are different types of 'Matter' (or physicality, if you like), within 'your' own Universe. It does not have to be like what you know.

BR- Within my Universe?

Yes. It is hard to be precise and explain clearly, simply because you only know what you Humans are used to. The atoms you are made of, as a body, are nothing like what other places (still within your own Universe of Matter) can be like. **That** was and is the beauty of playing with creating new material and new worlds!

So, those **other places have different textures, different aims, different needs, different results and different associations** with the other worlds, which could and can be created. All this is within the Joy of Creativity and the excitement of THINKING of something different.

199

However not all 'things' are what you would call things... simply because you Humans only relate to objects which in your eyes have no 'soul'— but you must realise that **whatever is created by Mind will have Mind Energy within it. Therefore it will have vibrations which have the potential to 'emerge out of their state'**, i.e. to 'think' in a way—perhaps not like you would think, but would have the Thought Power vibrations that created them.

That is Energy in itself that we need to, or can, buzz into a different type of action, but we are reaching topics which will be away from our main subject and also may confuse many readers.

So, we'll go back to the point where we'll say: Yes there are other worlds and Beings within your own 'known' Universe (which Humans don't know at all actually!) but within THAT type of Matter, there are Beings who have elected to become somehow 'something or someone' else, **just to be able to do more than being a Being of Thought and Light.**

As was explained before, yes, there are 'physical' (in the sense of what *you* call 'physical') places and Beings who have chosen a body of a different nature and aims to yours. BUT you would not see them even if you had the strongest telescopes. This is because **their vibrations do NOT link up to your own Earthly vibrations: you would not see, hear, sense** or notice them. You would think those planets are bare, empty!

Nature on them may be very different since 'your' Nature is extremely special and you may not always come to actually grasp and appreciate what you have in front of and around you on Earth. This is why we keep telling you that your Nature, your Earth is such a precious jewel, that it should be admired and respected...and far more than it is nowadays. It is a loving Being as a whole, but who has grasped that?

200

Made of Matter means 'physical' to you. But **some types of Matter are not what you would call physical** - yet to those Beings who experience them it is 'real', solid, usable etc. It is a totally different experience for them.

All this is to do with the process of emanating more Energies in different ways — in creating more in order to 'be' more — because nothing is more exciting than the Joy of Creativity: ever changing possibilities, stimulating ideas, trials and errors, improvements and challenges. This is what is in the nature of 'Existence'- 'being', existing. We cannot think of any other way of explaining this.

So, if you understand that the **Joy of Creativity is the stem of everything and every Being existing,** then you may begin to grasp what we are all trying to tell you and the world you live in. This new book is to attempt to put across more profound facts which would have been difficult to grasp had we told you all that in the first volume of our revelations. *(I asked several questions which crossed my mind)*

If we were to answer all those questions in one go, you would be very confused, because each answer contains many aspects and sidelines. If you permit us to carry on the way we plan to 'teach' you, you will eventually get those answers to your questions.

When your Earth was created there were many possibilities, which means it could have been done one way or the other — there were choices, which had to be decided upon and sorted out. Now you know the ones that have been decided upon since you live a life on that Earth. But some of the other choices still exist because whatever is thought out gets created somehow! **Their blueprints still exist** and even if it is not lived in the way you could imagine, the reality is nevertheless there!

'PERFECT EARTH' POSSIBILITY

So, those 'Humans' who have not made it as you know it, are still real and still live in their own world of Mind and also physically; they have not chosen to kill others, they have not chosen the path of mechanical and technological inventions. They have deepened their knowledge of the world they live in and **understand thoroughly the use of Plants** whether to heal or to sustain them, to help them survive there for as long as they wish. So that's one Earth that exists simply because it is a 'replica' in a way, but not really, more **an alternative during the many possibilities** to finalize and actualize. If only it could be easier to explain, it would be great.

BR- Where is it exactly?

It has no physical place as far as **you** are concerned, because the **vibrations are not the same** as the ones you see and emit yourself. So it is not 'on top' or 'under' your own Earth. Nor is it within the vicinity of any of your stars in your galaxy, say. But it is real nevertheless. That is what possibilities do and are: Invisible to those who look for them, unless and until the desire to have them actually created and actualized is SO strong that the manifestation takes place!

BR- Where would it appear if it was done?

That world needs a lot of focused desire but you would need a reason for it to exist first. Assuming it did become 'solid', it would and could only be so within the range of frequencies which would sustain it. And that may **not be your range, since the aims and results are different**. What would you possibly see is a similar Earth outwardly, but **it would not be the world you know because the Beings on it may have chosen to live differently**.

BR- It would be the same Nature though?

Similar probably, yes, but all depends on what is to be done on it and with it - We mean: you would **not be able to see it with a telescope** or even stronger instruments, because you **would have to break the barriers of Thought frequencies and understanding**.

So, let's go back to the original aim: to live in your world was a choice and you all made it. In the same way, to live in other worlds is and was the choice of Beings who wanted to be something different 'physically'— but not out of the same Matter as you are made of. What we mean is, what you know as 'substance', flesh, plants, air, water, all those are made of similar things one way or the other — say, some gases in most of them. But the new/different Beings wanted to be in **worlds which had no need for that**, unless they wished to visualize it. They could visualize a tree and imagine it is there, but they did not have to (*?... illegible word?*) or cut it or live off it... (*Unfortunately I fall asleep! Hopefully they will pick up the thread of their thoughts and teachings when I tune in again*)

WIDE SPECTRUM OF REALITY

Many lives will not be able to give you even an inkling on what is going on outside the Earth's influence and choices on it. It will have to be seen from beyond that 'sphere', that area. It needs to be seen from an outsider's point of view to start to grasp what is really going on and how it happened if it did, and how and why it did not happen, if it did not. Do you see what we mean?

So the solution to understanding all this — or at least one way to get a glimpse of what really is beyond the limited view of the Earth environment — is to be able to comprehend other realities, other happenings linked to, or caused by, or related or unrelated to it. It has such a wide spectrum that it **can only be attempted by those who are not on the Earth AND who have access to** far superior vantage points and knowledge.

This is what WE are attempting to do to help you all on Earth understand or remember what you really are - and why you have been helped to go there without being told you 'must go', nor have you been punished or banned to that place! It is all choices and more choices and possibilities.

If you had not been born on Earth in the 'cycle' of possible lives to live there, you could (and still can eventually) be doing far more, or as, interesting things and be other Beings of a different 'texture', let's say. It's all to do with preferences and there is plenty of 'time' to do other things. Nothing is pressurising you or anyone to be or do anything!

As we speak of Earth and other places, it may be useful to point out that the Matter all of you are made of is not dissimilar to other Matter- yet it is very dissimilar! It is simply the emphasis on one aspect, the intensity of certain elements, the quantity or the more **refined vibrations which may make one appear totally different from another one** — merely because it's like a block of ice which looks very different from mist, yet it still is water but in a different form, isn't it? So it is with other aspects of Matter and its reaction to its surroundings.

This is said in passing to make you aware of all the subtleties occurring, even purely in the composition of what surrounds you and what could be making 'another world' compared to yours for the time being. If you had more time to look at each little object in existence in your Nature, each tiny Being which exists, you'd be overawed by the complexity and astounding ingenuity in creating every single one! It is indeed awe-inspiring and mind-boggling!

So, you cannot imagine what we can see from our own vantage point with access to other realities which make 'your world' look quite puny in some respects - yet quite wonderful and awesome in so many others. This is to give you a glimpse of how things can be seen and considered. Now, we'll now carry on with the rest of our explanations:

When the first atoms of your present Matter started being put together, it was a gamble and just one of many experiments. It helped those creating them focus on new possibilities - that's what we want to bring to the surface of your Mind - **Everything you are surrounded with was a possibility materialised by Will and focused attention - the DESIRE to BE and desire to CREATE. That** is what makes things appear —at least to your eyes if we talk of the material life.

So, the Will of the Minds creating those things was very strong indeed because it was focusing on ONE thing at a time. That gave it power and potency. It allowed them to make things happen, gradually in a way, as there were various choices at each step. But it was only 'finalised' when one choice was made to stand out by the sheer desire to have that existence.

IF none had wanted to exist or be created, then all would be different. So it boils down to an Urge to WANT to exist, intense Desire to make something exists, concentration of Will Power and power of the Will to help all those ingredients become a certain shape and have a particular existence; **That's how Matter comes into being. Any matter from anywhere.**

There are and will always have been those **three powerful giants: Will, focused Desire and Urge to BE.** Whether a blade of grass, a speck in the universal cosmos, or a Being of any size and dimensions, ALL will have been 'made' via that method and process.

If we are to carry on with this, we need to make an extra 'side comment' to back the lot up: if there had been one Being (a 'god') creating all this and others whenever 'he' decided to do it, it would have been rather limiting! If every idea, conception and possibility had to come from 'his' Mind, those could not have been the gigantically wide range of choices which exist ad infinitum... Because **one** Mind though extremely creative, cannot produce what, say, millions of Minds can compute, design and create! **It is the extensive range of possibilities out of which more possibilities stem from, which give Reality and Creation's wealth and richness.**

Make the life you live worth living, because you have an aspect of that range of possibilities within your grasp; so it would be a pity to waste the chance to experience certain points: when you can learn what you can do with your Mind, find out what can be discovered when you open your Mind to higher levels of information.

SSS

CHAPTER 23

(Those past days I had a lot of problems with my computer - 'Windows' and the security programmes were fighting off the brand new printer I had to purchase because the older one started 'limping'- That non-acceptance was driving me mad, as the screen kept going blank or the pc refusing to obey and acting very weirdly, not giving me the chance to click or unclick what could help it work. I can cope with I.T. if things behave as should- But that obstinacy was getting too much for me! So I gave up, hoping it would change its mind...or I could get help; meanwhile I decided to tune in to let my Teachers carry on with their book- Also I wanted to ask them about the unexpected foreign writing which we received from a discarnate personality who reached us via Elli's trance last Tuesday during our 'APPEX' experimental séance. That unknown person did not speak but used a pen and writing pad available, suddenly producing 6 lines neatly written in total darkness! It is not European or Asian lettering. Looks more like Middle East lettering.)

BR- Please let me know who wrote this and why?

Lots of people would like to know what goes on in their lives and not have their material problems. We cannot help with all those problems, but we can say you have had your share at the moment...because you need to concentrate your attention on what really matters in your remaining life and your need to focus so hard that it will happen. So, your inner desire being thwarted, **you feel 'all at sea', rattled and**

churned...And this is reflected on your surroundings in your material and electronic objects!

BR- (Stunned by this totally unexpected declaration) I can hardly believe it! You are telling me I am affecting my pc's Windows programme? Anyone else would assume it's a technical hiccup!

You have far more power than you'll ever imagine! Your Energies are spread out, all intermingled and mangled with each other too! You are a 'mess' inside in a way, because you are not succeeding in what your Self and Soul are trying to do. *(Note- BR- Which is getting that book ready for publication!)*

You need to and must be more focused, then you'll see that achievement and successes will pour out of all this effort. You can explain this to other people too, because you will have experienced it. We can only suggest better improvement if the advice is followed. If you try, you'll find you'll succeed at once as you will have regained the focus you lost quite a few months ago.

We know it (the focus) will be repaired IF you can work twice as fast and as intensely. We'll help as much as we can. You had to learn 'your lesson' in a way it had to be shown and experienced. So now you know what we are talking about. It is ever so important you grasp the power of one's Mind over one's whole life and aims and surroundings! You HAVE affected your computer. You needed to know that and see it to believe it. If we had just told you, you may not have accepted it as true. *(Note- BR-I am astounded! But it is very true that I have been feeling 'out of sync' and frustrated for months. Perhaps I should sing jolly tunes to my pc from now on?)*

ANCIENT WRITING

So we shall now answer your question about the writing. It is essential to understand that centuries make no difference to people or Beings who have left the Earth. So we can now see a Being who has lived before in your world, who wants to make an impact in your lives by telling you things he has experienced. He could only do it by 'showing' himself in a way that would intrigue you. He had chosen the writing he was used to in his days on Earth. He has been 'famous' in his days because he was the leader of a group who wanted to achieve freedom for their people. He has been very well known but that is not so important now, as what matters is the message. He has written about the track record of his people.

BR- What was it about?

He wrote the story of their journey in an 'ancient book' long ago, about what they did to achieve their freedom. This book was kept very secret for a long time before others found it, because the record was for their own people to remember and pass it on- but not for the 'enemy' to know of their strategies or secret meetings.

So we can see the start of his tale saying that all Beings have freedom *'per se'* and anyone interfering with others' freedom is a criminal in a way—as it is an offence to affect others' liberty yet want one's own. So this is what those few lines are saying to open the door to his speech, to his narrative. That's why he wanted to present it his way, as he had prepared those words long ago to make the world sit up and listen to those who had been subjugated and finally shook off the yoke and freed themselves of oppressors, or so they hoped!

We know you can be concerned as to the veracity of our statement. This is what WE are seeing as we are aware of someone who came to talk to you all *(In my APPEX experimental group)* but could not communicate the way he thought of, so finally reverted to his 'old habit' of writing down everything for posterity.

We could not label the language ourselves, as these are human labels — but we think it has to do with the Jewish religion versus the Romans' imposition of their laws on a people who had been in that country for a very long time before they came. We know it is a well-known fact, but the man who wrote that had achieved fame when he told his people to fight for their freedom. There was blood on both sides eventually but the law of justice had to be maintained and re-established.

We have here that gentleman who has spent such a long time in a kind of exile in those days and wants to put across the necessity for Mankind to reunite its various 'parts' and sides. Mankind has been split up into so many varied and dissimilar facets that it has become rather frightened to contemplate it as a whole. There are not 'many' aspects: there are hundreds and thousands of packs of Beings who should all be one and are not! **They have been told** (by Human leaders) that they **"must be different** because the laws or rules and ideals are different from all the others, therefore **'that'** makes them stand out and 'superior' to the rest!" This is so wrong nowadays, he says.

(I was briefly disturbed by someone else but my teachers pulled me back, by saying, "You know it is important that you stay focused. It is most vital that you listen to us now in one long swoop and not be distracted - so we'll carry on...")

This man is of great importance for teaching Humanity what needs to be done if anyone listens to him.

He has started making himself known that night *(In my APPEX group)* so that you all knew he existed and he made a point by writing in his 'old' previous language, which is not used or needed by him nowadays!

He's been saying, as he repeats here: "There is a great need for Mankind to have their Souls' aims in front of them, i.e. that all Beings are equal, there should be no separation between 'tribes' or 'countries'. The divisions are man-made, yet the aims have always been to be One Being but converted into various 'disguises' for the fun of creation and creativity. So, the fun can be achieved if all are relaxed and not in fear of each other.

"This is why Humans have failed to let themselves enjoy the world they are in, without hurting their neighbours and themselves in the process. All should be free to do what they can do and discover, without feeling they are under pressure brought by overpowering other Humans who want to lead, crush or interfere with the Free Will of those they are oppressing."

This is his message overall - but the bottom line is that **freedom should and must be a paramount right of each and all individuals. No one should be in fear of others, that way no one will have any need to fight.**

These words are obvious, those ideas are evident but who listens? Who is applying them at the moment? Not many - Worse - too many have forgotten it is their **right** to be free and the **duty** of others to let them be free!

That is the vicious circles of animosity created by those who want to feel important and have all the material goods they can accumulate — amassing them before they 'die' and leaving the whole lot behind, often without ever enjoying the joys they thought they would have! Now we'll leave this topic if you allow us before we turn back to our book?

BR- Could I just ask: Has that gentleman more to say in our Tuesday APEX sessions? As a regular speaker or through me?

My dear, that man has been before but you did not notice him.

BR- Oh! Where and when?

He HAS come to talk to **you** before in our other book (T, L&D) **and he's been in the group but did not speak.**

BR- (surprised) Is he 'the Big man' my friends saw?

He was quite a large male when he was on Earth in that life. He has kept the impression left behind of an 'imposing personality' which comes across as 'a big man'. He has been before and may come back, you'll know him now as the one who 'spoke' by writing those Hebraic, Aramaic words as a token, a sign of his presence - *(Note- BR- I had misheard at first and thought he said 'archaic' but felt it was not right - then he corrected me: 'Aramaic')*

BR- Could he give me a name for him? I'll let my pen write in 'automatic'...

The pen started slowly tracing some letters - but as I was at the bottom of the page I asked him to do it again on the next blank page. So this time the pen wrote 'vertically' one letter per line linked to the next one (!): J O H N, followed by the words:

"All called me 'Yohannus', now known as 'JOHN'. My words were written **before** the man Jesus came along to preach the same thing, to encourage people to go away for safety, away from the crushing of the invaders. My 'book' was more words of wisdom and encouragement — because if they were clear in their Minds that they should not be enslaved, then themselves would not want to enslave others later. That was the main teaching: All free."

212

(NOTE- BR- I discussed with my APPEX group the idea of inserting a photocopy of the writing here, as we guessed many readers would be curious. But knowing Mankind and its narrow-minded views, after much pondering we reluctantly came to the conclusion that 'alphabet experts' who may see it, may not value the wonder that Yohannus managed to try and RECALL this language after millennia and do it THROUGH an Earthly person/medium who was unexpectedly used that way for the first time – Since in those ancient days letters/characters could at times differ from one region to another, we cannot guarantee 'experts' would analyze or recognize it correctly! So they may criticize if it did not appear 100% correct to them, instead of them appreciating the WONDER that Yohannus managed to not only RECALL one of his past lives' languages after millennia (he very likely does not think in those human words anymore!), but also do it THROUGH an Earthly person/medium—This could cast an unnecessary shadow on his genuine communication and on the teachings of my channelled book. We know it is 100% authentic and that's all that matter, since after all this unexpected writing is not what this whole book is about.

PART OF 'THE BIG BOOK'

(My Teachers come back) All will be revealed in more detail when we have finished our book. Now we'll continue if you don't mind! We have so much to say and you have so much to do to put the message across to the world that we both have to work even harder nowadays. You will really have to catch up with all this, my dear. We have been left dragging behind because you could not pull yourself together to attack what you need to attack and tackle. Get your action plan sorted out so that we can fit it in and be fitted into your life to make larger strides towards our goal and your success, as far as your life plan and our teaching the world are concerned. So we'll say this:

1) This is important and you need to think about it more: if you want to succeed, you will have to tidy yourself mentally and physically- i.e. rebalance your way of thinking towards your goals and give them priority. You'll find it will help you tidy your physical life and surroundings too by the same act *(My office need more sorting out- again! But... it is times consuming whereas I should be preparing the book for publication!)*

2) The layout of your new book (this one) will be helped by us: We'll dictate what needs to be put in the correct order so you won't have to worry about which chapter comes first or not. You will be helped. We'll break it down for you as best as we can to save you time.

3) This book of ours is an important section of 'THE Big Book of Knowledge' being spread across the world at the moment. *(They are teaching the world in many different ways and media, via various people.)* So it can't wait forever to be published, you understand? You will **have to** get it out as soon as possible- which means receiving it, typing it and sending it to the publisher whichever suits you best to get it done.

4) Our dictation is not a one person's job. There are MANY profound thinkers as well as knowledgeable Beings providing the facts, which have to be disseminated across the world of Humans. So we are 'inspired' ourselves: that means we are receiving more and more information for us to pass on to you.

This means you WILL have to be very receptive, relaxed and quiet and not ask questions in the middle of the dictation (but you can afterwards), as we need to keep our linked Minds free from disturbing sidetracking. It is essential to understand this point!

When you have received the lot we'll tell you: "That is enough for now, get it published." As only so much can be given at a set time.

If we tell you the world you know has been created by Beings from beyond it, that will not be new to you of course; but you have now realised **those Beings have nothing to do with the 'Spirit World',** as you call it, which is for us simply a part of what is linked to the Earth vibration-wise. That means:

• You have the Earth vibrations which have been created to make the whole physical world visible and acceptable to Life on it.

• But we also have the area of vibrations *(the Spirit World)* which have been created by the need of those who choose to live on Earth for a while and go back later for other experiences. They have to come over first to 'change tack', to refresh themselves, to sum up what they have learnt and experience and decide what they want to do next. Hence this level of vibrations is for those who want to go over to the Earth and come back to rest and reflect on that journey, then possibly go over again.

This is why we had to have those **'layers' of Mind focus made to fit in with the Earthly mentality** (i.e. from having been a Human) but also to reflect and **remind the Being who has just been on Earth, that he is also a Being of Mind and Light**! So, he will be reassessing his needs at each trip: before, after and in-between.

This is why we have that *'area of thinking'* called the Spirit World by you all. But **it is NOT inhabited by Beings from other planets or other worlds of Mind if any**. It is just for the particular planet Earth which you have chosen to live on as Humans. That includes any helpers and 'teams' of the travellers, as they all need a back up when making their journey and tackling their tasks. If it was not so, the Earthly explorers would be very lonely, lost, confused and no doubt most would give up easily, thus 'endangering' their original life plans.

So there we are, in this plane, looking out for you people 'over there'. **But we also have access to far beyond** that section. And 'far beyond' is all to do with subtle or **high levels of thinking or Matter that are unknown to you all.** Adapting to conditions and situations unfamiliar to Humanity - so far anyway- and mingling with extremely active Minds with a scope impossible for Mankind to envisage.

All this information is not helping you as you have not experienced any of this, so you will not be aware of what is and what can go on. If you wish to know more about those 'other worlds' you will have to accept that not everything is physical. So, your world of planets and stars and galaxies is nothing much to us, compared to what is and can be! We'll have to leave this for another time as your Mind is getting tired.

SSS

CHAPTER 24

What we could tell you about now is the 'sphere system'. That system is not a pack of big round bubbles of whatever size. It is only a way of speaking to put things in a kind of perspective for you Humans to get a vague idea of what can go on and is going on beyond the reach of your Earthly instruments...

The levels of Minds that exist are infinite. One can compose more and more by simply thinking or wondering in a different way on a different slant or topic. This very fact is actualizing many new stages of Energy. This is very difficult to explain, so please bear with us: it is not a 2 or 3 D topic!

It is about multilayers of subtle vibrations which have to do with infinite Minds, as Minds never 'die', never run out of power. Mind Power is the mightiest thing that exists because it is bent on constantly creating and it does!

So, the 'spheres' we are talking about are not so much areas of definite dimensions but **fine, subtle blending of ways of thinking;** and within each way of thinking, each thought sent out, resides that astounding power to create what is being thought!

Therefore, as thoughts are produced and sent out, **the power gets energised even more - and that generates even more shoots and thoughts** *ad infinitum*! So who says there are limits and dimensions of the Earthly type? We cannot put limits or define any limits to this ethereal power that creates 'physically' at times.

What we name **the 'sphere system'** is not what round balls or spheres are to you - but over lapping, **intermingling**

levels of thinking which, if let loose, go on at random with wild enthusiasm. If reined in by a strong and forceful **Mind filled with a goal** at the time, then the **thoughts are channelled** to create the goal as their 'product'.

If Humans imagine them to be spheres as round balls of whatever size, they definitely are putting dreadful and incorrect limits to something which has no physical or even ethereal 'walls' and boundaries! That's what we are trying to put across: you cannot measure a sphere which has only Thought Power as its source and product: it is impossible! Where are the limits within your own Mind and thoughts? They shoot out and spark out, mingle and have no boundaries or end! It is eternal. **Thought Power** has always been, is eternally lasting as **infinite mental combustion**- but not mental to do with any physical brain of course; there is no such thing.

Therefore, if you have grasped the infinitely and **extensively gigantic multilayers of refined Energy that Thought Power is**, then you'll be in a better position to grasp that the creation of 'other places' that are not physical to your eyes, can and do exist.

They exist in the sense dreams exist yet you can't touch them. You live them, experience them - you feel real when you live them and see those places or activities in them - yet you cannot possibly give them a 'physical place', can you! It is not 'all imagination' but it is **realms of creation, beyond your Human understanding** as long as you view them from your Earthly point of view. It is beyond anything and anyone who is not experiencing them.

So it is with those other realms and 'spheres of thinking' - not limited by any 'physical' boundaries; not seen by others who are not on the same vibrational link; and out of reach of any mechanical, physical instrument which could never measure the intensity of what goes on both 'there' and in the Minds of those living the experience.

So we can't say more than: "This is an example of worlds that cannot be spotted, known about or defined — yet exist, because they are the product of Mind Power. Mind Power is universal, ethereal and eternal. It cannot be limited and defined by any kind of calculation etc". This leads us to the next question:

WHAT CREATED MIND POWER?

Well, there is only one answer: **Mind Power has! Because it is the most extensively potent Energy that can exist - NOT out of a brain or a separate Being but as its own self.** There again not as a personality but as the fact it exists, has always existed and will always exist!

There is no reason why it should have a beginning. It is your Human Earthly way of thinking that gives you that slant in your assessment. In the world of Energy, or rather the topic of Energy we are talking about, there is absolutely **no grounds to have a beginning for an Infinite Power that:**

• **Never extinguishes itself,**
• **Is in fact constantly on the go,**
• **Is continually filled with the Urge of Creativity,**
• **Is pulsating with the desire to activate itself and actualize what it can conceive!**

It's all beyond any average Human approach, we know that. This is why we are trying to explain as simply as possible, step by step to make you feel the situation and reason out that we are right in passing this information which it is great time the Earth population tried to understand.

It is no good looking for little people or big ones on other 'local' planet around the Earth. There will not be any visible 'Human looking' (or even similar) Beings — and the

219

ones who could be there you would never see with your own eyes, or detect with your instruments. So it is rather a waste of time looking for them. *(Note- BR- I started asking a few questions but my communicator stepped in)*

What you are asking is what we are aiming to get round to. You really need to be patient. We have to take it step by step so that everything makes more sense. We can only tell you in passing that tales about the creation of the world abound enormously. Every tribe have their own story. But if you want to know the real details you need to go into the 'Eternal Facts Box' *(BR- Note: Also known as 'Akashic records')* and look into them to see **which possibilities** of creation and creativity took over the milling of ideas and **'won'**. So not everything is correct in those tales!

What you really need to know and have explained will be and is given to you NOW. We do look into all the facts there are available. We have done our 'homework' so you need not wonder or worry whether we have got our details right. You have been shown before that we aim for Truth and Perfection as much as can be produced. So we shall not give you incorrect information.

If we can carry on now, we'll tell you that the same questions have been asked over centuries and millennia! It is one of the quests of the Human Mind: "Where do we come from, why are we here?" This is what we are working on and telling you.

Why us rather than some other book written about it no doubt? Because we have given you evidence that we can explain obscure topics and make them clear enough. We always endeavour to produce true, correct facts out of all the information obtained by delving deeply into the 'Memory Box of All Times'.

So we have a clearer picture and we chose you to do the job of receiving it because we know you only want the Truth and nothing but the Truth. You would not clog your Mind with preconceived ideas, because you cannot bear limitations and brainwashing!

BR- True!

So we shall carry on with our way of publicising facts across, as they need to be explained for better understanding.

NO SINGLE BEING AS A DEITY

If there had been one deity creating all this, who would have create It / Him/ Her? It is the old question. And if / He/ She/It "has always existed" then in that case you are accepting that it is possible and feasible to exist forever with no beginning.

So if a deity is an ethereal, Energy Being, then it is on par with what we are trying to put across. Except that the **idea of a single Being** making all there is and can be, **is still limiting it** and the results.

Therefore we'll turn to the immensely gigantic Power residing in everything and being the Source, the 'bottomless, wall-less Source' of constant Energy to power into any kind of Reality what needs and wants to be actualized.

(As you look at us, see us in your Mind as a bright spark or light, pouring light into you with exciting information. You will not fall asleep then! It is essential to be alert to receive all this, otherwise you can't take it down on paper). So the main points are:
• Where does that Power Source come from? Nowhere in particular, everywhere if you wish to see it that way.
• Why was the Earth created? It has already been explained in our other book *(T, L &D)*.
• How was Mankind created? Partly with the Will of those who wanted to go to Earth and therefore help build a suitable

221

vehicle of flesh for themselves. But **also by a consortium** of great powerful Minds bent on creating more exciting venture. **All those Minds come from various 'areas of thinking Mind Power'**— areas in the sense of various levels, frequencies, degrees of subtlety and creativity.

The blending and the auto-generated excitement produce and produced many ideas and possibilities, which were tried out or rejected. It was a kind of ball game, tossing ideas and seeing what would happen. Those Minds were **'Beings' in the sense of focused Minds with more accumulated experiences**, which gave them extra knowledge already tested.

All that supplied some 'ground work' for the production of a new world made of Matter utilised in a different way— with emphasis and intensity put into production as usual, but accentuated in certain ways to make it different from before (if ever used) or simply 'different'. That's what your physical Matter is. As the atoms' energies were played with, the results came out differently and were juggled!

CREATIVITY BY-PRODUCTS

The many stages it took for one single world, such as the Earth, to be created, have been astronomical i.e. tremendously gigantic by all standards. So please be patient and understand that you all see things from your Human point of view as we have repeated many a time before.

As the world of this type of Matter was thought out and created, there were many others which were thought of as well in a way, because there were either by–products of what was being thought and thus got into part or whole creation - or were rejected, not completed- but **if they had been thought of, they will have had some kind of Life Force put into them** by that very fact.

So this is where so much Creativity produces so many products: ideas float about, fired out of curiosity or simply intensity, and it will produce something out of the Matter produced by the thought! You need to constantly remember that thoughts are productive, thoughts have results - whether they lead to the final result or not. So we have **hoards of mini-creations, mini possible worlds 'half-baked' as you would say, which may not have been finalised in that particular plan, but still exit and float about!** They can still be used in a 'backing up capacity' as far as their Energies are concerned, because they could and can still help maintain an equilibrium. But not all are used for that.

We are saying that the first thoughts regarding the creation of your Earth were millions no doubt, of random thoughts gradually crystallised into Matter and infused with Life Force: the Life Force of those who thought them out into 'being', existing, then the rest.

JOY OF CREATING MATTER

We have several people who want to speak to you tonight - You'll have to pay great attention to what they wish to tell you. We have a 'senior, superior personality' here, who has been very much **involved in the creation of many smaller worlds to give them life and structure** so that they can reach a satisfactory development.

(Change of communicator)
This is what I wish to say on the matter of 'Matter'... There are many types and there will always be many more kinds of what you call 'Matter': That substance to make things out of, somehow. If we wished to be finicky, we could say there will always be far more 'Matter' than you Humans could ever imagine.

223

So, this Matter you know of in your Universe has permitted the creation of 'solid' (to your senses) objects, sceneries and even worlds apparently not invisible to you all— yet many parts of them are invisible to you all! This is the conundrum of wanting to see and sense with physical senses - you want things to be tangible and visible, yet you cannot do it properly because your senses are very limited!

Therefore, to come back to what we were saying: The fact that something can be visible and sensed stems from the delicate structure of its anatomy, its construction, its inner elaboration. It has to be constructed in such a way as to being indestructible as far as Eternity is concerned — yet be limited in its very existence as a visible physical object, because the physical world is limited and temporary. This is why my interest in Matter stems from its creation by Minds - THAT is what is **so** exciting about it.

Mind is not physical, it cannot be 'touched' and so on— Yet **it can create simply by pulsating out its innumerable outpouring of thoughts. That gives LIFE** to what can be created, according to the **Intensity** of the thoughts and **Desire or Urge** behind each one of them! **That** is really something to be admired!

So, once you come to terms with this point and accept it as part of your everyday vocabulary, you'll come to understand the significance of wanting to create even more at every step of the way. The excitement is so intense; and the juggling of thoughts and new ideas is astounding, as they seem to present themselves to our Minds as if they had always been there — yet are 'new' since they had not been thought of.

This leads to the next point: once the main thoughts have started elaborating a basic structure for a possible 'new world', **the combination of other Minds** joining in the 'discussions and projects' is very essential, because it adds

224

clarity, innovation, serenity but also joy and excitement. All those emotions are very creative by themselves, so you can imagine when they are all joining others it means an exuberant and constant fireworks display of superb creative thoughts!

What we are trying to put across for you all to grasp is the **sheer Joy of Creativity** at its constant best, trying to outdo itself all the time as it goes along. It is not stale, it is not limited, it is not slow. It is constant bursts of newness and wishes for 'better and different'. And that is what is shown on your physical world in myriads of ways—but what is also shown in other levels of existence which you cannot possibly ever be aware of, as long as you are on the Human physical plane.

When the rest of the physical world was on its way to 'being' (and there were many huge possibilities of turning those creations into umpteen types of other dwelling places if need be!), **the ultimate aim** was not so much making 'homes' for new Beings, but rather making things and Beings and mainly seeing how one can expand oneself into other 'dimensions' - not only physical sizes but also dimensions and levels of Mind—**how one could broaden and expand one's Mind towards and into spheres of Knowledge.** There is no limit to Knowledge: the moment one thinks to become more aware of what is possible or impossible, at once one expands one's Mind so that it triggers the possible creations of those thoughts.

One is trying to examine or consider the possibility of something new, and THAT automatically gives it Life as mentioned before. As those levels of thoughts expanded, their creativity meant they lived before they had completely manifested themselves in a possibly physical world! In fact they existed fully as 'invisible', never or not always becoming realised into one type of Matter or another!

225

THOUGHT ENERGY: FASTEST THING

There are several points we need to make in order to specify what needs to be learnt and understood before one deals with worlds other than your own:

• There is the lightness and speed of Thought.

• The temperament or way of thinking of the Being sending the thought.

• The ease or not of manipulation of those Energies and the impulses every thought sends around itself as it creates more happenings.

So, the main points being laid out, we need to give a fairly brief overview and explanation to make sure all is well on the comprehension level!

1) The lightness of Thought vibration - Thought as a result of Mind activity has absolutely no limitation. Its Energy can transcend everything, pass through walls, even travel round and though the Earth. You have no idea how powerful and malleable **Thought Energy is the fastest thing ever in existence!**

2) Making sure the personality or Mind sending or creating each thought is true to themselves and not sending mixed Energies. If you send a mixture of anger and joy or anger and love, it will not reflect a very clear message, will it! **Clarity of thinking and feeling is paramount to produce perfectly balanced results**. That may be obvious to you but it has to be pointed out.

3) If the personality or Being has not done their 'homework', has not planned out in their Mind what they wish to achieve, there will be quite a lot of hit and miss activities in the direction thoughts will go in their actualization, or half results possibly fizzling away. So, clarity of Mind is essential and an aim, a goal is vital for perfect results.

If Creativity is left to play on its own without a clear blueprint, there will be lots of shoots all over the place, before it falls down in a definite line. That shows one needs to have a **clear Mind with a purpose** to create and invent anything new, otherwise randomness will not achieve anything which could definitely progress satisfactorily.

As the world of Mankind grew into what it became and what you now know, it exemplifies **the need for responsible construction.** It is not enough to build, it has to be done responsibly **with vision** of what it could lead to later on. If left at random, the Urge for Creativity will take over and the shooting thoughts will materialize somehow without a definite plan forming itself at the same time. So **it** needs sensible, **levelheaded willingness to exist for a purpose,** whoever it is or will be!

If the Will is not there, it will not drive the construction of the materialization or actualization; the **Will is essential to any creative act!**

Why discuss this? Because the creation of this world or any other world - whether of 'pure Mind' or of a particular type of Matter of its own - has had Will imbedded in its formation. Otherwise there will not be 'new Matter' or 'new worlds' or Beings... Therefore we always need to bring back this point.

If you wish to talk to other possible Beings, you need to be familiar with the way they can be formed, as they are not produced without them knowing!

𝒮𝒮𝒮

CHAPTER 25

If we told you the need for more Knowledge in your world is increasing, you would not be surprised indeed and we feel the same. This is why we are so keen on passing knowledge of facts that have to be understood, as they have been lost over millennia. It's all very well to want to know where you'll be going after your body 'dies'—but what will happen when you decide to no longer hop on the wagon and conveyor belt of human reincarnation? This is when you need to know what's behind the whole thing!

If there had *not* been any Beings wishing to fill a new world (= The Earth) with new temporary passengers, there would have been no Earth! So where did all those Beings come from? You probably all thought: 'The Spirit World', but is not quite correct!

At the beginning **the first individuals as Humans on Earth, were CREATED by those from beyond that new Earth,** in order to experience a new exciting trip in a novel, different world of Matter. This is what needs to be put into perspective, as it seems Humans have got completely confused regarding the creation of their own world and of themselves! This is why we wish to put the record straight and attempt to make you all open your Minds to much more clear-cut facts than all the imaginary fables poured at you over centuries. There had been people who had understood or had been inspired, but they were crushed by those who did not want their own 'inventions' and tales to be shown as utter nonsense.

BEINGS FROM BEYOND THE 'SPIRIT WORLD'

When the dust settled after the physical creation of your new Earthly world—i.e. when the physical crust of the world was more established and ready for Beings to arrive and investigate it and enjoy its newness—there was quite **a** crowd of **willing travellers!** All they had to do was **willing themselves into appearing there. At first there will have been such Beings 'from elsewhere'** let's say, who simply *visited* to see what the new creation looked like and what had been put on it. But they were not really the 'first Humans' because they had not chosen a flesh body—not yet anyway. They were just passing, or were some of those involved in its creation, because there had been myriads of them projecting their ideas towards the 'new Invention and Experiment'.

When those had been on and off, there were some who **decided they wanted to try and be there longer,** hence the new body... since that was part of the Experiment in the new Matter! So they did and the results are now known to you, of course.

But it is essential to recall and realise **they were Beings from OUTSIDE the environment of the new Earth's Universe—and NOT from what you see as the' Spirit World'.** Because 'the Spirit World' came into existence so to speak, when the need arose to receive those travellers back and help those going again.

What is needed is a clear understanding of what that 'half way' world / 'Spirit World' is.

Picture **a level of vibrations with multiple layers according to the states of Mind of the travellers.** As they will be creating for themselves the reception area, then 'progress areas' which they will be travelling through with their Minds, they will *eventually* gradually move away mentally from the mindset of having donned a flesh body as a Human and all its consequences!

(NOTE- BR- Readers be reassured: your loved ones WILL be waiting for you and receive you when you pass over - The explanation above is to do with much later evolution).

The original Beings were not unlike what you imagine 'Spirit Beings' to be, i.e. **Beings of Light and thinking and sensing Energy.** There are numerous types of such Beings, but those who have come to Earth **were interested in its creation and its new Matter** - so they will have eventually fashioned themselves the physical bodies you know.

But the original ones of the early days did not have to 'dress themselves up' (with a flesh body) nor do they need to do it nowadays either. **Those who were part of its creation and design have been back many times and can still come and help or try to! And also help realign Energy fields out of place, or attempt to calm other areas.**

Those 'creators' have the **well being** of that plane at heart because they were so involved and part of it at the beginning. That is what you sense at times, when some of them come to visit and make an impromptu adjustment to some field and vibrations. Those trips by original Beings are **what you call 'UFO' lights** etc, but they are not evil Beings with bad intentions: They come to check what needs doing, to rectify certain situations.

BR- Why were some cows, say, found as if operated upon or dead etc?

Those kinds of incidents have **nothing** to do with what we are talking about! *(Note- BR- suggests to anyone wondering about such as the cows etc. to look into declassified info on secret work by governments' defence and army programmes!)*

We talk of original creators and designers coming to HELP their creation remain stable and in good form. Whereas

230

you are talking of intrusion and interference with some of the Earthly inhabitants i.e. Animals in this case. We only wish to discuss for now the fact the original Beings are still concerned about what they made and want it to work well, in spite of Mankind's stupid and reckless interference, all the time it seems nowadays.

All those involved have always been interested right from the beginning of its creation, but that has not always been understood. Then it got 'diluted' and distorted by umpteen religious leaders. So we are saying: do not fear the UFOs you may see or sense. They will **not** be evil Beings ready to have a war with you and 'conquer' you. Those are the ones at the back of it all, ready to support your world's continuous formation.

But if you know of 'other planets inhabitants' then you could ask us about them individually. We have no information about 'evil and nasty conquerors' planning to invade the Earth!

What you need to put across to people of your world is that originally they, as Higher Energies, wished long ago to try and see what it would be like to live as physical Beings disguised as Humans. This is what you have all forgotten, **you have never realised you were Beings from 'beyond'.** Beings from far superior and more refined vibrations than the slower vibrations of the Matter your own Earth and Universe consist of.

So, if you see the latter as a closed box, so far limited by its own levels of vibrations created by the type of Matter you know of, then you'll comprehend better that the 'creators' of that huge box and its contents of Matter were **outsiders from much higher levels of vibrations**.

Those levels will be hard for you and other Humans to grasp, as long as you are in the Earthly flesh, because you will not have experienced and will not recall any other levels, much higher than yours. So we have a dilemma: trying to put this across to Minds who cannot technically relate what we are saying to anything they know of - but we will still try.

To sum up again: the Beings you have on Earth as 'Humans' were originally and still are of course, Beings of Mind and Light, i.e. Beings who had no need for a flesh body but thought it intriguing and challenging when the project was started!

BR- 'Where' and how did they see themselves? All on the same level of vibrations?

If we were to explain using the example of lights or a light: if you were a light where would you be? A light in your sky, say, because we cannot make you imagine non-physical realms. The light would be free to travel; would be self-igniting and powering; would be agile and enjoy its freedom and its own abilities to travel as fast as it wishes; that light can also think and feel. So there would be added qualities. As to 'where' exactly', there is nowhere exactly! It is more what 'it' (or whoever) **thinks** it is doing, or how or 'where' it **imagines** it is doing 'that' (i.e. whatever its activities are). That is the type of Beings we are talking about.

So, the Minds of all those from that level of thinking, and no doubt from others at other levels of thinking, had joined and exchanged thoughts about the possibilities of creating a new experiment for fun and challenges—challenges only in the sense of **testing one's abilities about manipulating *that* new type of Matter**. It is always so much more exciting and exhilarating to find new ways of doing anything not done before!

So that's where **you ALL are from - a level of complete freedom, speed of Thought, Mind Creativity and a desire to overcome little challenges set by yourself** and the conditions you find yourself in. Usually to do with your Matter which is still largely a mystery to most of you!

232

Moreover, most of you have completely forgotten why you CHOSE to be here, and how much your Mind and its creative force can influence not only your body but all material conditions! If only you learnt or re-learnt to apply it properly! That's what we are coming to again: Use the Power of your Mind!

MORE ABOUT OTHER WORLDS

BR- Please tell me more about Other Worlds and "Beings from beyond"...

If we had tried to tell you all this when we first started our books, you would have found it extremely difficult to grasp. It had to be given in gradual doses, as done in our first book *Truths Lies & Distortions*.

Now we'll tell you that the whole of Humanity is lots of 'people' who are primarily Beings from the Ultimate Energy, i.e. who are and have always been Beings of Light and Thought, but not always remembered it, hence all the troubles on Earth.

So we'll start with the reminder, brief but true, that the Earth being an Experiment was *only that*. And it is not and was *not the ultimate goal of existence*!

If you had been told you came from 'beyond the stars', you could have thought we were telling you a lot of nonsense and you may not have listened anymore...

If the world of Matter you know was not as it is, your world would obviously be very different. Your world of the Earth is part of your Universe and that has astronomical dimensions seen from your point of view, but puny from ours. That means when you focus on the vibration of this type of Matter (yours) you will see - if you can - hoards of places, planets, stars etc. But they are only varieties of the same thing - they are **all made of this same type of Matter** which has many facets, yet created things that can be sensed on this Earth vibration.

IF you reached *beyond that set of vibrations*, you would then sense far different experiences, which are not quite analogous to yours.

The worlds BEYOND your Universe have slightly more refined or less refined vibrations and slightly different frequencies. This will mean that tracking them can only be done by those who can focus on that type of vibrations and receive them clearly.

Your physical Universe is of no different Matter than what is in or around your Earth, so you have a good sample there. But the **materialisations** are at times different, depending on the emphasis put on the main elements. So if you have 'gassy people' *(mentioned in my Tuesday APPEX experimental group)* they won't quite be the same as some other 'fluid like' Beings' (let's say, so that you do not automatically imagine them to be with two arms and two legs like yourself!). So the 'gassy Being' who comes to talk to you has that 'appearance' or consistency if they choose to sense themselves 'physically' — i.e. with senses other than Mind and Thought.

But those gassy Beings can travel in ways you could not do with your flesh body, which is why you have there a big difference to start with. They can **use their Minds to fly** off from one place to another. You can do so in your visualisations but **Humans have lost the know-how to make your body of flesh transcend the weight it has.**

You can still send thoughts over to others and some of you have retained the knowledge and understanding that this is not only feasible but very useful and advisable — in the same way as some of you have understood that healing of the flesh body is primarily done with the Mind, for the good reason the

Mind has caused the problems in the first place, thus causing diseases!

But you need to try and grasp that giving you a 'list' of places where there may be others in the same flesh or not, or in a different type of 'outward condition', i.e. visible or not, is not going to solve your problems!

What we are trying to make you all understand is that you can only see things via your five senses which can be extended by additional instrumentation *(NOTE- Such as, X-rays, gamma or ultra-violet rays detectors, for example)*, and that means you cannot see and calculate those existing beyond them.

If that was not so, you would see all those other Beings and places and what is on them. But because you only 'see' with your eyes – or even your microscopes and telescopes - **you do not have access to vibrations which are beyond their reach.** Therefore, we are here trying to fill the gap to make you comprehend what you cannot get to.

So yes, such as those 'gassy Beings' communicating with your group, have an existence *in areas of your own physical Universe*, BUT **not on a particular planet or star,** or whatever you may try and spot with a giant telescope. It would not be possible because **their world is MADE UP BY their Minds** i.e. made of what their Minds imagine. And that **can change at any moment** as we told you before. When they project themselves towards you, it is via the process of Mind to Mind links known as telepathy and mind blending.

So theirs is of not much interest to you. If you want to look at other remote planets and stars etc., it is not much use looking for Beings like you, as you are unlikely to find them.

BR- Why are we unlikely to find Beings like us Humans?

What you could see is possibly similar but not 100% the same. What would be the point of experimenting and doing the same thing twice or more? *(=When they created THIS world of Matter)* So we are saying: you'll find other Beings (yes within your physical Universe) BUT that would mean difficulties in spotting them even if you had extra powerful telescopes or cameras. It is not that you would not be able to so much as **you could not recognize them,** as they would not be what you would expect. They might be 'lights' or 'shadows' or 'shapes' or nothing physically noticeable.

BR- But such as radiations, or radio/ electromagnetic waves, would be spotted...

Ok, but would you link it to them being 'Beings'? It is not that easy to make sense of it when you don't know what to expect. What you see as a planet is not always a living place, a place to live on. It is often just a complementary force to balance the Energies of your own world. So don't imagine they all have to be populated, or some other use than being useful to the rebalancing of all the Energies!

We need you to accept what we are telling you. Then discuss it if you wish. Rather than breaking our flow and cutting bits out of context. Could you do that please?

BR- Of course, I am sorry. I keep forgetting you need to focus very hard to keep the flow of information flowing.

If we now have 'carte blanche' to get on with it, we'll add this: **What you see in your physical world is only ONE aspect of what goes on in it!** The visually physical aspect is only for YOUR eyes and senses (and therefore your instruments if they can see better). But the truth and reality is that **this physical Universe is only one of many** that exist. *(Note- BR- This is indicated by Quantum Mechanics!)* Not necessarily physically as you imagine it to be, because you Humans, sadly label things according to and in relation with your five senses, as mentioned before.

So the label we would give is to go beyond those senses. Then you would 'see-sense' far more: **That's where the dilatation of Time and Essence come into play.**

What is seen as 'Time' is non-existent as far as the concept you Humans have, because you see it in relation to your sun and stars. What we see (We and others from Beyond the physical Universe!) is a fact that has many aspects. **That fact is that Eternity, in all directions, is constant! Always is, has been, will be!**

INTENSITY: THE KEY

So you cannot think in terms of Time. But you can then **sense** the **Intensity of Focus** instead, as a parameter. It is when Intensity is put into action and considered to be in play, that you will grasp things differently. Because **Intensity is what makes things HAPPEN,** no matter what. IF there is no Intensity in Thought and Desire, there will be no result. IF there are no results, then where will creation be or take place? You have to have Intensity of Desire and Focus. Then the whole thing makes more sense because this is what causes actualization — and actualization is the process of 'becoming', and 'being' and moving into action. That then implies a kind of direction from 'not being' to 'being', from not existing to existing.

But the **moment the Intensity diminishes** or vanishes, then **the actualization will instantly start fading**. If it can be recovered 'in time' before it vanishes completely, then one can recoup the creation and rebuild or reinforce whatever was on its way out, or nearly out.

This is where there is a feeling of 'time' in YOUR eyes, but to us it is more a lack of Intensity, a loss of Focus and Desire.

URGE TO EXIST

Once that is understood, then the next step to grasp is the NEED for anything to exist! The moment there is no Need, that means there will be no existence, because with Need comes **Urge to BE.** No Urge to Be = no Need to Be = no existence.

And that is how everything exists anywhere, at any level, *in any world*, whether of Mind, Light, Flesh, Earth or other planets and stars.

So this being considered, now is the next step to take. If the Need is there, and the Focus and the Intensity put in the creation or in actualization of the thought — because all needs and urges are thoughts somehow — then the Energy is available all the time to make it progress. THAT is when you'll see proper actualization in its making: when the Energy within the Thought and Urge has enough Intensity and Power to make the Desire become 'real', the personality to create itself or increase its own potential and abilities- or objects to take shape.

But objects in creation are not what you think of as 'dead things'. **Everything that can grow has Life Force within.** And that is another difficult point to grasp when you are stuck within the limited viewpoints of Humans.

When we put all those coordinates together, you'll see that somehow nothing can be created which is not wanted and has not got an Urge within, whether put as an Urge to create that xyz, or to be created. This is all so complicated to try and explain because it boils down to various types of Energies, aspects of Mind and emotions. An Urge to Be is an emotion. But a very creative one of course, as that is its aim.

So where are we going with all this?

The point is: The Earth Experiment (as we've explained previously in *Truths, Lies & Distortions*), has stemmed from an URGE TO BE DIFFERENT; to try different things; to assess differently; to be on a par with some other feelings of existence.

What are feelings of existence? Some are excited, others are calmer. Some are creative and procreative, others are receptive. All those are part of existing. This is what the Earth was about and the Beings on it, as explained before.

Now you want to know beyond that Earth. As previously mentioned, in your physical Universe you'll find many places with no 'Life' on it — i.e. no Urge to be, no Desire to exist. But the planets themselves, say, would be there to be useful to such as the balancing of Energies to maintain the overall equilibrium.

As to other Beings existing 'farther away' it is not vital for you to know really—even though you all want to know! - Because **those Beings would be other aspects of materialization or actualization** of Thought and Desire. If they exist for the sake of being in that state and condition, they will do whatever suits them and they fancy. It may be, and is very likely to be, very unlike your Earthly life, so you may not accept or comprehend those concepts, so why worry about knowing them?

CREATIVE LIFE FORCE

It is far more useful to know that every little spark of Life on a planet, or on yours, has a tremendous Energy within it. That is a Creative Energy, a Life force - And a Life force does not necessarily mean water as some imagine! It is a Light of Creativity, but not so much 'light' as you think of it with bulbs or sunlight - The Light of a Creative Force has no

239

boundary, no limit. It does not fade. **It just IS.** It acts as soon as it is triggered into action by Desire and intense Urge to Be or Do.

So **those are the criteria** which lie behind all types of creations, whether in your physical world and Universe or elsewhere. "Elsewhere": That is where we are coming to. What is 'elsewhere'?

Elsewhere means 'other than the world you know' and the world you know is extremely limited by its consistency, its weight, its outward appearance! As you get into more knowledge of the inner world of the world that you know, your scientists will start to understand a little more of **the fluidity and timelessness of what lies therein**.

If or when they grasp more about those aspects, they will comprehend much more what we are trying to explain. What may be glimpsed then will be nothing or hardly anything, in comparison with the Reality of what IS and really exists beyond the physical world. And THAT is when we shall have some common ground. Why?

Because the 'world of the invisible' to you, Humans, is the beginning of what can be understood of the reality of what EXISTS 'elsewhere', what IS all around, all over, for 'Eternity'- i.e. no 'time' as you think of it; no space or void as you think of it; **nothing is as you think of it, or at least what your scientists think of it!** *(NOTE- BR- Quantum Physics is coming round to this way of thinking!)*

That is what we are trying to 'creep' towards, to open Minds and doors towards the link between worlds of the 'invisible' with the 'Earthly visible'. What is needed then?

At first an understanding of an **eternally existing Life Force underlying and permeating every single thing** one can think of. Everywhere. Nothing is 'suspended' in oblivion, in emptiness. **Nothing exists that has not got that vital Energy of Life within it**. Whether put into use or not, everywhere is Energy and that may have been grasped by now by your scientists.

It is essential Mankind understands they have not been born 'of the Earth Matter' - nor 'been in Spirit World forever' before coming to the physical world as Humans. It is a big step to make and grasp for anyone who has never thought of such a possibility.

If we told you that **all physical Beings have been other 'Beings'** before, you may have a shock. But we had to give the information in graded steps, so that it can be absorbed and assimilated gently, instead of giving a huge blow, which is most likely to be rejected.

What we look at is a mass of Energy turned into physical objects and Beings who chose to go and visit those 'places'. Those in dissimilar 'places' would be very different from your creation. What you want to know is **why there are Humans on Earth and not on other planets etc? That is because it is where they chose to go!** It has been hard enough to create this Earth and balance it so that it can do what it does - you want us or others to repeat the same experiment elsewhere is rather crazy, since there is no need for a copy!

What has been and is being experienced is a unique opportunity to feel as you do, and encounter whatever you chose to go through or face. So, it is to be enjoyed, cherished and valued. It is not to be ignored and thrown out, as all Beings are valid, all are special and unique.

This is what you people don't seem to enjoy and appreciate. **If you all respected the other Beings who are going through their own experiences, you would be more in harmony with yourself and the rest of the world around you -** all doing the same would mean peace and quiet for everyone. Instead, it has sunk to an appalling level of depravity, selfishness and greed! We are all shocked to see what goes on in the world.

The Beings who are **now born and reborn (on Earth) to come and help rectify the situation**, know they will be facing an uphill battle, with little help of succeeding 100% —

because of the inequalities and imbalance created by the current and previous residents. So, we are here to try and open your eyes, all of you, so that the task is as reduced as can be...

WHY CAN THOSE BEINGS COMMUNICATE?

If you looked at a Being from our world (which is not necessarily from the 'Spirit World'!) you would see a difference. **Our** world is the one we are talking about. We are emissaries from the other side of the coin, **BEYOND the other aspect of what is known as 'Spirit World' and the physical world**.

We have access to Minds when they listen or pay attention to ours. **We are Beings from 'past the stars and planets' and past the vibrations of the physical world.**

We are attuned to **you** *(me BR)* through the kindness you show to Animals and other Beings in suffering. You have altered your attraction to the physical, your physical vibration of the Earthly world, in order to polish it to the higher vibration of Compassion, and that is your forte: the caring and love and compassion—not the rest.

This is a very special vibration, which **allows us to ride on it**. That vibration has a lightness, which cannot be sensed on Earth as much as we sense it where we are.

What you wonder is: how can we be in touch with you as a Human on Earth, if we have not been born or are not Human and don't know your words... Well, it is simple: If you think of 'higher', kinder thoughts, and have those thoughts when you are the compassionate Being we know of, **you are transmitting much finer and higher vibrations** than when you think as a Human in their everyday life.

This is why the vibration is easily recognisable and we can use it to convey thoughts. **Our thoughts are instantaneous thoughts and ideas. They are sent on the line of 'colours'** *(vibrations)*, **which represent you in that caring state**. This is what facilitates our link.

242

When the line is lit up or maintained, we can send our thoughts and you receive them in that vibrational field.

If you were to lose your concentration, you can be helped by those who care about you and stay nearby to adjust the link *(i.e. my Team of Spirit Guide & helpers)* this is really all there is to know. The details are far too complicated to explain, since you cannot see what goes on. *(NOTE- BR- I feel very embarrassed to have to publish those kind words, but there are fortunately millions of compassionate people on Earth, so they can benefit from reading and understanding this).*

The words are what your Mind knows to translate the impressions sent by us. We have to think 'simply' enough, so that you can get impressions, rather than 'facts' of a nature you would not know of. So, the words come from your Mind to express what you feel OUR Minds have sent to your Mind as we are trying to make you sense and understand.

We are indeed Beings who have NOT been on Earth but have understood the need for helping those there.

If you want to help others, you do your best, so we do our best. We are not 'solid', in as much as *we can see ourselves as solid or ethereal as we wish*. So, that is the advantage of not being a 'Human'.

If those qualities or abilities did not exist, we would not be different from any other physical Beings. So, the ideas is that you receive our thoughts and 'words' and understand them, then you can pass them on to your peers, your crowds, your co-workers. That way you'll be able to help the world in your 'corner'.

My function as the 'mouthpiece' or spoke person of those interested in talking to you is to make sure you know that you can/one can/ have a link with those beyond the world of the flesh and physicality—and also **let other Beings come through to explain things which are beyond your normal concepts.**

243

You are bound to be stunned and doubtful as we say those words. We know you would wonder whether someone else is pretending to be us, but we will do our best to try and show you or prove to you that you have a link with 'beyond the stars'. It is not your ego, it is not lunacy, it is simply a fact.

FROM WHERE?

Of course, you want to know. If **you can receive links and information from 'beyond the stars' where is that? Well, it is within the vibrations of the Earth world, BUT that level is NOT physical.** *It is the layer of Compassion and Love for all*, **which is part of what the Earth world was made out of.**

That creation (the Earth) was conceived out of love and caring and interest and excitement and urge for discovering new adventures and experiences.

So, that line of vibration is very strong and exists throughout the Universe you know — but is also on the vibration lines of that Earth world you live in.

So, the line from you to us is via that vibration which crosses and bathes your Earth and reaches us as we are at the 'other end' of it, if you like, except it is not necessarily an end. It is simply part of it. We exist on the same 'line', on the same 'frequency'. When we feel compassion, you feel it. When we feel sorrow, you feel it. When you feel those feelings, we feel them and that is why we are linked to you (and many others who care as much as you do).

What you can do now is trust what we tell you, until we can prove to you that we have genuinely spoken to you. So please do not block or reject what we say so that it can be said or taken down.

244

BR- All right. Thank you, I am very touched.

We know you wish to know why there are Beings who come to your world to readjust the Energies... We say 'why', because the Energies have been so disturbed and shaken, they need urgently to be redressed and readjusted. You already know that.

Yes, it is one of our 'jobs': we choose to do so out of Love and Compassion for the creation we and many others have put efforts into—for success, not failure. So we try to help its readjustment. It is not easy but it has to be done.

It is simply a question of sending our Power of Thought towards the Earth. It is so potent that we can adjust those Energies, because they have emanated from us (and similar others) in the first place! It is not complicated. It is just special skills and it works if we are not hampered in our efforts.

CROP CIRCLES & VISITORS

You have heard of places where patterns show on your ground.

BR- Yes, 'crop circles'?

We are responsible for them. It is not because we like pretty patterns, but because they are **the equivalent of the rebalancing needed for that area.** There are areas which cannot be reached as easily or be as visible to you, but we all do our best to fight off the lack of equilibrium—equilibrium which is so badly needed for the world you live in to stay where it is in the cosmos, so to speak.

As to other patterns which you have not seen, they are underground! You would see them if you lived there. They try to adjust the forces fighting each other where they should

245

really be in balance with each other. And that is another mystery for Humans who are not aware of what goes on there either! So we've answered that question.

The other is: why are there **Beings coming to Earth 'disguised' as Humans,** when they do not come from the human race? *(BR Note- As we've been told by the Being who spoke at our APPEX group).* Well, it is because at times we really need to try and influence Humans as well as Earthly Energies —so, coming as 'one of you' is easier sometimes. It cannot always be done and is only executed when necessary. We have ways of 'pulling strings' by **appearing as the kind of persons who would be needed** there, or would be accepted in particular cases.

BR-How do you become 'solid'?

We have great knowledge in the manipulation of Matter and Energies, my dear! This is child play for us really, considering we had a say in the creation of the Earthly world and helping Humans have flesh bodies! You cannot doubt we have the ability, can you! Some do. It's far too complex for us to even try to give you an idea of it, since you Humans don't even know how you were helped to create the flesh bodies you have at the moment!

We know you now need to stop linking and leave us for a while, that's fine, as we have said plenty for now. You can think about it. Please do not doubt. We'll come back to talk with you as soon as you are happy to do so.

SSS

PART 3

CONSCIOUSNESS

****

"Knowledge of any kind...brings about a change in awareness from where it is possible to create new Realities"

(Deepak Chopra)

CHAPTER 26

BR- Could you tell me more about expansion of Consciousness?

The matter of Consciousness is a very important topic because we are more aware of it than you people on Earth. **If there was no Consciousness, there would be no Reality constantly created around those who experience it**. So it is very essential to be aware of what can or cannot happen when one is or is not aware of one's Self. This is the crux of the matter: **Being aware of one's Self as a separate, or rather individual, entity**.

When someone chooses to go back to Earth, let's say, this personality has usually already experienced many lives 'before' and now wishes to expand on their knowledge or improvement of their own attitude, mindsets and inner goals. But when they come back here to this level of vibrations (called the 'Spirit World' by Humans), it is simply to recap what they have learnt and experienced, and review their overall plans for the further improvement if need be. Yet this is only one little stage of the whole process. As they look at their recent and also 'previous' Earthly lives, they can **compare and check** where they now stand in their development.

This is all to do with making Progress – as **Progress** is getting more and more **aware of you as the one who is 'at the root'**... And the root of one's Self is the almighty Power one is, but perhaps one has not developed and polished or extended enough. Because the Creative Power is the very essence of everything and everyone, wherever one finds oneself throughout

any and all Universes, it is still the same Energy, the same Force which has that built- in Urge to do more, experience more, create more.

That's what happens when one expands one's Consciousness, because the 'Spirit World' (as known to those who chose to go to and come back from the Earth) is only a tiny, puny part of what else one can do, be and has been.

If you looked at the original spark of one Being (let's say, to try and give you an overall aspect), you'd see that the intense mental activity within it is fantastic! The word 'mental' has been chosen purposefully because **the Mind of any Being is what drives it**, as it is its tool for expanding and progressing as well as creating around and for itself.

So the Minds of all Beings have a lot to do when you realize every single thing or creature has that tool (a Mind) working for and with them, at any level of conscious development.

If the level of Conscious Development is not very advanced yet, it could simply be because the Soul in question is still finding its way around what it can or cannot do—more likely trying to focus and limit it to one activity at a time—so as not to be showered with creations all round itself and ending up not knowing where or what its Self is and is doing!

STARTING POINT

Therefore **the basic 'starting point of a Soul' is to become aware** of its own Power: that is using and reacting to the Inner Urge to 'BE', an urge 'All That Is in existence' has.

So the Soul focuses on one particular 'feeling' or aspect and helps it open up doors to more discoveries—whether to do with this Earth world or others in other Universes at various levels of vibrations unknown to you all. This is only a start, as said before.

If that Soul, that Being in the process of developing itself, acts upon its Inner Urge, it will provide itself with various experiences which may satisfy its needs or curiosity. Curiosity comes later when inquisitiveness is accentuated and comparisons can be made with other states. When the personality grows within the Soul is when the extent of Consciousness has developed or is developing itself enough, for the individual to **recognize 'they' exist as a particular entity, instead of being part of a 'melting pot' of Energies...**

This is when such a Being may decide, among many choices to **appear on Earth as a Being of Energy** acting through and directing a flesh body and a physical environment; because by doing so, **it empowers itself** with conscious or even unconscious decisions of its Mind to react to and manipulate the physical Matter of their surroundings.

It is a feat to be able to do so, starting with consciously **designing one's own flesh vehicle** so that it is suitable and geared to the purpose of one's physical trip. It does not deny them the use of their own Mind Power. On the contrary it helps them use it more and be able to see the results. Whether they are aware of it or not is another story - as far too many **Humans are absolutely unaware they actually create their own problems by projecting their Mind Energy towards the rest of the population** and towards their environment!

If the Mindsets were more balanced and constantly compassionate, there would be no problem on Earth, whether within individuals or within countries. It is when the Beings are on that Earthly path that they will all individually **develop their Consciousness at different speeds and different degrees**; because once focused strongly on one personality, one tends to forget the other facets one is composed of and part of. If the focus was not there 100%, the personality may have problems manipulating the current Reality it believes it is in.

When they arrive back in the 'Spirit World' after the so-called 'death' of a particular flesh body, they may at first feel they still are on Earth, and thus confuse themselves a little, because their Mind focus has not detached itself from the physical body and environment. But when they gradually open their Minds to what is around them and pay attention to what is presented or explained to them, then they should be able to readjust to their new surroundings, which were theirs in the first place before they left for the Earth trip.

As the sun rises, you usually see clouds scatter to make way for the warm rays to light up the sky. As the Mind clears, the Consciousness becomes brighter and more focused and centred on what it is sensing and dealing with.

When one's Mind has been focused on Earthly matters, it takes a little (or long) while to focus back on Higher Energies which are part of the whole Being one is. So, as it is focused on Earthly matters the Being has a cloudier outlook on its Reality.

As it gradually clears and lets the reality of inexhaustible Mind Power step back in focus, then **the Consciousness of that Being explodes with Joy at its new challenges but also abilities and opportunities!** That's the joy of being real and eternal, because there are no deadlines and limits to what you can do!

MIND & DEGREES of CONSCIOUSNESS

A Mind is a tool for living Beings of whatever kind. Any Being of Light has a Mind by the very fact that the Being 'lives' so it has a Life Force within: whether a stone or a blade of grass, it exists therefore it has that Life Force!

Mind is a Creative Force therefore everyone and **everything has it, BUT not all necessarily USE IT!**

BR- Why not?

251

Because they have not quite learnt to process the patterns **within** themselves. They could be aware, or not, of the fact that they have atoms which can think in their own way - **atoms know** where they are and why they are there. It may not be quite known to all your scientists yet, but it will soon be a fact for everyone to recognize this.

Since atoms know what they are doing, a stone should know—but it could be that the process of **putting this knowledge together has not quite gelled yet: that is where Consciousness comes into.**

If the stone has NOT developed its Consciousness (of being a stone and existing within that environment), it will delay its using its Mind Power tool.

BR- Perhaps it does not need to, as it has nothing to do?

The Matter of which the stone is made, has been created by those who created the physical world you live in. That is sheer Mind Creative Force used to the best of their abilities. So, since All That Exists has that Creative Force as a fundament, then it means they have it in them and can use it, IF or WHEN it is grasped and realised.

So, whether a stone or a blade of grass, they do have that Creative Force called 'Mind' in them as a tool of their own Life Force. **Whether it is used or not is the only difference.**

That is **where degrees of Consciousness come into.** It will allow and encourage/ boost the use of that tool when realisation takes place: conscious knowing of one's existence.

Make the world realize there is not 'one deity or force' creating or ordering those created. It is a Self-Creating 'world' — or rather **STATES of Self Creating** - which allow All That Exists to move forward, if its Urge pushes it to do so. Always for improvement, not a retrograde direction.

ANIMALS' & PLANTS' CONSCIOUSNESS

As the Creation you know of is to do with Humans, Animals & Plants, we'll hasten to say that **all Animals are conscious of their own existence** but usually **in a slightly different way from Humans**. If it is a larger Animal it will have chosen that body for a different purpose from a tiny Animal's aim. All have an awareness of themselves as a Being.

Their **extrasensory perception abilities are far superior** to Humans' overall and they use them constantly, unlike Humans nowadays. In the 'olden days' Humans could use them too but have now lapsed.

When Animals pass over and come back here after their Earthly journey, they are aware they have been a cat or dog or lion or elephant etc. but, **unless they are a pet who wishes to stay close for a while to those Humans they loved on Earth**, they will blend their Minds and Consciousness with others of the same species to add to the Pool of Knowledge this species has accumulated.

BR- Do they lose their individual 'identity' then?
What happens afterwards?

What you see as 'identity' is only a cover, an external habit and garment to have during one particular life. It is not necessarily the identity of the Soul/ the Spirit/ the Energy that has chosen to be such a 'cat/ dog' etc.

Its identity is not the outer physical cover, but the Inner Light which stems and emanates from that Being. That Light never gets extinguished, nor vanishes. It can melt with others as mingling but not disappearing. So the same Being of Light is not bound to any other outer external garment it wore for a while.

Plants have a certain kind of Consciousness. A plant is not a 'dead object'- it is an object filled with Life Force— that is Energy with a tool for creation. It creates itself from within itself & absorbs outside Energies and vibrations. It has an Urge to grow and experience various things such as weather and climate, absolute freedom to grow or constraints.

(NOTE- BR- As the book dictation brought up the topic of expansions of Consciousness, I am including here some conversations with other people in the 'Spirit World', which focus on Humans' and even Plants' Consciousness.

I received/channelled these from members of my family during the same weeks as my Masters dictated their teachings (I have been reporting those family exchanges for the past decades in volumes of my published diary 'I'm Not Dead I'm Alive without a Body') – Why this particular dialogue happened now is obvious once one has read it.

Yesterday was the 15th anniversary of Mum's passing - so I tuned in to my guide with a query.

BR- Could you kindly give me some news of my loved ones in your world if they cannot come and talk themselves? It seems a long time since I had some info.

This is going to be a long 'bit of information' section then, as you have quite a lot of people here! We have your mum here who wants to be remembered. Of course, we are aware that you know it was her anniversary recently; but to her it is only the time when she left you all which she is sad about, if she thinks of it too much. And yet she is glad about it, because she was reunited with her family over here, met new people and discovered all the fantastic things she encountered, as you know; but there are more, as she has not told you everything happening to her recently. Your mum is here - she has quite a lot to explain...

(Change of communicator - Mum joins in!)

If you were me, you would really be happy to be here, darling! It's so wonderful... You have been told I have been very busy indeed. We have so much to do when we start delving into our Selves! It is so incredible and astounding! My view of myself as the little lady on Earth with nothing much to do *(during her last years there)*, except suffer from her body or sort out house problems, has 'gone' in a way, as I can see I have been and am far more than that.

Here we know we are 'people' but **we also become aware that we are made of Energy,** and not flesh as we used to think on Earth. When I say 'We' I mean me, my dad and your dad etc. Even Pierre now *(her first son and my eldest brother)*, as he's been approaching me much more and asking questions and seeking to understand.

He had been overwhelmed by his arrival here. *(NOTE. In 2009, after weeks of agonising pain and fast spreading paralysis, from some kind of tetanus, he speeded up his certain death by breathing in some chemicals. When he passed over, Mum & family were there to help him come to terms with his new situation)* So, it has taken him some time to overcome the reality of being here, free from all the troubles that pestered him on Earth. He is more a free agent now, doing his own thing as usual, but this is carried out as happily as can be because there are no constraints and obligations. Only fun to do if one wishes to do it.

That way his Mind is developing more towards freedom of thought and a greater understanding of the totality of what surrounds him. He is aware that everything is linked up; whether on Earth or here, and that **all our Minds can be linked up as One** if we wanted it.

So, he has begun to sense and grasp that whether Nature/ Plants, Animals or People, the 'whole lot' is one big Mind Power, not so much 'divided as those Beings' than disguised as various shapes and individualisation. We have so much to discover! There will be enough for ever...

I have been particularly focusing on my other facets because that has given me so much food for thought that I am somewhat addicted to **digging into all the layers which compose the 'Me' I feel I am**!

We are not separated you and me, don't worry; I am not leaving you to be 'someone else'! I am just looking at what I have 'already been' we could say, though by saying this I am aware of the **error in labelling those lives as linear. The 'line' is in our human Mind. The reality is, the past of one life would be the present seen from another angle!** This is when it becomes complicated!

But I don't have just that. It's become more a recreational pursuit than necessary work, as the more profound aspect of my 'time travel' has been to focus on many other aspects we had not discussed before.

If you want to know, I'll tell you there are many instances when somebody's Mind can go 'out of the window' and focus elsewhere. That happening occurs regularly because their focus had relaxed But the point is, the very fact they switched off my place, say, to see themselves elsewhere means they **changed levels of frequencies of thoughts** and they will be 'broadcasting' on a different frequency, like changing channels on a radio set.

This is why you may have **'departed people' appearing in your Earth world and then disappearing,** because they may have briefly thought about it or mentioned a memory and that could have projected them to your world for a moment.

It is not always possible to prevent it, because one needs to be aware one is doing it! It is very interesting to think one can so easily become visible and vanish, or at least make a trip there and elsewhere and reappear in ours!

The pleasure to talk to you my little darling, is always as wonderful as before and ever. I am so pleased and happy you are still on line (after all those years) to speak to me, as well as to all your kind Teachers. You do have a lot of work ahead. They showed me you will be talking to many a crowd in other places where you've never been before. They say there are lots of plans ahead to make you more known, so you can be asked to go and talk and share your knowledge on the Afterlife — and that's what you have come on Earth for, I am told. So they are very pleased with the way things are turning up for you and your work.

You can only do one thing at a time and not worry about others. You have to focus on what is important for your chosen life plan, because in the end it will be YOU suffering and being miserable and regretful if you have not achieved it. We are told you'll be able to fulfil it, you'll become known more and more, because those plans ahead look as if they may well come to fruition.

It is all a question of patience and hard work on your part of course as usual! But you can be a hard worker if you don't let yourself be distracted and that's one of your weaknesses. You can be sidetracked too easily and lose the intense focus you need all the time to plod on in the right direction. *(Note- BR- Sadly true!)* So now we'll answer your questions...

MIND TO MIND TRANSLATION

BR- Who is 'we'?

My Mum and I are watching over you as we speak. I am speaking (me your mum) but my own mum is there, your Grandma. We have realised you are getting this in English as well, though we are thinking in whatever way we are thinking... I don't reckon I am using words, it's very strange! I feel I am thinking in a 'non-word language'... It's as if I am saying something in, say, Chinese, and you understand it in English or Russian! Weird indeed!

BR- Can you explain how you are not thinking in words?

When a thought comes to our Minds, there is an instant interaction by our Minds and yours. That means the **thought we send is included and interlocked with your Mind mechanism** — in that it translates in whatever language you may be happy to think in. So we need not search for words, we just express our feelings or pictures of what we want to say and it happens at once as words in your Mind, so that you can understand it.

That's what I am being told to tell you! It is not easily understandable from our end because we do not realise it is happening; we just 'think', the thought's gone and you react.

BR- Thanks- Have you been anywhere new or done anything different?

When we think, we **need to focus very hard all the time; that's what gives Intensity to our thoughts for them to produce results.** I still like to go to my quiet place now and then, though it is more a mental place than a 'real' physical one

- So when I go to there as usual, I can find myself rebuilding my own momentum. I feel increasingly more relaxed and I focus more and more on what I am thinking: that way I can create a totally new set of adventures. Not necessarily 'fake adventures' like pretend films, but finding out all I can about *those people I have been in other Earthly lives and also finding myself on different levels of thinking.*

GRASPING ANIMALS' THOUGHTS

That happens when I decide to understand more complicated things. When you are a Human, how can you understand what a bird or other Animal thinks and feels? So, I make myself go to that level of thinking to grasp what it must be like to be a cat or lion, or insect like a butterfly or dragonfly... Then I feel the reactions to events as if I was one. I am NOT one of them but **I can reach that level of thinking**. If I fail it's because I have not focused enough or got distracted.

BR- Tell me more: which Animal have you "felt like" that?

I have **not been** the Animal, I repeat to make sure you grasped that. I went into the thinking mode or level of thought, or frequency probably, of that Animal. You feel they have lots to think about on the spot, they need to react at once to the 'now', the event of the moment!

The language they use is their own and that has much more sense when you see it from their point of view. It is not just tweeting or meowing etc. We know they mean something but Humans can never really understand Animals' language, unless they can do what I have had fun doing and I can still do now and then. It's just a question of focusing on to a different level of thinking, that's as much as I can say. I feel, I sense the Animal, I go into its Mind and feel like one as it is expressing its thoughts and feelings etc.

259

It is quite an experience, which you will enjoy when you finally come over here! (But you still have far too much to do on Earth for now, for allowing yourself to come here yet! You must finish your chosen life plan, that way you will be free!)

Which other experiences could I describe to you? I found myself in a rather difficult position, as I was trying to help two people who arrived here and were not very happy with each other, because they'd had problems on Earth. So I've been the 'devil's advocate'...I tried to be the referee to help them relax and realize the Earthly problem were not so important after all, since they were both here now!

All they needed to do is grasp that all that one puts up with on Earth is to do with material gain or things, and **what really matters is love and proper friendship**! So those two men still fighting over arguments they'd had on Earth over a property was so ridiculous but to them it mattered!

That's why I was invited to help them sort it out as the arguments were pointless, since the Earth was gone out of their lives and "who owned what" was not really what they should be concerned about... since they had in front of them the delight of Eternity to enjoy and they could not even see it, silly 'boys' yet grown men!

I had a laugh in a way but I found it sad to see they were so serious about it. What we did, my Mum and I as we were together there, was to make them take stock of what they were doing and why—and then compare it to what is available here- and we gave them examples of Mind Power and peace of Mind and fun of all kinds.

It eventually worked, but it took them a while as they had **locked their Minds** on the anger and frustration that had built up for years on Earth, it seems. Such a stupid argument! We could not believe people could be so silly and closed-minded. But we won in the end!

BR- Well done, Mum and Grandma!

260

AWARENESS OF FACETS

What we can also tell you is that your Dave *(BR- my husband)* has had a lot more 'work' to do lately, as he has been discovering he too had had other lives! That's stunned him and he has been doing just what I have been doing - looking at them and studying why and how it is happening. It is quite an experience, you know, to think and realize and have the evidence that you have been many other people of all kinds!

Incredibly interesting but also mind-boggling to have them as if they are real, yet you know they are not 'solid' since nothing is 'solid' in this world. You have to be on Earth to imagine things and people solid - Once you are here you **know** it is not 'solid' even if it seems to be! Because, here, the moment you stop thinking about something for long enough, it will gradually fade away, hence the definite lack of solidity!

So, that's what your Dave has been inspecting and still does, I think. He's been with his mum and dad and newly-arrived brother it seems *(Raymond Rix)* - There was quite a big gap of understanding between the two — I mean understanding about the world here. The new one was not up to date at all! At least you had talked a little about here to Dave, whereas his brother had no idea as such.

He was lucky to be met by Dave and his family as that's given him some grounding: the brother knew where he had 'landed'—he grasped that since those loved ones were 'dead' so he must be too! But all is fine there, I think. I have not been to disturb them but I know 'all is quiet and happy' on their level.

My own dad has been busy. He is still around now and then but not as much as used to be, because I don't really need his help. **He has been "investigating many deeper levels of focus and consciousness"**, he said, when he came back from one of his inner trips.

GRASPING PLANTS' AWARENESS

From what I understand he has been looking at what other created things feel, Plants for example. He liked Plants though was not a keen gardener as such: he never had the time if I recall. He said he' s seen that Plants which have short leaves feel somehow different from those with long leaves... What he meant was: **A Plant wants to be a Plant because it feels the urge and need** to be one, but the small leaves ones are often not as excited about being that than the long leaves ones!

BR- (stunned) Am I hearing that correctly? Weird! I am wondering about mighty palm trees and pines!

What transpired, it seems, is that the desire to be a big tree with long leaves is an impression left by many long leaves trees or other plants. Seen from here, the smaller leaves ones seem more focused on themselves than on their environment. This is what my Dad told me; he's seen more but I think he should tell you himself...

BR- Yes I need to know more. Could Grandpa talk to me, please, as all this sounds so strange!
(Sudden change of communicator! Grandpa Léon comes online!) ...

What we have here my dear, is the intriguing **attitude of Plants as I saw them behaving on Earth but seen from here**, of course. I studied their reactions to sunlight and warmth. I could see their Energies expand and absorb it and have a great affinity with it. But when I looked at and compared the various kinds of trees and other Plants, especially leaves types, I noticed there was a definite difference in their 'mental' attitude!

BIG LEAVES

We know Plants do **not have** the same level of Consciousness as Mankind or Animals. But those Plants with bigger, heavier, longer leaves have more avidity and excitement for Life around them, than those with smaller leaves or no flowers or buds. **The leaves did seem to make a difference to their awareness of their surroundings!**

That mattered because awareness of the environment, enjoying the sun, wind, rain, place where they are, plays an important part on the inner attitude of the Plants in question. The more they can focus on those 'feelings', let's say "on that awareness", on noting the difference between types of weather, the more their **Consciousness (seen from here as lights and colours of various shades and intensity)** seems to grow, flourish or simply stagnate.

That is my impression as I plunge into their 'feelings'. I'll say feelings to help you understand what may be going on inside their Energy fields. It is quite extraordinary to think and realize **Plants DO have lots of inner reactions as 'Beings'**, rather than as 'things', as one may be tempted to treat them on Earth!

So, as I was saying Plants (whether trees or small bushes) have a Consciousness developing at various rates, according to what they are. **It is an individual choice** to be a tall tree or a little bush or some small flowers somewhere- but the aim of their Mind it seems is to become more and more aware of where they are, what they are, accept the state and enjoy it.

The moment they are not happy, they will definitely leave the Plant shape and **come back here as Energy,** a Light which has had an experience of a particular kind. **That Light shows its experience** by shining in a way different from other Plants' lights. So each has its own way of expressing and storing it within its Energy Field.

BR- I am astounded. Please can you tell me more about Plants in your world?

The Plants that I have seen here—which have been on Earth and have 'died' as far as the Earthly Plants were concerned—**were blobs of Light of various hues. Lights to us are Energies.** We see that around us all the time. So those Lights (ex-Plants) are assembling or simply 'being' and seem to revel in the joy and experience they have had. They don't seem to travel anywhere.

BR- What do you do to see them? Do you go to a particular 'level'?

My task (as assigned to me by me!) was to inspect the happenings of those unusual Beings—because we do not seem to give them enough importance, yet they are very special on many scores. So as I felt the urge, the attraction towards Plants of the Earth as they left it, the Energies that have been a Plant, say a tall tree, came or rather were visible here near me, during my tuning in or focusing on that subject.

I saw them in my Mind's eye and saw the whole spectrum of what was going on in those Energy fields. What struck me was the variety of 'feelings' I must say (or at least 'impressions' may be a better word), which was impressed on them as they lived their lives!

The tall tree with **long** branches was full of joy, excitement and importance in that 'it' had **FELT PART OF his environment!** It felt its own place, it realized 'it' was there; 'it' had a place, a need or a use to be there. We could say 'it' enjoyed it. I don't dare to put too many feelings into a tree in case you thought I was mad or exaggerating, but that would express it quite well.

264

Therefore my conclusions were: the tall long-leaved Plants had absorbed their environment and their place in it as a meaningful thing to them. It had mattered they were there. They felt they 'belonged' to it, if you see what I mean. Whereas the small-leaved Plants/trees, no matter how tall they may have been, were not so visibly excited and interested in having been part of their surroundings. Isn't that strange? I would have thought they would have all been the same.

They all come back here in a state of Lights, Energies pulsating and the experience they went through are like throbbings in their fields. They have lived it. So that's something for them to 'digest' or absorb. I don't know whether I should say 'ponder about' but it could well be in a special way!

TO BE USEFUL

My understanding of **their aim is to be of use one way or the other.** There seems to be that underlying need to be useful at the 'bottom line' of their existence. Then, **as** they exist to become 'real/physical' on Earth, this attitude or Consciousness varies into many possibilities. They could be very conscious of their surroundings or simply just there, 'get on with it' then leave it for the trip back.

My thoughts on and understanding of this is that the little **Plants you eat** have chosen to be of use as such, because that was their **basic instinct to be useful**, let's say—so they became 'carrots' etc. and let themselves be eaten; then they do not focus on the Earth anymore once eaten, as their Energy is absorbed and reabsorbed by the overall Energy field of All That Is.

It is a simple externalisation of *Energy turned into something useful as meant to be*–and that's it - No need to give it a spiritual Mind of its own. (And don't forget: Plants do not have nerves or a nervous system, so they do **not** feel pain as such.)

265

But if the Plants of the forest have a long stay on Earth, or as their basic Urge 'want' to be there, to be useful somehow, but also to be aware of what they are doing, or at least aware of their surroundings—then their Consciousness seems to develop itself more and produce some 'thoughts' (let's say) in the sense of actually accepting, recognising and enjoying the experience.

This is where I think the creation of Energy shoots produces shoots of Consciousness. Those levels of Consciousness are still simple—primitive enough we could say—because they are buds in the Mind Energy of 'All That Exists' all around. That inner Energy is experiencing **impressions** that had not been felt before by those particular buds or shoots of Energy, when they first became a 'Plant' or future big tree. And that is how I think it is happening... But we may have to look more into it.

All I know so far is the Consciousness of bigger leaves has to do with the fact the Plant is enjoying more what it is doing—or at least is much more aware it exists and it has a rapport with its surroundings. That is interesting to check and observe. You may start to think about that on Earth next time you look at Plants!

What is relevant is the apparition of leaves. **When the leaves come and grow, the whole plant is waking up.** As it grows it usually absorbs more light from the sun, doesn't it, and it grows in stature. The more and taller it grows, the longer the trunk will be as a tree. So it will absorb more and more sunlight and moonlight and Cosmic Energy. But the very fact it is very tall is NOT the factor for its acceptance and recognition of the fact that 'it' is within a particular environment. Its surroundings are not what matters to it if the leaves are smaller than usual, let's say.

You can see it on your trees in your garden, in your books, look for small and long leaves and understand what I am telling you.

266

BR- Could you give me a clearer idea of the size of the leaves?

I cannot give descriptions of sizes. **I see Energy fields** of varying shades and brightness of light, colours and **intensity of Intention and Consciousness.** That is what I see, you understand?

So we'll have to come to the conclusion that you have heard something unusual and hopefully unheard of before, haven't you?

BR- Definitely! I have never heard of or read that before! Amazing. Thank you!

Well it's been worth talking to you then! I am pleased if I have been of some help to make you discover or rather, understand something new. Maybe I'll find out more and I'll come back with extra information for you, my dear.

BR- Thank you so much. Am I talking to Grandpa Léon?

Yes you are, my dear. We have always been watching over you all your life, remember that. You are never alone. Our hearts are with you all the time, so that you do not lose courage and carry on...till you come back here.

§§§

CHAPTER 27

NOTE- I discovered that the following unexpected conversations bringing more profound thoughts and knowledge took place for a reason, as usual. It's because my Teachers and Masters from the Great Beyond had asked my Mother and Grandma to share their experiences, in order to crystallize the teachings on expansion of Consciousness and Awareness.

My Mum started her explanations.

What your Mum can tell you about her life here is always interesting too. There is constantly the nagging feeling one may not have done one's best when on Earth, so it is one of the reasons one tends to look at one's life as a 'film' to check whether there were some lapses.

If there are any, the amazing thing is that you can use the Power of your Mind to **redress the situation** and erase the mistake and **replace it** with the correct actions, so that your **Mind and Soul see that result** and absorb it as a way to act and 'live' if there. It is not to punish oneself, it is to redress the direction of things that went wrong.

So your Grandma (my Mum) was discussing this with me once and we saw how we could redress some little things which had gone slightly wrong between her and me! We never had any big war, feud or disagreement but it is part of life to have hiccups. And those were useful as examples to read just what could have been said, done and felt.

This is why I used to say to you - when you were kids - to do your best, as I was **always trying to do my best and not to let myself be influenced by others to do otherwise.** If your conscience feels you are on the wrong path, you have got to listen to it and straighten yourself up as far as that is concerned.

THOUGHTS NEVER 'DIE'

The path of thoughts is obviously well carved as we live whether here or on Earth. The amazing and intriguing thing is that they never 'die'! Thoughts are such powerful projections that they exist the moment you produce them and **they never disappear**. How about that? They keep on going towards whatever... It's impossible to 'suck them back' into your Mind and say: "*I did not think that*". It is done, bad luck! So we may as well try and **keep them sane and healthy so that we don't clutter the Universal Mind with that rubbish.**

When thoughts are produced by a Mind there is usually a lot of emotion behind them. It is rare not to have any emotion linked to what one thinks. So **if the emotion is strong, the thoughts will be even stronger by the very fact their actualization will happen!** *The result of the thoughts will exist somewhere* or other — either in your own world where you thought them, or shooting out in the 'Mind World' that surrounds and bathes all – so, they'll create themselves there as a little 'world' or creation of their own. **Those little packets are floating around CONSTANTLY!**

BR- Surely, those zillions of zillions must be a messy hotchpotch of thoughts as Energy parcels throbbing on various frequencies?

The web of Mind Energy is never ending, ever extending to infinite 'length and width' so to speak. **The Web of Thoughts has always existed and is the basis, the framework in which other thoughts build up**—thus creation of mighty ideas can happen, fuelled by that self-created and replenished Energy. The contents of the thoughts do not matter too much, it seems; it is the *Energies, and emotions and motivation behind them* which colour and influence the whole structure!

It is in the interest of Humans to know all this because they are the ones creating their own framework all around themselves! They have to be conscious of what they do while on Earth, as they ARE fashioning the emotional surroundings which bathe them all...

If the 'air' and Mind Space around them is filled with hatred, it will be very difficult for each and everyone to feel happy and relaxed!

So we need to tell you to be aware of what you are creating around yourselves, like we are getting more and more aware of what we create around ourselves here. It is more straight forward for us because we see our thoughts actualized instantly—whereas on Earth you may not be aware of this as easily as we do here.

This is our message for all Humans struggling on Earth: **Be conscious of whatever crosses your Mind, as it will shoot out and be part of your everyday surroundings!**

So, make living easier for yourself by having gentle soothing and happy thoughts, because the moment you have anger, hatred and depressed thoughts you are **building a framework of dark depressed or nasty energies** that foment, pulsate and spoil your 'breathing space'—or rather your Soul's breathing space to be more correct. Will that do?

BR- Excellent! Many thanks Mum and Grandma.

We were asked to express our thoughts and knowledge on that kind of topic, to help you with your presentation talk and especially with teaching the world of Humans what they do with their Minds, as THAT greatly influences their lives, all of them including the Earth's atmosphere and balance! Now we'll leave you to let your Teachers take over.

FROM 'ENERGY BLOB' TO CONSCIOUS BEING

BR- (Sending a thought to my dictating Masters)- Please tell me more about Consciousness?

As a Human you have the Earth as a centre of attention at the moment, of course - But the centre of the Universe is definitely not the Earth, as you well know by now. You have to comprehend that the centre of anything implies limits to the site, i.e. it should have sides and other dimensions so that you can pinpoint the 'centre'. This is geometry and mathematics.

We know there is no end to the scale of Eternity or to the Universal Mind Power that creates everything, as this is a fundamental point. So the centre of something that does not exist physically is very difficult to pinpoint!

That's why the whole idea of anything conscious being limited is ludicrous. **No conscious Being or Entity can be limited because it is pure Energy**. It can be smaller or bigger but it is the kind which has no limit, no end and no start. What we mean is that Beings of Energy of any kind and strength do not need to have a start as such because they are pure Energy – and **Pure Energy does not begin or end**, no matter what some Humans may think. It is pure vibrations that have their own life, aim and direction and as such will grow and expand.

Pure Energy of Mind is the basic, fundamental power of All That Exists. If the Energy is directed or directs itself towards an Urge, follows one particular Urge, it will develop accordingly.

The Urge of any Entity is its driving force. Therefore any Consciousness has an inner Urge. It may not be as developed as others, but it will be there, **latent and ready to go full guns** when it is let loose and allowed to develop itself.

If one lets one's Consciousness develop, it will be because it will do so by itself. It is not something anyone 'decides'. As said before: the Consciousness of anything has that inner Urge—but which may hold it back if the Urge is weak.

What helps an Urge grow is the motivation, the aim. If the goal is tempting or satisfactory, the Urge will develop. An Urge is not a thing, it is an inner Energy, an emotion for 'more', for 'bigger', 'for better' - therefore that built-in Yearning will always exist because in all Creativity there is that push to 'make it' and 'improve it'.

So, back to **Consciousness of Beings**: when a Being wishes to improves itself, this will trigger and light up its inner Urge which will fan the flame of its Desire by acting upon itself, following what is felt - like drops of water attracted to each other and sliding down a slope to form a puddle.

What we would like to point out is that **any Urge for improvement,** and certainly **an Urge to 'Be',** is to **come from the inner part of the Being.** So its Soul is to feel the need and the push—that's how interest and desire propels the Soul towards finding out and **understanding more what is around itself** and what else can be found.

If we were to give **examples** we'd say this: **When one 'personality' has chosen to exist - out of the mass of original Energy** that has always existed - it will have been produced by the inner Urge for actualization of that mass of Energy. Within itself there is a 'Desire to Be' and do and create and change and improve. So **that 'blob' of Energy will follow the current flow of the inner Urge pushing it.**

If its tendencies grow as should, there will be even more Urges and Desires within it 'to be' of a certain shape or intensity or texture etc. If it chose to follow the path of inspecting the... *(As I relaxed and focused even harder the concentration makes me doze of... When I wake up my Communicators are*

272

fortunately still there!) - As you regain Consciousness (!!) we can tell you that your Mind slipped its focus towards our world. There, we were able to impart much knowledge into it, which hopefully it will now be able to convert into words!

So with this we'll say: **If a future 'man' wants to exist on Earth** when he has not been one yet, ever, it will have started "at some point", (let's say, so that you can visualize it better) as part of a mass of Energetic Power which has shoots in all direction—because its inner Urge is desperate to exist and recreate itself into different states.

So the state of Mankind, being one of many states, will be the Urge for that particular creature. It will then ponder more on what it wishes to achieve. It may not be a 'pondering' like you would do with pros and cons, but a **pondering of various degrees of intensity** which weigh each other up and sense which one is the best for the current project created by the inner Urge!

So the 'blob' acts on itself and 'thinks' towards being in existence as a separate Energy, one with a Will to Be. As the Will to Be excitedly decides to grow, the framework/ the grid of possibilities form itself by the very fact that **thoughts are creating themselves - as the Urge projects its 'possibilities' into blueprints of action.** Finally when one is stronger than the others, it will take shape.

BR- Where does Thinking, Intelligence, Consciousness come from?

As you think, you exist. As you exist, you think. As your mass of original Energy started to split from the original 'motherboard', it throbbed with an intense Urge to Be. As that Urge grew stronger it automatically developed the power of thinking/sensing actions. Its actions followed that inner Urge and tendency.

273

The idea of pros and cons come later. It is first a **notion of 'Existing'** and **that Consciousness is** what is known as **the basis of evolution**. When you hear news saying people "lost the Will to live", it's because they were aware of their situation and could not cope with it.

So **Consciousness arises from day one of wanting to exist**. But as said before, it is also to do with Intensity of Desire. So the two pooled together give rise to a mighty Creative Force, which is Mind Power.

Mind has no problem existing. **Mind has always been part of the eternal throbbing Mass of Energy** which is a 'sea', a 'world', a constant state, but which is also constantly ready to shoot off into actions of creation!

The Desire to Be and to follow that Urge gives rise automatically to possibilities and that develops more and more into 'comparisons'... You could say 'calculations' (but **not** mathematically) of possible other states and happenings. This is where Consciousness develops more as the Urge starts looking after itself and at what it is compared to and could be.

Consciousness is a latent state slowing waking up, as the actualization develops and triggers other states and surroundings.

The moment the 'new Being in actualization' takes stock of itself as 'in existence', it has opened the door to its own Consciousness.

SEARCH, DISCOVER, EXPAND

If you want to know more about Consciousness we'll say that the more one extends it, the more one discovers, as one becomes aware of far beyond one's limited view points. It's like that at any and all levels of Consciousness.

If one does not focus on just one thing or view, but let the Mind roam around like a flash light or lighthouse light,

274

searching around for more interesting things, or simply to discover what else there could be nearby or what else one could do with one's Mind, **then the doors open automatically** and one sees, senses and knows more. It is as easy as that.

It is not limited to the 'World of Spirit' (as you call it) which has its own limits in the sense that it can only show people what they need to discover before or after they have been to Earth.

Once they have gone beyond those stages, they can then transcend those limited views and reach for deeper or more refined and elevated states of understanding. That comes with knowing one is more than one has just been or known oneself to be so far.

If a Soul, who has been a Human many times on Earth, reaches the understanding that everything it has learnt has polished the shine of its Soul—or has nourished his Real Self with even more understanding and knowledge—then *the next step will eventually be to look further.* This is usually done of course **once all ties and desires for Earthly conditions have been dealt with and vanished.** Then the Mind of the Energy Being is free to move on for more adventures, more discoveries.

You could try doing this when on Earth, by going into very, very deep meditations, transcending the usual states, but it usually takes a lot of practice. As the thinking Mind always evaluates what it senses or sees, it is valuable to carry out such things when possible—even just for the pleasure of possibly reaching a more even state of inner stability.

When one expands one's Consciousness, one becomes one step closer to the original state of Oneness, as everything and everybody, i.e. every Being, stems from that one 'ocean' of deeper, inner realisation and Self-realisation.

All are One as you know, but as individual Beings you often forget it and feel separate, unique and at times 'lonely' in the sense of lost in the mass. **No one is lost, all are connected,** that is the secret! All can get recharged and re-boosted by simply **linking back mentally with the original pervading Oneness. That Energy IS LIFE and has Life**! That Energy has the impetus for everyone to be recharged and redirected on their chosen pathways. Therefore, no one gets 'lost'. All Mind Energies are linked up, all can find themselves in the connection.

WHY SOME FEEL 'LOST'

When a Soul is 'confused' on Earth, it is because they feel they have mislead the connection to their Higher Self, their Oversoul, their Real Self. That is why they have lost their bearings as to their chosen path.

If they feel forsaken, **all they have to do is go within** and search by simply immersing themselves in the peace and smooth guidance of the Higher Energies bathing them—but Energies they had forgotten they were surrounded with. That will redirect them via their own intuition and inner knowing.

When a Soul needs help, help is all around: all that is needed is to show them that is so. Therefore guide them to quiet times within rather than pills!

When the bond is re-established the Soul will regain its footing in its right place. The personality will remember or understand the importance of what they have chosen to experience and learn from. This is where **Healing takes place - when the inner Energies are rebalanced, when Mind, Soul & Spirit are reconnected as one 'thread', so that the directives of one are not rejected by the other two.**

All this has a link with the expansion of Consciousness because it is the link which binds all aspects of one's thinking. The moment you think and all Beings think one way or the other, the connection to **all the other states** are available. They just need to be focused on and gone more deeply into. Then you can step from one to the other and find out much

276

more, and rejoice in the newness of a more refreshing, enlightening horizon-stretching state—and also dimension. Because the dimensions of Mind are unlimited therefore, you can look into myriads of possibilities, myriads of probable events or states not activated. This is the joy of Creativity as each step has its surprises.

What is needed is for people to realize all this exists. Because there is more to it than going to Earth and be a Human, possibly enjoying the pleasure of a flesh body and physical activities! **THAT does not fulfil a Soul!** Those are only passing states which have to be experienced since one is a Human, but which are **not** the ultimate aim of existing.

The Soul needs to know how to guide itself in numerous situations, so the challenges of Earth are one way of testing oneself, learning and achieving. The joy of having created and designed a flesh body is an actualization no one seems to comprehend on Earth nowadays, because they have lost the knowledge of it: they don't remember they had planned that body. All they seem to think is to satisfy its needs!

Satisfying the needs of the flesh is NOT the aim of being on Earth, no more than spending your life waiting on the demands of your car and polishing it. You need to understand the body has only one function - to navigate yourself physically in a world in which you could have lived invisibly as an Energy Being!

Also, your Mind being very active, **its creative Power makes your emotions and thoughts visible,** without your realising it most of the time. *This is why your environment (as events and happenings) is constantly affected by what you feel and think...* so this is what you **will** see! You all affect each other with your thoughts, unknowingly it seems. Yet as a Being of Energy you knew it would happen before you went on that trip.

FORGOTTEN HUMANS' AIMS ON EARTH

The ultimate aim is and was to have another 'new' experience in a totally different state from being an Energy Being. That has eventually caused troubles when those very Beings forgot their reasons for the trip and made their vehicles the centre of their attention: whereas **originally the wish was to discover and realize what you can do with your Mind in a different way.**

The fact that events can be constructed and physical surroundings maintained by simply living in them is an aim people have completely forgotten, it seems! You can have a home and live in it because you believe you are in it, you see it and expect to see it. It is far too complicated to try and explain in words but this is basically what happens.

Yet we do not see your home and car or even environment like you do! We can go through it all and not see it as 'solid' as you see it.

YOUR THOUGHTS' FOCUS CREATE ATOMS

It's all to do with focus of thoughts and beliefs engendering particular vibrations that create atoms of so-called solid objects, but the **atoms are not solid and the physical sensation of solidity is an illusion,** as many of you already know.

So, if you want to live your life to the full without impinging on your original life plan, as you were meant to do, make sure you always remember you ARE a Being of Thought Energy. You are floating around with an Energy body, which is disguised as a flesh/physical body, which others also see as 'solid'.

But you must also know that body is not really solid, and is changing all the time. And - most of all - **your thoughts and emotions are making it what it is** (as will of course what you do with it: how you treat it and feed it).

278

Therefore your aim was to experience feeling 'solid' in a world with other Beings of Energy feeling 'solid'.

And those are also disguised as Animals of various types - and Plants- which have not all got the same degree of Consciousness and self-realization as you Humans have, but which have an aim too, as that has been discussed already. Therefore enjoy your trip to make the most of it.

What must be understood is that the Beings of Energy who have put their Minds together to **create this Universe of** physicality were only focused on what can be done to create new 'Matter', new ways of existing.

It was not to have particular desires fulfilled, or even to possibly extend the population of those going there! It was to see what could be created if one did this or that.

But the Beings who decided to try it and experiment with it, have enjoyed it so much that instead of making it a passing activity, it became a more important focus. And that has been caused by the attraction to physical looks, tastes, feelings.

The **emotional links** built among those coming to inhabit the Earth world **were originally Mind links** - Mind vibrations linking harmoniously with each other. But as the flesh 'came into being', those Beings getting together felt the Mind links too, but may also have enjoyed the physical side of it and other physical attractions.

So the greatest blend is two people with good Mind links as they understand and fit in with each other, but also some physical attraction, which maintains and consolidates the partnership for the time being on Earth. **As physical attraction disappears,** once back in our World of Mind, **it is the Mind link that survives.**

LOVING BOND

What needs to be grasped is that **the emotional bond between two Humans or Animals, stems from the loving bond that exists between ALL Beings in Eternity.** All Beings have that caring, compassionate state as part of themselves. So the break of that bond on Earth is usually caused by 'physical' reasons: reactions to, say, greed, wanting more of something physical such as food, objects and sexual needs of the flesh body. But the loving caring bond is at the heart of every one.

BR- Yet, Compassion is not the same as being in love or loving?

What you call 'being in love' is simply attraction to the other Being via the Mind AND the physical attraction.

When the physical attraction wanes, there may be the Mind link left; whereas the love for one person by another whether a child or an adult, is different but not really... It is still the understanding of that person, the knowing you are on the same wavelength as Beings of Energy and the enjoyment of knowing and feeling it. Wanting to be close and wanting that other Being to be happy and at peace. It is not an extra sensation, it stems from the very fact you are all Beings of the same original Energy of Creativity and caring.

SSS

CHAPTER 28

We have already explained to you that the **Souls** who decided to be 'Humans' **are part of the Higher Self of each individual.** They are the *identification as a Human,* each time. That's simply said as 'pictures' for you to visualize the process- yet it is not quite correct in as much as the whole process is multi-sided and not linear: it **can be viewed as an explosion of lives from an original decision to try the Earth Experiment.**

This is just an example or an image, for you to try and grasp that the rule of the Universe is the Power of Mind, with its multi-facets eternally spurting out new ideas and therefore new actualizations.

A Soul who has not achieved its chosen plan for a life is not punished—but is perhaps hesitant to go back and do that again out of fear of failure. That is more important to get over than the actual plan it may have chosen: **fear of failure should not exist because the aim is chosen by you!**

So you should not punish yourself if you have got distracted and learnt or dealt with something else on the way. That something may have been part of the probabilities in that particular life!

As for the life or existence 'BEFORE' that: the Being of Energy, who has recently chosen to be on Earth, may have been many other 'aspects'. Those aspects depend on what the Being chose to do, learn and experience. If it chose to experience 'speed', very high speed, as a Being of Mind it will be easy because Mind and Thoughts act very fast! It is not enough to 'BE' and do nothing: **The Inner Self wants some**

kind of action, and the actions depend on what is in the Will and wishes of that Being.

When a Being has many ideas but does not know which to actualize, 'he' (let's say) simply needs to 'be' and thoughts will happen around him. 'Happen' means being alive, **becoming as planned**. They show themselves to that Being and the very fact of existing will produce even more Energy as the actualization is in progress!

What that Being needs is a greater FOCUS. He has to maintain that concentration—just like you need to do *(NOTE: That's a little dig at my 'dozing off' as I get in a deeper state!)* —to find the strong link to what is most important or urgent for him. It does not matter if several actualizations happen 'at the same time' because they will not feel and see it like that. It is of no importance really because the aim may simply be, to feel 'in existence'.

So, if you wonder what you may have been before you chose to exist as a Human, as part of your vast range of possible experiences, it may or could have been something like that - being a Being of Energy with various 'happenings'.

BEWARE OF 'INFLUENCED' REPORTS'

BR- Could I have existed on some other planet of this physical Universe?

What you are wondering is whether there are Beings on planets within your own physical Universe!

BR- Yes and me possibly being one at some point?

We have told you that everything is always possible and this is just one example. There is no need to have created similar Beings looking like Humans on other places. But there will be Beings of various types which would be so totally different that you would not recognize them as such—or else would be vibrating at a totally different set of frequencies that **you would not be able to see, sense or know of them, because your vibrations would not match!** So please stop 'worrying' about other Beings in your Universe!

BR- What about (as read on the Internet) alleged conversations with "Beings from stars or constellations" who supposedly cohabited with Humans or "came to improve the savage original Human race"?

If you have heard of "Beings from stars or planets" communicating with Humans, it is not always certain *who* is talking—and it is usually through a Human who may have his/her own ideas which will and could influence the communication. This is why **WE are very careful** about what we say and **we check your** *(Me, BR)* Mind is not interfering, which **it has not done so far**, fortunately.

What has to be said on that is: Why would some 'physical' Beings from your own Universe go to your Earth to make Earthlings better when they are of some physical constitution themselves? If they had been the creators, it would be understandable - but **they will have been created themselves FROM OUTSIDE that physical world of Matter** - or else they would not be able to exist! It HAS TO be made (and has been made) by sheer concentration of THOUGHT POWER like everything else.

What you are asking is not really possible or probable.

When a Being from **BEYOND your physical Universe** wishes to contact, communicate or act upon that Universe, it has a whole range of ways and possibilities to do it because it does NOT belong to it — it is not part of it.

If you had someone from within your own Universe trying to contact yours and your Earth, it would be on such a different set of vibrations you could not know they are doing it... Why can't you believe what we are telling you? It is not to trick you, it is to make you understand how it works.

BR- It is not that I don't believe you, I just want to make sure I get the facts right to reply to anybody else with those questions. One can read on the Internet of lots of claims of such alleged conversations...

There are a lot of inaccuracies made up by Humans! *(Sadly I am suddenly interrupted by a visitor whom I had to deal with - that makes me stop tuning in for now.)*

GENUINE SCOLE EXPERIMENT MATERIALISED VISITORS

I attended on numerous occasions the astounding, respected and genuine 'Scole Experiment' (Norfolk, UK). These extraordinary séances were tested over years by such eminent and highly regarded investigators as Professor Archie Roy, Professor David Fontana and Montague Keen, all seniors members of the prestigious Society for Psychical Research (SPR). They attested to the genuineness of the mind-blowing phenomena and reported meticulously their positive experiences in 'The Scole Report': recorded conversations with departed people, messages written on sealed film, influencing material objects, even spirit forms materializing.

The scrupulously kept and fascinating diary of those five years of paranormal events - titled 'Witnessing the Impossible'- was kept by Robin Foy, leader of the four psychic researchers who started this series of experiments.

On authentic video stills of some of the latter years' astonishing séances—which unfortunately I was unable to attend—we can see their actual 'Visitors from Other Realms'.

One 'face' was the nicknamed 'Blue', but there were also other Beings actually walking and touching the team in the room.
Today I want to ask a question to my Teachers:

BR- Do those videos still prove there are Beings from 'other planets'? Please explain. (My hand feels compelled to doodle numerous lines creating patterns overlapping and blending with each other - I let it happen.)

The Beings experienced in your friends' séance were indeed 'real Beings' i.e. not imaginary. But we need to remind you that we told you there would be some Beings in 'Other Realms', but it would not be easy or possible for you Humans to sense and see them. This is an example: Becoming aware of these particular ones was not done by scientists with mighty Earthly instruments. It was **done** *(in Scole)* **in special conditions, which allowed the 'teleportation' of some Beings**. They have to prepare themselves for those visits. Those were special cases rather than 'routine visits'. They were very carefully planned and organised, so that the Humans who were experiencing them were open-minded and ready emotionally and physically to receive them.

It had been mentioned that there were other worlds, but they won't be like your Earth and nothing much was said of 'where' they so-called 'lived. Those *(in Scole)* were not 'run of the mill visitors' popping down from a planet next door! It **was vibrations transmuted to fit in with your Earthly vibrations**, so that those Beings could be 'experienced' by some Humans who could cope sensibly with it. It was not every day you could get that sort of happening!

How they came was to do with the enormous Energies the *(Scole)* Human group had managed to create over time— and the intense Will, Desire and Dedication they put into the work. This **produced the right pathway for any such contact**

285

and communications. When the first one reached them it was a great joy for all those concerned!

It is possible to invent any kind of 'outer body' one wishes. This is what Creativity is all about, so the outer experiences and presentations *(the 'looks')* are of no great importance.

What they achieved is trans-communication between worlds of the Universe. But we repeat: it is to be remembered as a 'one off' more than a 'run of the mill'. **Your scientists will not succeed doing this UNLESS they could create the same level of receptive vibrations.**

So the Beings' appearance is of no concern because it could just be they showed themselves that way, to be more accepted as 'living entities', than if they'd been floating around as lights or vague shapes. But the Intelligence and thinking Minds behind the disguises is what needs to be accepted, recognised and admired. **THEY have succeeded in reaching the Earth too!**

Why we drew those lines earlier *(doodles before they spoke)* was to focus your Mind even more deeply on the topic you wanted us to answer. It had to be a calm receptive Mind to listen to us, not one churned with a barrage of thoughts.

What you can see in those lines is the kind of **multitude of superimposed and intermingled levels of vibrations and dimensions, all in one yet all separate!** And that is so at whatever level you look at things, within your own body and your world, or ours or other worlds, **there will always and constantly be that mingling and mixture** of paths.

So be wise and understand it cannot be looked at as if it was one single picture, and it cannot be described in detail. All those things exist non-stop and multiply and divide and change and do not 'sit there' to be looked at and analysed, so that you get a description!

We hope we answered your question...

*BR- Can you tell me more about those visitors'
appearance, the big eyes etc.?*

If you saw some Being with no eyes, no face, no shape,
how would you know you are seeing a Being. If it was a large
or huge blob of light, would you, Humans, think of it as a
'Being'? To you or most of you a Being is someone who at
least looks like, or nearly like, a Human, or some kind of
"Animal'. It has to have a kind of shape you can identify
enough with, even if it is not completely like yourself or things
you know.

Therefore a Being of Light of whatever colour with two
eyes is more a 'Being' to you Humans than a blob of light, isn't
it? So this is what happens and happened: They had to show
themselves somehow, so that you people could accept and
'identify', even though you were all (in that group of people)
willing to accept any kind of shape, so to speak, as long as
what was said made enough sense.

EXISTING FOREVER & SEEING BEYOND

If we told you **those big eyes are a symbol of being
able to SEE BEYOND what you can see and sense beyond
what you can sense,** would you be happy enough? That's what
it is: those Beings were there to help prove there can be links
with those existing beyond your physical Earth and Universe
as you know them.

Those Beings are not so much 'from stars' than from
'spaces between and beyond stars.' This is where it becomes
difficult for you Humans to grasp, because 'between stars' to
you means a physical space—whereas it is not like that. It is
**between the vibrations, between the wavelengths and
frequencies** at a level you Humans are not used to deal with.
It is at a level of **infinitely refined vibrations, which
you Humans cannot reach easily.**

This is why those who came had made the great effort to **adjust themselves and their Energies** in such a way that they would **become 'visible'** to your friends' instruments, because it was important the Humans knew who was there and who they could reach, if there was a certain concordance of Energies.

Those Beings came in order to be recognised as existing, so that the world of Humans could be told there exist other worlds and Beings **beyond** the physical world and Universe known to Humans.

That level/ plane/ sphere/ (or whatever word you want to use) is of infinitely refined vibrations, which allow pure Mind to play with its own Power. Thus all Beings there are Mind-Energy made as 'xyz' - i.e. whatever the Urge of the Being created.

If your instruments were powerful enough, you may be able to sense something there, but you are unlikely to reach them as such, as you would not perceive them as 'Beings'. Therefore, we explain this to obliterate the idea that such Beings sit on stars or planets and 'live a life' even just a little similar to yours!

They exist, they ARE and they 'live' forever in that **they do not 'die'** since their bodies is not really a body and certainly not made to end like the flesh body.

They exist and change shape if they wish because they ARE Beings of Mind Energy. That means OF Energy= which cannot be totally destroyed and OF Mind which is Energy and at that a Creative Force—so this indestructible creative Energy cannot die. They can change their 'appearance' if they wish to have one, but they are not really bothered with 'looks'. They exist, enjoying 'being' and experiencing whatever their Urges and thoughts take them to or into.

288

BR- Are those 'big-eyed' Beings the ones (or part of those) who come to rebalance the Earth Energies- those you said we call 'UFOs' etc?

You mean: "Is such a Being as talking in your own *(APPEX)* group, or seen in the other group with cameras *(Scole),* **part of those who come to rebalance the Energies** of the Earth they created?"

Yes, they are part of those, only 'part' because there are myriads of Beings who took part in the creation of the Earth Experiment. But it is not that which matters.

What matters is, that they are seen as existing, therefore people on Earth realize there is more to Life than what they imagine in their silly, limited, materialistic ways.

We have to come over to your Mind *(to me, BR)* to explain all this (as it is also done to other people in your world who are receptive and willing enough), because that is one of the seeds planted to try and open Mankind's eyes to what Reality is really! Not the physical world you Humans have buried yourself in.

CREATED TO BALANCE

BR- Why were such gigantic numbers of zillions of stars, planets, galaxies created? Surely not just to have the Earth there? So why and how and who else?

'When' the plan to have THIS type of Matter put into actualization and manifestation was started, so to speak, it was not an overnight decision, as you know. So the thoughts, built-up gradually and put together, became the big plan for this physical world experiment. It was not a 'new' thing in one way - and in another it was!

It was not the first time some things were created on a huge scale, but the first time, so to speak, for THIS **type of Matter to be made so successfully that it could encompass many, many different types of creatures,** including Plants and the Earth itself as a 'rock' in space (This is just an image of course!).

So the decision to carry it out was an exciting one. That's why all the ideas were constructed one on top of the others, so that the whole concept was safe, well balanced and successful. Then it was built upon so that Beings could choose what they wanted to be and do.

Not everyone wanted to 'Be' and 'Do'. Not everyone wanted to 'do something'- some just wished to simply 'be', to exist and enjoy the feeling and sensations of existing there as Energies within a 'physical enclosure.'

But the rest of the planets and other bodies were not 'abandoned', they were part of the whole concept of balancing a very intricate system of Energies counterbalancing others, as some of them would and were wearing out; therefore some new ones had to be created to replace them.

There were and are Beings of Energy linked to those or some of those places, but it is not in the way you imagine, that is the problem! You all look for 'Mars 'little aliens' or Saturn's population or whatever... It is not like that!

It is only where there was a **need for other outside Energies/ vibrations to be located in certain physical places,** that you would have some Beings of Mind **focusing** on those vital places: this is to keep giving them renewable 'fuel', to keep their 'fire' going — fire in the sense of constant energetic sparks, constant creative Energy.

What you all need to grasp, is that the whole Universe you see and live in, is ever so small to us compared to what is infinite everywhere else! What is not understood at all by Humans is that whether the world they live in (the Earth) or the

290

rest across 'light years' as you measure it, it is **all to do with MIND POWER!** All the little and large physical 'things that float around' are created with Creative Mind Power. THAT is WHY it was created! A new game, another fun way of making something new.

So this Energy your Universe is based on and made of, has no end as such. It will replenish itself, or change itself, or be changed into something else; but it is not 'solid' and limited. What you think you see with your instruments is only a very small part of what could be seen. What you perceive is simply an area **where all the bodies involved are there to maintain each other and create the necessary velocity power to keep the whole area going.**

Many parts of anything built are often just there to help keep the rest going, not to be an aim in themselves. So it is with the physical Universe and they do it. They are not meant to be a world where one goes and live like on Earth; most of them would not be particularly pleasant probably!

You being **within** your world makes it very difficult for you all to see and comprehend the vastness of what you do not see—and the intricacies of the mechanism of your own physical Universe.

Being 'outside it' as we are (and as are other Beings from beyond your physical Universe) means we can judge, observe and realize what is going on. Therefore please try and believe what we are doing our best to explain.

You have in front and around you a marvel of Creativity with the slightest detail seen to meticulously, so that the whole 'machinery' works like clockwork. It had to be so or else the whole Universe, including your Earth, would collapse into no existence. It has all been done with the mightiest Power that exists: the Power of the Mind - the Universal Creative Power that bathes and is within every conceivable thing and Being, forever!

So this world of yours is only one little marvel out of 'zillions' of others that you will never have time to discover through Eternity, even if you wished to! Because Mind Creativity has no boundaries and thoughts forever create... So how do you think you'll be able to see every single little and big creation that are or have been created?

BR- Is there a limit to our Universe on this vibration level? Yet it seems to travel through our Space, so it is unlikely - or else the limits are extendable!

What you asked cannot be answered properly in Human terms because you may not grasp the full meaning. If you create something which 'moves' forever, it will need its own space (physically) to advance, travel forward. So no, there is no limit because of that—BUT it is within a particular set of vibrations and 'level', so by that very fact it is 'limited' to that level of vibration... Yet not limited on how much it can keep expanding. Does that make enough sense to you?

BR- Yes it does. Thank you.

WATER IS NOT 'LIFE'

We can also tell you about **more about** water. You Humans think because there is or might be water on other places, you will find life there. *That* is viewing things as if everywhere has to be like Earth life - But they don't understand that 'Life' is not always needed in some places, and that 'Life' is not water: What gives 'Life' is not water, but the Energy from the Eternal Source which is what we call the limitless 'ocean of Mind Creative Energy'.

What you can tell your people is this: Consciousness which is within everything has various degrees of Intensity, whether a rock, a tree, an Animal or a Human. In the outside

292

Universe there is Consciousness but in a different kind i.e. it is the Consciousness of the Beings behind the existence of those created things and places.

So, if the Sun shines, it is because its Consciousness is the one belonging to the Beings in charge of its existence, who keep it going with their own Creative Mind Power.

If the Moon goes round, it is because there are Beings in charge of maintaining it. When the physical object of the Moon wears out, or is so damaged that it cannot do its work for the Earth, then the 'satellite' is removed, dissolved and replaced by another one more suitable—all this is done by Beings in charge of the world equilibrium. Yes, the other planets, galaxies etc. are in the same boat. They are useful ways of creating in this physical Matter world/ Universe.

Yes, there are Beings in charge of the constant 'fuelling' with their Mind Power attuned to the various needs, whether chemistry or physics as you'd call it. So, you must not think anything has happened 'by chance'! Nothing has. Everything is and has been planned. And Consciousness being awareness of one Self, where one is, exists at many different levels as explained before.

WHAT AND WHERE AFTER FINAL TRIP TO EARTH?

BR- Could you please remind me: once Humans have gone through all the Earthly lives they wanted to experience what can they 'go to'/ do?

What we can tell you again my dear, is that the 'Earth going' Beings have a pattern to follow to a certain degree, as they stepped on a ladder which means there are automatically numerous steps to follow, since the **aim of all trips is to discover and grasp more and add one's own Creativity to the adventures**, to see how well and how much one's Mind can create!

293

So, this is the aim on Earth with all its possibilities.

Yet, after all, you cannot be on that Experiment for Eternity — as you'd get bored, or you would fulfil all that you wish to extract from the experiment. So, once that has been achieved, you can choose: there is so much choice constantly available! It is just a question of: "In which direction does your Mind focus? And then once done, how deeply do you want to 'travel'/ enquire into that area?"

And most of all it will lead to realizing more and more (and therefore reminding you!) that you **have always been more than a Human**—which was only a temporary disguise even if it has lasted several of your centuries! You are a Being of Mind and Light, you are a Being who existed before the Earth was born, but you may not have realised it.

HOW DID I START AS A 'BLOB'?

BR- There must have been a 'starting point' when, say me, was only a blob of Energy in the eternal pulsating 'ocean' of Mind! A 'blob' who eventually developed into me as a Being? Therefore there has been a point when I did not have any Consciousness of being a Being?

What you are asking is a very profound question indeed. Yes it is true, there will have been a point when you were not aware of your Self as a Being, as most Beings will have been this too in a way. But it is difficult to put a 'time' to it, as this does not exist as you think of it. So, let's not talk of any 'time' but the fact that you will have been a 'blob' of Mind Energy detaching itself from the pulsating Mass ever so keen to exist and develop itself!

This is where you have the dilemma of understanding where/ when Consciousness is present.

Being conscious of one's Self as a separate Being is a very tenuous happening, which *develops at its own pace.* What each creature does may be very different from what others do. So, we cannot give you set rules. But what can be said is that **the Urge to 'Be' is usually followed by a dim Consciousness of Self, growing more and more as realisation of Self expands.**

This is how it basically works and that **starts at the Mind level of course - it has nothing to do with any physicality,** since you cannot have CHOSEN to have a physical state if you did not know (or hardly knew) that you existed!

BR- What about you, my dear Guiding Friend?

We all have that ability, you included - the ability to have help from Beyond our own world. You are helped by me and your Team and others, because you are on Earth temporarily. We are aided by those who have created the Earth and its 'life sequences' — so they are BEYOND the physical world and the 'Spirit World'. They give us input and Energy, and even guidance when needed, to help us help you — and certainly providing us with information to pass on to you in this case.

But **the Energy World you think of is not just the 'Spirit World'** — which you know is only the 'level' of vibrations you come to when you have left the body and will probably leave again for a few more trips, i.e. the level for those who go to and come back from the Earth indeed. The Energy 'World' is the infinite 'ocean' constantly producing and reproducing itself into myriads of creations as said before. So, WE CAN tune into it (and so can you, if you tried more by having pure Peace of Mind!) and thus refresh our own Mind Power. It is all a question of FOCUS as always.

If we focus on that level of extremely refined vibrations (that 'way of thinking' you could say), then we can have a breather and replenish ourselves with even more vigour and depth of understanding. That way we are **constantly expanding our own Selves and our knowledge, and we better our access to even higher, even more enlightening information - more depths of knowledge**, of understanding of this unbelievable Reality, which is constantly creating and developing itself, simply because it is pure Creative Mind Energy forever 'on the go'.

It is unfathomable, therefore offers forever new insights into more detailed knowledge. It is very difficult to try and explain that to you Humans, since most of you only know of your physical and others may only just about grasp the state after death of the body.

Yes, you can always expand your Consciousness of what is going on and what you can be, because you really never 'just ARE': **You are CONSTANTLY EVOLVING AS BEINGS OF MIND,** hopefully becoming increasingly **more conscious of what you CAN BE and become, and do** with your Inner Power—since fundamentally you are a Being of Mind Power, and that's it!

So it is up to you, each one of you and each one of us, everywhere, **to play with your own Awareness and seek to expand it,** all the time: therefore **never be stuck in one Mindset, but searching and opening inner doors out of sheer curiosity and interest!**

SSS

CHAPTER 29

Each of you needs to be conscious of the fact that **you are a Mind on the go**, a Mind that throws thoughts all over and all around. By doing so you affect every small and large aspect of your life... and others'! It is so important to know and grasp you have this bulldozing and spiralling effect. One thing leads to another because you thought of something in the first place. This is what makes your world the way it is!

So don't complain or blame a god or a devil. You Humans are doing it. You are like a fireworks display, shooting out thoughts which will carry on existing—and most of them will materialize around you as events that you will like or dislike, or dread or suffer from... simply because you thought them and of course, you are under the influence of other people's thoughts too!

It was **not 'meant'** to be unpleasant happenings - if everyone thought genuinely pleasant, warm, caring thoughts, none of you would be suffering. But it **has become this constant barrage of resentment, greed**, hatred, thus leading to a considerable amount of stress for all of you. Hence unease and diseases reflecting in the flesh body. That's what you have all done with your world by just not becoming aware of what your Mind constantly fabricates and emits— when instead you could all have been happy.

You all have to turn around and change your way of thinking and start afresh, wherever and whenever you can; otherwise you'll still be going downhill fast for hundreds of your years!

The 'desert of a Mind' does not exist. The Mind is always fertile, always shooting out thoughts. The Mind never stops.

MIND: ELECTRIC TOOL!

BR- A silly question: Is my Mind now as Brigitte, the 'same Mind' as in different 'past lives'?

You all **have a Mind, which is your individual way of creating the world you think you are in**. Each Being has its own Mind. The Mind TOOL used when you were in a different situation (what you see as a 'past life') would **possibly not be the same way of thinking** but **will be part of the same Energy of your Higher Self—the Real You**.

Your own Higher Self has the power to produce and create. It has various personalities or Souls, to experience different happenings as 'lives' on Earth. Whenever a 'person' comes to Earth as a specific Human, that person has an inner power suiting **that** particular Self. It has the same kind of Energy, i.e. Creative Force, as the whole Universe and Universes, BUT that Energy is fitting the particular Being as, say, a woman, so you are thinking in a way suitable for the woman you wanted to be for a while. Intrinsically it is the 'same' Power of Thought but **it is not the same line of thoughts** you may have had as a man, hundreds of years 'before'.

Your way of thinking now is already different from your way of thinking as a child or a young person, so you will have adapted your thinking, your attitude to people and situations. But the 'electromagnetic power' (let's say) of your thinking tool (i.e. the Mind) is like all electromagnetic powers, i.e. all Minds elsewhere. The Energy of Creativity is the same, because it is universal, but the details and the attitude in this life are different from your attitudes and your way of thinking in other lives.

There will be a thread of similarity in some cases as you have the whole Being, the Higher Self as common ground;

but your Soul as a woman has directed that creative tool to think and act in ways different from, say, the way the man whom you have been at one time, was thinking.

A Mind is not a Being. A Mind is an electric tool, plugged into the 'Universal Electromagnetic Energy,' let's call it that. So when you think, you are using your own wires to bring in the current from elsewhere—but what you do with that current in your wires is up to you and your own attitude as a 'Spirit Being', as a Being of Energy, **as a conscious Being** who should be a Being of Compassion but with Free Will. This means if you directed your Free Will to commit acts which are not compassionate (but instead are selfish, or against the one universal Law of not hurting other Beings), you would lead yourself down unpleasant roads and states!

That is where your Mind would be firing out thoughts– and therefore creating events which will surround you and others—good events are up to you, bad events are up to you...

BR- But it could be bad events hitting me because of other people's bad thoughts?

Indeed. Your Mind affects others just as others affect you, but you can **use your Mind to protect yourself** by blocking any kind of unpleasant influences.

It is simple and effective. **Mind Power is electromagnetic** as you call it. **It ATTRACTS events just like a magnet.** So when you think negatively it attracts similar negative attitudes and events. If you think positively it attracts positive, acceptable, suitable events and of course people.

Therefore, do not think, negatively, **do not dread** things or happenings because you are creating the very situations you are dreading or fearing. It is so simple and obvious - yet most of you are not aware you are doing it.

BR- What do you suggest we do to 'protect' ourselves?

You know how to do it! Simply use your Mind Power to visualize and **believe in the visualised picture** you create: imagine a blockage to the assault from external sources. **Build a protective 'wall' or 'bubble'** or sheath to surround you and yours with — thus not letting nasty, unwanted Energies from other people or events. It is so simple. You can do it all the time at any time and keep reinforcing it.

VISUALIZING BIRTH OF CONSCIOUSNESS

BR- Going back to grasping Consciousness, I need to be able to visualize the whole picture...

As you imagine a colossal Expanse of throbbing creative Energy spurting and spouting out shoots of 'INTENT TO BE', **those shoots have no concept of what they are** or will be yet. They just have an Urge, want to exist as 'something' in a way different to the gigantic Expanse of Eternal Existence. The Huge Expanse is Creative Energy, remember, **intelligent by the fact that it has always been and is aware it exists.**

BR- Doesn't being aware mean Consciousness?

It is aware but it does not ponder about it. It is **aware that there is a built-in Urge which pushes it to want to BE more** and DO more. So the Urge drives it, an irresistible Urge to Be itself, to become 'more'...

When that Urge explodes within a particular 'blob' (let's say), it shoots as a 'flare' - "I want to 'BE'!" It does not know what to be, but it knows it 'is' something detaching itself or shooting out of the general Expanse of Creative Energy.

When the individualisation of that shoot takes place, the only activity or sensation is that Urge. As there are others doing the same thing, connections of awareness of being different from others arise, awareness of not being part of and blending with a 'big mass'...

While all this constantly happens, the general 'feeling' is simply an Urge to shoot, an Urge to seek out for more. As that Craving is satisfied by the creation of individual shoots, those spurts of individual Urges separate themselves by their own individual Intensity of Desire. The **Desire within is the new drive= an extension and improvement on 'Urge'— because the Desire may then become more** orientated towards an aspect or the other.

BR- How would they know what to wish for/to be?

Those are innate 'feelings', desires acquired from the powerful Creativity built in their own Selves as shoots, since they come from the Universal Creative 'ocean' of Energy. So that latent Creativity has the power to 'invent' the various possibilities of different states of being or doing. Thus **built-in Creativity leads the way and pushes towards one possibility** or the other.

As the result starts building itself up, the whole of that 'new creation' senses it is changing for the better, in a new way, from its original state as part of the 'Big Mass'. That's how it **starts developing an awareness of being itself by encountering other shoots,** crossing Energies with other 'shoots-cum-creations'. The whole system builds up more and more that way.

BR- Do 'Intelligence' and Thinking come later then, or being a 'shoot' of Creative Energy (whatever urge, desire, sensation it has), builds up into shooting new creative happenings?

What you think of as Animal or Human Intelligence is not what we mean. **Intelligence** is by definition the way you think up things, work out things, to make them fit better using knowledge of happening, to improve next happenings.

Whereas **Mind** is the very Creative Power which resides in anything and any Being. What Mind does is *create without analyzing* whether it is 'good' or 'bad' in your terms.

MIND just creates;

INTELLIGENCE analyzes;

AWARENESS senses what is around or within;

CONSCIOUSNESS is awareness of Oneself, whether an 'object' or a 'Being' — but that means it **can be at different levels and can increase and progress.**

So if we get the same understanding of the words used, we'll be on an even footing, otherwise we'll talk at cross purposes. Your Mind 'thinks' because it is a part and a tool of your Energy Being. You cannot 'not think'. As your Mind thinks, you as a Being of Compassionate Energy nowadays, can direct your Mind not to think 'that way', not to give importance to some things or others. Throughout, you as a Being can direct your thinking Mind since it is your tool - it should NOT be your leader; you are in charge, you must be strong!

If you are weak, you may let other things influence you, like the needs and desires of your physical body – a body which has reactions caused by its very nature, its own structure, its nerves giving sensations which may be pleasant for example. So if you give in to those over and over again, you'll be ignoring the calls of your 'Other Nature', the other side of your make-up: the 'spiritual' side, the side of the compassionate Being of Energy.

WHAT IS 'THINKING'?

BR- Could you please explains more what you mean by the Mind 'thinks'?

The Mind does 'think' as long as the Being whose Mind it is thinks, of course. The thing you call 'Mind' we call Mind *Power*. Or if you prefer 'Creative Thinking Power'. It is creative as soon as it thinks. 'Thinking' is not so much cogitation and pondering, but more having an idea coming to the 'Mind'...

The idea comes because of and by the very nature of the natural **ability to create the moment something is 'thought'** / appears in the Energy of the Being. (We say 'Energy' to try and avoid the word 'Mind' which seems to confuse the issue).

The moment a new idea pops to the surface of the 'idea-making-level or area' (We describe it so to help you visualize something!), the Energy of **the Creative Power sets into making it happen, if the intensity of the thought is strong enough to maintain its actualization.**

So, the Mind (i.e. tool of the Soul or Being) is not a personality but a useful creative instrument which can produce 'thoughts' by the very nature of its creative force.

Understand that all things and Beings which create themselves out of the Mind Power Mass of Potentiality have that Creative Power within themselves. So **it is just a question of how much intensity can be generated by Urge and Desire and Awareness.**

As those progress in their intensity, the **focus on new 'goals'** increases; that is when the creation of new settings, surroundings and animation of the thought takes place. All to do with the focusing and concentration.

BR- A while back you said that when you dictate you send your thoughts to my receptive Mind and 'close' my thinking Mind... Could you elaborate more please?

As you think we listen to your thoughts. So as we think, please listen to our thoughts! Then the blending of Minds will create what you obtain as 'knowledge' because **we can access your Mind by simply blending with its receptive part.** This is only an image to help you understand what goes on.

There are layers of comprehension and absorption within the Mind, like 'sponges' taking in some products and not some others. So when we talk of profound topics, **the absorption of those points is made by the *layers prepared and nurtured* to be able to accept and soak up those subjects.**

This, in your case, has been built up for years of your time on Earth. If you wanted to speak and understand, say, Chinese or Hebrew, you would have to start tackling those languages from the basic level and build up on it, until you are fluent both in comprehension and in speaking it yourself.

Similarly, we needed to **help you build up your own receptivity to concepts you had not encountered before, so that your Mind did not reject them as 'nonsense'.**

So, when we speak to you by **sending you our thoughts**, we send them **towards the finer vibrations of your Mind's receptivity,** if you see what we mean. We reach the deeper levels of your understanding which go beyond those needed for normal everyday Earthly life.

What Mind does is act on impressions or ideas coming from itself or from surrounding stimuli. So, when you are constantly bombarded by such things throughout your day, you cannot easily receive what is sent to your deeper 'layers of receptivity'. Mind being a Creative Force wants to act constantly and create, create, create...

This is why we need it to put the brakes on when we send it some nutrition at a deeper level, some knowledge on topics beyond its daily activities on Earth—which means we need to **focus our thoughts intensely and aim them at your more profound and receptive areas** (so to speak) **and calm down the daily activity/ routine strata**.

It is not easy to carry out because you all have Free Will to do and think what you want! But **your** willingness and desire to reach us and acquire more knowledge, helps this to happen more easily. So, focus on both sides (yours and ours) is vital—and deep and strong intention and desire for success and knowledge absorption help the process every time we meet in Mind exchanges. This is very summarily explained to give you a faint idea of what goes on, more or less...

TO REACH 5th DIMENSION: RISE ABOVE MATERIALISM!

BR- Has what is named the 5th dimension anything to do with the Expansion of Consciousness?

The higher the vibrations you reach, the more refined they are: you can sense many Beings, many thoughts which are there or beyond. Once you elevate your thoughts beyond the level of vibrations and frequencies emitted by those on Earth, you'll reach higher levels of thinking- because everything is bathed in that Creative Mind Power.

The expansion of Consciousness you all talk about is what **constantly goes on anyway** but at many various levels. It can only be **improved once you have learnt to reach more refined levels** - you can only reach them, you don't want to retrograde or stay at some 'lower' level of thinking, because you have experienced far better.

305

So the "5th or 6th or whatever dimensions" (which are simply Human terms to mean just that) are simply 'levels' of thinking which are based around the very fact you are Beings of Mind Energy and you can feel what you experience to a higher degree: so if you feel free, the feeling of freedom will be practically ecstatic, far more wonderful than you get on Earth.

When the freedom of thinking and freedom of feeling are one within you there is no inner boundaries. So that limitless existence is sheer Joy in itself. *No limit is what all Beings aspire to so that the Creativity within them all can expand more.* That is what happens when you 'reach' more refined 'Levels of Thinking' which encompass everything that could be done—even what has not been thought about yet!

As we said before, what you Humans label **'5th or 6th dimensions' are simply more refined levels of thinking, more advanced creative levels** as Creativity has even less boundaries that you may have known... You have all limited yourself on Earth within the boundaries, or seemingly limiting boundaries of Matter.

But once beyond the constraints of your own thoughts, once you've elevated yourself beyond and shed the Earthly attitude and way of thinking, you can re-establish yourself (within yourself) as the Being of Light and Creative Mind which you have always been.

What is needed for you all is to think of a ROUND OBJECT, say a ball- then realise it has limits all over by its very nature of being 'physical'. Now if you **imagine a ball made of JOY, where would the limits be?** There are none. It can only expand itself more and more if it chooses. Well, that's what all feelings are like when you have shed the Earthly way of thinking, the way life there has nowadays become for you.

There used to be far more Freedom and Joy on Earth when the Experiment was created and Beings chose to investigate the intriguing fact of having a flesh body. Since then, things have become more a nightmare than a joyful experience! For the simple reason that those in charge or those living there have fallen under the spell of their own physical experience, their bodily needs, their fears constantly emanating from them...

What we could say about those 5th & 6th dimensions is that they are certainly **not physical**, not on a star and not in the 'Spirit World' as you call it. Because by the very fact of existing, they have surpassed that level and gone far beyond in vibrations, not in physical distances.

ENJOY, ADMIRE, RESPECT NATURE

IF you wish **to 'go there' you need to work on your sensing:** sensing the fact that you are a Being of High Energies which has a need for expansion, constantly reaching for better and more refined ways of existing. Therefore make the effort to **rise above all materialistic ways of thinking** to appreciate the wonders of the intricate Creative Power, which displays its work all over your world. Then go within and sense more... and more...

You can admire the Earth world, you can enjoy it but do not fall under the demands of the flesh needs, or the absurd rules of any man-made society or organisation bringing you down to a lower level of thinking and sensitivity.

If we had a piece of advice to give, we'd say: "Look for the best in everyone and everything, look for improvement in yourself. **Enjoy what is in front of you in Nature** and admire and respect it. That will help open your inner senses to better avenues and eventually 'dimensions".

There is something else to tell you about Consciousness. It is the fact **that if there was no Consciousness available, the worlds would stand still and even disintegrate.** It is the

Wish and Urge and Desire to progress, to get better, to find out more and BE more, that keeps Creativity going. Creativity will go on, but if the created 'things' do not become aware of the rest around them, what will happen? They will just stagnate and eventually dissolve back into nothing, if there is nothing to 'go for'.

Consciousness is part and parcel of all those creative Urges and activities. Sooner or later they will become more conscious: THAT is part of the thread of Life, it has to become so.

(A few days later, my left ear suddenly started ringing for no physical reasons! I had learnt to recognise the sign. My Teachers' shortcut to draw my attention — their way of 'phoning' me when I am not tuning in! So, this made me take my pen, just in case, even though I had not been asking any question ... I was amused and intrigued 'they' had something to say.

You may be asked this: What can be done to improve the development of your Consciousness? The only way is **to WANT to feel more conscious and aware** of anything and everything you know you have not noticed, or you know you may be missing or are weak at.

If you feel the Urge and Desire inside you, then go ahead and want it more, wish for that awareness to be more developed. Make sure that you aim at that side of things and have a constant wish built in you, so that it becomes a driving force. And you'll find the result will come! You will be able to do more, receive more, sense more.

Do not let yourself down thinking 'you are not good enough' and others do better... You CAN all do anything you want if you can build up that awareness. First, focus on that intense Desire and Wish and build up that alertness. This is to be worked on. That is what we would like to add to the advice and knowledge on Consciousness: You can all constantly develop your own!

SSS

CHAPTER 30

BR- When Mum (newly arrived in Sp.W.) decided to send a thankful thought to her 'guardian angel/ guide (or whoever looked after her when she was on Earth), she suddenly saw a wonderful 'Being of Light', who swiftly appeared and disappeared and reappeared to her. Who was 'he'?

What you call Beings of Light will be all those here, as we are all Beings of Light! It is understandable that for your mum who had just arrived in our world, this was extraordinary, because you always feel like you did on Earth when you arrive here. Only after a while do you get round to shedding Earthly appearances — which are all imaginary anyway — and realize that everyone is a Being of Energy, of Light as you said.

We can tell you that you all have a helper backing you all along your Earthly trip. That personality will have been chosen by you and will have accepted to be by your side throughout your Earthly life. That does not mean he cannot be a 'Being of Light', of course he is. But there is a difference between:

1) those who have been to live 'some time' on Earth to experience it and be better prepared to help those who are there as Humans — *(our Spirit guides)*

And 2) those who have never actually been in a flesh body because that is and was not their aim and purpose. Humans who want to imagine an 'angel with wings' will see one – especially if they were brought up to believe in them.

What we can tell you is that the Being your mum saw was her life-guiding companion. He has always been by her side in particularly tough times on Earth. 'He' was the one she saw because of 'whoever' had helped her in her life.

Whereas whoever helped her with her arrival and settling in was part of her team of 'helpers'. It's one job we all 'chip in'!

When you arrive here you are on your way to becoming again—or rather remembering again gradually—that you too have always been a Being of Light, once you've stripped yourself of your mental and emotional garment of that latest human life. **So the radiant Being of Light INSIDE YOU eventually shines beautifully** and all can see it so. This is what needs to be understood.

When the 'Human side' steps back and fades away from his / her outer shell (with all the little habits and memories and attachments), then **the true Being you are can step forward** once more and be true to Itself, as it has acquired more knowledge through the experience of that Soul as a recent Human.

That is not done overnight and will take time unless the Soul in question is so experienced and **'advanced' 'he' knows at once where he is.** This is what happens when Beings from Beyond this Spirit World have to go to Earth to help those in need or the Earth itself - they will quickly shed the 'human garment' when they come back!

So if you **think of your own Soul as a snippet from your Oversoul and Higher Self** *which is your real Spirit,* you'll see that the Soul has been on Earth—but the Oversoul has not done so as a 'single Being': your Oversoul **has experienced it through the many lives of those various facets**. This is how your Higher Self acquires more knowledge and develops itself. We see this as very simple even if you don't.

The Higher Self is the very ESSENCE of your Being—and your Mum's Being... So each of you and us is a

Being of Light and Energy, a limitless Being of Creative Energy, who enjoys being in many 'places' and states, and loves multiplying the opportunities for its own development. So, we know what it is like.

The very fact of **going to the Earth is only a minor aspect of the constant development** of the "Being of All That can Be"; and this is valid for each one existing.

Therefore, regarding your Mum's visitor (the Being of Light): she will have **seen the very core of HER (Higher) Self**, as it shed its other aspects and showed itself as a fundamental radiant Light, radiant Energy, the Compassion of which had to be felt because it was always there! This is a tribute to *her* caring personality, as she should now have seen throughout several lives she has become aware of and had a look at. (*Since that vision Mum has been examining other facets of her Oversoul by grasping and viewing many of her 'past' lives to understand and discover her 'Real Self'- as related in "I'm Not Dead" etc. Vol. 1 & 2*)

Pleasant as it may be to think you have an 'angel with wings of feather', you'll all have to come to terms one day with the reality of what goes on here in this world.

We all have the same Energy: the Creative Energy of the Energy SOURCE that has always existed, ok? So this Energy—being 'divided' so to speak into various personalities, Beings, entities, or whatever word you wish to use—means that you all have that One Source embodied in you as your Creative Power driving you to do more, to create more and discover more. This is all very well if you accept it. If you question or doubt, it will make it more complicated for you.

So, the basis a 'Human' come from is that Energy Being which is/ 'was' in your terms, an Energy Being who chose for their own purpose to go and experience the new Matter of this Earth.

That's why you have all appeared as Humans because of this 'transformation'. But **the need for guidance in that unusual world was set right at the beginning of Mankind wanting to stay longer on Earth.**

This is why the guidance from a 'guiding personality' (known as 'Spirit guide') has taken place, because it had to be people who had lived and experienced similar events to yours, so that you could be understood and guided- or at least reminded of what you wished to achieve.

This is where we 'guides' come in. We too are Beings of Light and Mind BUT it had been agreed by us and you, Human protégés, that we would help you individually as you went along. So what you sense now in life as you are helped, is the 'guide' who spends his 'time' with you to assist you on your path while you need it.

ABOUT YOUR HIGHER SELF/OVERSOUL

Your Higher Self is there as a **Thinking Creative Force which knows where it is going on its path** but has all those other facets to handle too. If you wish to see your Higher Self, you would have to be very relaxed and know how to tune in to your Inner Self to find the key, the core. It may not be quite possible now if you have not practised this enough...

(Throughout I feared my concentration was going, yet the dictation carried on! But now I doze off once more and fell asleep for good...)

I tune in again but a few days later. Since receiving the previous dictation late that evening, I had not read it again and had gone to bed not knowing what was written, because of my peculiar 'altered state,' therefore I did not recall at all what the answer to my original question was!

I am now concerned it might have been 'rubbish', because I recall my body was struggling keeping my eyes open and kept dozing off- thus possibly interfering with or distorting the explanation. So, I decided NOT to look at that text now, in order to prevent the risk of influencing my Mind – and instead ask my Communicators to kindly reply again and explain once more, even just briefly, who or what my mum's Being of Light was. Poor Teachers, they need to have a lot of patience with me!

We can tell you again what we told you last time. It is not so much a Being from your world than a Being from our world. That means from the world which includes your 'Spirit World' but which is in fact far vaster than that. That Being your mum saw was the kind of personality who looks after you throughout your individual lives.

First of all **you all 'have a Being of Light WITHIN you'** because you all ARE a Being of Light yourself. But this vision was NOT so much a 'separate guide' (i.e. who had been on Earth to learn what it's like to be a Human- then decided or accepted to be your guiding voice throughout a particular life). That Being of Light was the epitome, the ESSENCE of what you mum is—just like you are one too—The Being of THE Light she is 'made of'.

That is what you may call your 'Real Self', your 'Higher Self', or 'Oversoul'. You know she did see 'it' in more detail later on, but the first time she could only be shown that much without risking confusing her. She saw it as the one who guided her in her decision during her lives. And that 'who' is your own/one's own/ Higher Entity, one's own Being of Light which you all are made of and ARE. This is what it is. So no need to worry about not grasping it.

That is why your mum saw it as, throughout her life, **she was guided by the very Essence of her Self,** who cannot go wrong as to what is needed for the particular Soul in a particular life on Earth. It is its guiding force she felt, it is her inner Kindness she saw. All Beings are kind and compassionate at root. It is the Humans on Earth who often forget or shut off the voice of their Inner Self telling them they should, or not, do such and such...

BR- Is it a 'shoot' off the Universal Eternal throbbing Mass of Creative Force—a shoot, which 'eventually' chose to join in the Earth experiment?

What you need to realise is that the ginormous immensity of all this Power of Mind and Creative Force has no limits! So this makes it very difficult to explain. The main shoot of an eventual 'defined' Being (as you would think of it) is in a way coming from that original Mass, yes. BUT maybe not exactly as you may imagine, because you have to be continually aware of the **superposition and *intermingling* and constant outpouring** of more and more other 'shoots'... So, this is why we have to try and simplify those ramifications, so that your Minds do not get lost in all that!

My dear, your mum is a very kind Being as 'your mum' and as all the other Beings she has been 'so far' (by your way of thinking and seeing all 'other lives' in a linear structural way!). But you must know that you are all like that at the Source.

Your Source is a big mass of Creative Power, which demands to be 'more', to be creating extra possibilities, pushed by the intense Urge within, which has always existed. So, that conscious Power (conscious of its inherent, innate ability to create, as its 'gift', as its being 'that'), this conscious Power is not going to be able to stop its abilities, therefore the result is those shoots...of shoots...of shoots...spurting out and pouring away from the Source, so to speak, to make more of Itself, improve Itself, discover more ways of existing and 'being'! That is what it is all about - the Joy of Creativity, as always.

314

BR- What if I asked my audiences: "What is the most potent Energy?" and they'd reply: "Love"? How can I rectify or relate it properly to Mind Power?

What is difficult about that? You know perfectly well that since you think, you create - therefore since you feel, you create. This is a double-sided Energy! **The Energy of Love is part of the Creative Thought Power as it has Thought and Creativity in its make-up: loving to help, loving to create, loving to improve.**
So the loving feeling and thought is the ultimate of Thought Power because it adds to its creative side, the emotion and the caring, which is fundamental to all Beings of Compassion.

BR- I may be asked, "Surely not all Beings are compassionate?"

The fundamental Law of the Universal Energy and of Creation is: *"Do not harm (wilfully) any other Being"*. Won't you call that loving or compassionate? Not all Beings are aware of such feeling as such but no Being tries wilfully to harm others... except 'distorted Mankind' since it has got off the rail of the original plan for the Earth Experiment.

SSS

CHAPTER 31

What we can now convey is the summing up of what shall soon be the end of our new book. Summary: the sum of what it's all about, a kind of synopsis and conclusion. It's important it gets out soon. So the sooner we can get it done and you sort it out, the better!

As one who knows what we now are talking about, you appreciate the importance of the information we provide in it. It has to be made clear for 'the average Human' who may read it. So we cannot be too 'complicated'.

It is simple. **If Humanity does not realise they ARE special Beings from Beyond the physical world they know, they will never get to progress any further**. So we need to make them take that big step, grasp it, then step back to look at the mess that has been made of a wonderful experiment gone wrong! Gone wrong simply because Mankind overall has got the wrong end of the stick, and has done so for some considerable time!

This is what those Beings from BEYOND the physical Universe are saying to teach, or teach again, those on Earth: Wake up to the wonders you are in and on; see all this with new eyes. Not the eyes of the deluded people who think they actually own the world they exist in—and who think they can do what they want without harming that wonderful Nature and all that composes the Earth itself. You cannot keep plundering it, it will not survive that and neither will you—or at least neither will you be able to carry on living as you have been doing.

So, **stop the pollution**! That cannot be switched off completely since it's gone so far—but it can be reduced a very considerable amount. Stop the digging for minerals, oil and gases, as it will have **such a harmful effect that you will all suffer in the end.** We can see it from here and some of you Humans have understood it—but not the ones who are actually doing it.

Have a heart. Where is your heart and compassion? Why has Mankind sunk to such depravity, such cruelty? Such horrors created by Mankind for some of Mankind - whether torturing Animals to eat them later in some ridiculous dishes—or 'playing' at killing them slowly after agonising torture! What has got into you? All you have to think is: "Would I like to be locked up, tortured, burnt, etc?" You are mad if you think you get away with it, because your own Souls know what you are doing or have done—and **you are the one who will punish yourself SO harshly in the end that you wish you had never acted in that manner!**

You are totally unconscious of the extent of the horrors and tragedies you are perpetrating and perpetuating—but all this will burn you as gigantic remorse which you will not be able to switch off, as your WHOLE Being, your own Oversoul and Higher Self had been revolted by it for a long time. Then you will suddenly realize what cruel fools and wicked self-centred creatures you have been and still are, as long as you continue those depraved ways of eating and living for the 'joys' of flesh pleasure which cause harm and suffering to others.

HELP TO THE CREATION

So, we'll start again: The joy of being 'superior' Beings stems from being in charge of what one can do with one's own Mind Energy and constantly grasp the magnitude of one's own power.

You all have that power on Earth but you have relinquished it, totally forgotten it (most of you anyway). It is such a pity, such a disaster even, because what was meant was for you all to discover the extent of your individual power over whatever you wanted to create in that life in the physical.

You also HAD A 'TASK' in as much as **you were there, as part of the creation of that Earth world, to help it keep its own Energies balanced** and functioning correctly throughout its existence!

What you can tell those who ask, is that the composition of your Earth is different from the composition of other planets so that it is not an exact replica—but they are 'physical'.

What some Beings have done (who have chosen to go and experiment on those places) is to sense what the planet could offer and what they could offer it. If they are there as Beings of Minds without a 'solid-looking' body, then they will be doing different things from what you would be doing on Earth, say. If they go there as 'gaseous' bodies or other ethereal type of textures, then it will again be a totally different experience.

So it all depends on what the Beings can contribute to the planet and what kind of practice they can have there, according to what that particular planet can offer as an experience. They are all different. And many planets are not inhabited but are just there for the balancing of Energies in that Universe.

Therefore, as we were saying earlier, the aim to be of help to the continuous creation of the Earth has been thwarted and distorted. And now we are trying to instil some sense and some knowledge into the ignorant section of Mankind (unfortunately the majority) to get it back on the right track.

STONEHENGE

BR- Could you give greater details about such as Stonehenge circle of boulders (in UK)? And why did those 'Ancient People' need such huge stones marking the straight path in Carnac (Brittany, France)?

What you all see there are only remains of what has been a mighty building or mighty road, which was constructed with a definite aim in mind. The Minds of those doing it in those days were closer to the Energies of the Earth and their companions than it has been since. The mightily heavy stones of the Stonehenge assembly of rocks has the answer in its design: the **circular design was to trap the amount of Energy that was pouring out of the Earth** at that particular point. It has to be circular to send the Energy round and round to each stone so that it does not get dissipated: it helped to concentrate it in one such area.

As to the inner design and setting of other stones rows, it was to accentuate a certain curve from the Earth; it was also meant to match with some stars Energies above head at a particular time of the year. So **all those points put together helped the use of what the Earth was providing free.**

What needs to be understood is that the aims and goals in those days were far different from the way of thinking nowadays, so those enlightened people, who could sense the Energies pouring out of those Energy points or lines, were far more aware of what was going on or what could be used. They knew how to tap into the Energies pouring out nonstop because they had the Enlightenment!

They were indeed Advanced Beings. No doubt many of them had come specifically to that special Energy cross point or centre point, to help those living in the country learn to tap into the vast amount constantly pouring out—so this helped

319

Mankind and Animalkind in many ways. Healing Power of course was number one—but also help with the direction of crops culture and assistance with the re-energising of all Minds coming near it or focusing on it.

All that was needed was to know there was a large source copiously offering 'Energy food', pure Energy, so those in the know would help novices come and experience the Power. They learnt to rebalance their own Selves, or tap into it to open up again to their own spiritual enlightenment, their rekindling the spark that was always there—since they were all Beings from outside the physical Universe who wanted to bathe into that fundamental Power.

Why worry about how it was built? They had a mighty power there pouring out of the ground! Don't you think they would have known how to use that to lift some Earthly stones? After all the stones are made of atoms with empty spaces within. Since any of the **Beings had superior powers** as they no doubt had, then it would have been simple for them to sense the Energy fields, make it gather to one spot by moving it and **lifting the stones** with it, as a kind of supporting/ lifting net. The Energy can be sensed to vibrate, so any vibrations provided would have accentuated the process. This is where **sound could have been used** as well.

REACHING THE SEEKERS OF TRUTH

What we now need to tell you is that the main point of this new book is to be of help to those who WANT to understand "what all this is about": why they are on Earth and WHO they are. But they will never be able to grasp it by following Mankind's distorted ideas of evolution from an amoeba or some other silly notions!

It is vital that Mankind can make the mental leap to see itself as **coming from beyond its own Earth** and more - from

BEYOND its physical Universe! Otherwise it will keep going round in circles for more millennia and getting things even worse. We have to stop this one way or the other.

The word has been planted here and there in other ways too, but we need to talk to the 'man in the street', so that they breed new generations of children who will have been taught correctly from birth not to forget **their lineage from other levels** than the flesh lineage—not to forget and not to ignore their Inner Self, their Inner Voice and most of all their Inner Power! This is ever so important that we cannot stress it enough.

Now that you have understood it, you'll have to manage to put that across others - to those who will listen, think and realise that this makes more sense than any of the other assumptions and so-called 'facts' based on no solid foundation, but just on vague theories which don't add up if you look properly into it. Mankind teaches far too many distortions of bits and pieces twisted and entangled together in the vain hope to create a 'reasoning', which is fact, has no proper real base.

So this is where we are with this: it will have to be 'out', published very soon, so that you can reach more people and touch upon that extension of the topic of our other book *('Truths, Lies & Distortions')*. It cannot be 'left in the air' and it needs to be out before the Earthly catastrophes increase and the world and Mankind panic with no hope and no understanding of their situation.

Read it well, know it well and make people at least understand they all have a say in what they can do, as they all have **chosen** to come. There is hope because **many Superior Beings have been and ARE coming to help rectify things as much as can be done and rebalance the whole grid**, so that the Energies flow freely, happily and without hindrance. All the drilling and digging is definitely harming that world of yours.

321

BR- Any suggestion for a different type of Energy to use with our Earthly machines?

The matter is in hands. We have a few things to say regarding new ways of getting Energy for you all to benefit from, yet not keep destroying the Earth. It has to be thought out carefully and planned gradually. You'll all be better off with it, but this is for a different chapter. When we come to it you'll know but for now we must first finish this chapter, to say the advice given to Mankind is for its own good.

So, dear Readers, please do not dismiss what we have been trying to explain to you—because in the end the losers will not be us the messengers, but you the receivers. If you understand the importance of our message, you will reactivate the Inner Knowing that you **all** have: THAT will produce waves of positive, constructive and creative Energies all over, thus conducive to successful ideas to help the Earth and those on it.

As you think you **will** create.

As you believe you **will** create!

As you relax, you will absorb even more knowledge, provided by those who have the bigger picture in Mind—those like us who can see what was and is going on.

So, wouldn't you prefer to be warned, explained and shown that you have a Power within you (The Creative Power of your Mind), which you CAN tap into with successful results? But results will only be gained if you follow the advice of being very calm and tuned in — and if you never create anything that will be harmful to ANY other Being: People, Animal, Nature/ the Earth.

USE WILL POWER TO IMPROVE THE WORLD

This is so simple when you think of it—yet it will take some **understanding and dedication to WANT to turn things round for the sake of Humanity, Animalkind and the Earth itself**. Want it from the bottom of your heart and put it into action. Intensity of Desire and purity of goal (i.e. not harm others and help all). When Man wants something badly he can convince a thousand or a million. **When a million want the same thing badly, the Energy pouring out of their Minds and whole Beings will help the creation of that wish—it will materialize**. Have faith in this, **your own Power.** Not in some incomprehensible invention of some 'bearded man' floating in the sky to make things happen IF he decides to do so!

YOU are the ones with the power of a Will which itself creates as it affects all Energies around—as long as it is for the good of all concerned on Earth, not just for a small minority.

You Readers have the key. Use it to open doors for yourself but also to help others understand what you have now understood. Pass the word round so that Mankind turns round and becomes again what it was originally - compassionate and creative.

Why is it so hard to make people want to become gifted again and switch on their Inner Light, instead of remaining plunged in inner darkness?

Knowing how to make machines, cars and toys has NOT made you all really happier and has not brought Peace to your world, has it? So, you need to find and reach to your own **Inner Power - the power of a calm, focused Mind concentrating on useful goals with no selfish aims,** no self-centred reason, not excluding other Beings from the benefits obtained.

If only you could see how wonderful your world would become when you ALL do that, from the bottom of your hearts! No need for wars, no need for poverty. All equal, all happy and safe-and that includes **giving Animals the freedom to exist as what they fundamentally are - free Beings who chose a different outer structure from Man's.**

Let Live. Gain your own Inner Peace.

Remember, when a large group of people gather together in peace and harmony with no other thoughts and desire than to create a wonderful, useful and peaceful goal, that goal will come into actualization! They will create what they wish for simply by using their own visualization, their own well-focused intense desire. All well focused - THAT is the key!

YOU ALL have that power. THAT is what makes things happen. You have no need to dissipate it by 'passing the buck' to some invisible deity to ask 'him' or 'her' to make things happen! **What makes things happen is YOUR own intense wish, as you all have Minds creating outpouring electromagnetic thoughts?** It has been demonstrated many times before. Do not doubt, just practise doing it! The more people, the better, "All for one and one for all!' as the saying goes.

NEW ENERGY?

BR- Before I have to stop, could you tell me briefly whether you really have a solution for 'new energy' to use on Earth, instead of coal, nuclear etc?

What we'll suggest is the harmonization of water from the sea with air from the sky. The sea has power; you can harness it effectively, like you putting turbines in it and then blowing air in it.

BR- How to blow air without using expensive electricity?

The sea has an immense power from the Energy 'lines' ('fields' to be correct) it is over. You need to trace them and *tap into them* by looking for them and adding magnets to those areas, so the power is attracted to the magnets, then inflate 'balloon-type' objects to blow air into those areas. That will produce a force that can be continuous as long as the 'lines' stay there—and they are staying so there is no problem.

Now we wish to emphasize again something very important which you need to concentrate upon, to help us achieve what we need to do and for you to achieve what you have or chose to complete. The following is to be put in this, our new book.

When we look at the Earth and its planets from our dimension, it seems incredible that anybody could ever imagine and impose their beliefs that this planet is or was the centre of the whole Universe. It was such a ludicrous and egotistical idea and concept! But since Mankind has learnt better now that many evolved Souls inspired it to open its eyes more, the view is much better; yet they still have not got the concept that nothing ON Earth gave Life as such - nor anything coming physically from elsewhere.

This is still floating in some 'scientific minds'! So we need to reiterate that the only thing, which gives Life, is Life itself; And Life is the Energy of Life, the pure Energy of 'being' and enjoying 'to be'. To be whatever one CHOOSES— not what one becomes because a rock or an amoeba evolves in drastic ways.

NO RANDOM CREATION

What we have to put across is the need for the public to open its eyes beyond what had been inserted in their Minds since childhood and school days.

If the Earth had not been placed (We do mean 'placed') where it is, you would indeed not have the results you know, because the sunlight and the influence of its planets would have been unable to do their work - balance all Energies. Therefore it has been carefully positioned as we have already explained many a time before.

But the construction of a flesh body is not just something happening at random without some meticulous planning beforehand. All this has already been elucidated and clarified, but we need to remind you all that **if there had not been that PLANNING, you would not exist! Nor would all the rest of the Earth creation and your Universe...** including the voluntary, self-creation of 'Animals' who choose, just like Humans do, to have a body of flesh but with a different shape according to the species etc.

As if it was not enough, we'll add that the construction of all the Universes, which exist, is taken care of in the same way, because nothing can be left at random, nothing can be 'thrown in the air' hoping it will fall the right way up! All this was definitely planned as far as the 'construction' is concerned, why and how was made clear before.

We cannot in this book go over the nitty gritty of each item because you Humans will expect human terms of physics and chemistry and we work differently! The day you Earthlings learn to consciously create using just your Minds, then we'll be on the same wavelength—and you will **understand how your world was put together as the visions of inner workings are fabulously astounding!** But 'normal flesh eyes' do not see all that...

SEEING FROM 'BEYOND'

What we 'see' is what is emanating as rays of Energies in all directions. Some will look 'physical' to you and some will be totally invisible to you, whereas we'll see them.

326

They are the rays of anything created. So, **those Energies shaped as 'Humans, 'Animals'** or any other things (labelled or not by you) still exist even if you do not sense them.

But the question "Are there any physical Beings elsewhere in your galaxy?" actually means: "Do we see Beings who, to you Humans, would look physical or solid?"

We'll say: yes, there are Beings of all kinds in many 'physical places' in your galaxy or others; but it is not whether they exist **which matters - it is why and how they exist.** If they have chosen to be made of a particular type of Matter or shape, it will have been for a good reason since no creation is without a reason behind its being there.

So, anything choosing to be seen or sensed 'physically' can live that way for a while; whether they have the same shape as you or not is not really of any consequence or importance. We would like to stress again the fact that you Humans see things in limited and totally different ways from what we see from our perspective. If you were in our place you would laugh at the questions you expect us to answer, simply because at a higher level of thinking, free from the Earthly ways of measuring everything, **we see deep WITHIN vibrations and Energies. We do not see the shapes you** *think* **you see** and you think are 'solid'! So, it makes a great difference!

Yes, there are 'Beings' nearly everywhere, but not always what you expect us to tell you. There have been 'inhabited' places, which now are dried up, and 'dead' from your point of view, but does it mean there is nothing? There could be 'Thought' lingering there and your instruments would not pick them!

So, our present aim is to pursue what we really want to tell you. **What does exist is constant Energy of the Mind, i.e. a Creative Energy. It does not have to be 'a Being' or personality.** It just is there, ready to activate itself into action.

The thought of 'being' is the ultimate and constant emanation all over all Universes, whether seen as physical or not. All 'worlds' or rather 'states' are based on 'being'- just 'being'! Then each time the Urge rises, that state of 'being' wants to 'be' a little better. It is THE fundamental state that has always existed and will always exist.

So 'being' *(verb)* is what everything is. What 'it' does with it is up to 'it'. And that's how Creativity and Creation progress and expand. If nothing wished to improve itself, then it would lead to a dead end and a full stop.

By 'being', one can then sense a minimum feeling of existence. Then the innate Urge to 'grow', to become more, gradually increases: becoming aware of others in their state of 'being' triggers awareness and helps to expand.

Therefore, this is enough for you to know as a basic fact. Why and how each may change is up to that state, and is not essential or important for Humans to improve and grasp what need to be known for their lives—as **all those states of 'being' changed and improved**: some veered towards sheer Mind Power expansion and actualization, remaining pure Mind Power producing states and activities they enjoy. Others may (or have done so) choose for a while to create what you would see as more 'physical' states.

This is not so essential to delve into because it will be very difficult for you, from an Earthly point of view, to grasp states that you are not really familiar with or aware of.

SSS

CHAPTER 32

One of my keen readers, Emyr Thomas (who gave me permission to use his name), asked me this question: "When, say, a soldier dies in battle, is it pre-ordained before birth for that to happen?"

Instead of thinking over my reply, I thought it would be better to ask my dear Teachers from Beyond to give the answer - They promptly did so - and in far more details!

What you want to know is whether a young man who chose to go as a soldier is going to a 'premeditated death' or suicide. We'll say that **it depends** on what his motives are.

Before we say more, may we remind all of you Humans that **no one leaves their temporary flesh body unless their own Higher Self decides to do so,** for their own reasons that can only be understood on the large scale of Eternity! Of course, the departed will no doubt be mourned, but the Higher Self/ Oversoul is in charge of its particular facet known to you as the current Human, a 'soldier' in this case.

Therefore, there could be some lads who have chosen to die as 'martyrs' so that their loved ones will feel better to have lost him "doing his duty in order to save the country (or whatever cause)"... But he would have left his body anyway!

OR, there could be some lads who have been 'silly' enough to join the Army 'with great visions'... but then find themselves disappointed in their dreams of 'adventures and glory'! So they decide to get out the 'easy way', without having to explain why they have given up. Yes, it CAN happen! Of course it is painful for the families, but sometimes the 'family honour' matters both to the boy and to the parents. So that way it is saved!

But there is also the possibility of some lads actually **wanting** to be in an army and **wanting to fight** others, because their Souls have not yet understood that one really MUST NOT kill... And that urge may still stem from other (previous/'past') lives when they were soldiers then!

So, they see it through to whatever end, whether they come out of battles safely or not—depending on what their original 'life plan' was. Or else that **'plan' may have been open ended...** and the decision to leave the Earth that way may have been taken due to circumstances, or (sudden) lack of will to live—Or possibly as a gesture, a new awakening that one "should not kill": Perhaps he may have suddenly realised he was being made to kill others and his **Soul awoke to the repugnance** it felt doing this—So he chose to leave his body and not be forced to do this anymore! He hopes the lesson may also be to show in a small way how futile those 'mutual murders' are—how many countries have fought each other for years, then after all those deaths (even millions of deaths over centuries) now those countries are on amicable terms! Isn't that ridiculous and criminal to have acted that way in the first place?

So, you have quite a choice of possibilities according to the wishes and the Free Will of each soldier in question... Never forget that the person you cherish as a Human, is only ONE facet, one aspect of a multi-faceted Being of Light on his journey of discovery and experiences - his Oversoul knows better and sees 'further'. You are such a Being too...

SLEEP PARALYSIS?

BR- Following an email from another of my keen readers, Martin Crossley (who gave me permission to use his name), about his experiences of suddenly feeling 'paralyzed' when in bed, in an 'hypnotic' state or during sleep—and waking up in terror—can you please try and explain?

You have there a problem experienced by many people on Earth as they have not come to terms with controlling the effect of having a 'spiritual' / Energy body and a flesh one. It has to be explained in detail or else none of you will understand what is going on.

If you leave your flesh (as you all do at night or during any sleep state), it is bound to feel different from having your Consciousness focused onto the flesh, as you do over most of your daily life. So when you are 'out if it' you are ever so free indeed—YET your Mind has an enormous impact on what happens... And that is where the problems arise usually.

As you feel yourself as an Energy body leaving—or separating your Consciousness away from—that flesh body, you accept it at first most of the time.

But if you have a Mind full of emotions or problems to do with your Earthly life, you may compromise the smooth exit. That is what happens. You are not quite 'prepared' or ready to leave even though your Mind and Spirit know perfectly well that you have done it umpteen and thousands of times before! That is where the weak point resides:

If your Mind is *unsettled by the slightest thing*, you will be affecting the smooth transfer from one state to the other. So, hesitation, 'looking back', dreading forward for whatever (minor even) reason, **will** affect the activity. If you feel happy to leave as a little 'break/ holiday from being in the body, you will have no problem. Yet most people have things on their Minds. That's why this happens.

There will be more to it because people are different and cope with their worries in different ways. We know that all that said above is correct because it affects numerous people, but you can reassure your friend that he is not 'going mad' and is not being 'possessed' by anything or anyone - This is not a physical occurrence and it is certainly not a 'spiritual' one i.e. no kind 'Being' would affect him that way.

The question of whether an 'unkind' Being would be attacking him has not been asked but may be assumed—or be at the back of some people's Minds? So we need to tackle it as well.

As you well know, no Being would force himself onto another person unless the Earthly person was too 'open'/ weak/ in the sense of lacking resistance, and definitely had a wish to be linked with or approached by 'other Beings' that s/he would like to be close to, even if this is done subconsciously. So there always is the possibility of such a predicament. But in your friend's situation, this is not the case. He has experienced those happenings before and he is no stranger to them.

The answer is not always straightforward and black and white. There is always a grey area in all people's Minds. So, if you are not sure what happened to him, you would need to know what is 'bothering' him, even only slightly. Of course, you cannot ask him to reveal his life and inner thoughts. But you can pass the message on, so that he (or anybody with the same problem) thinks of testing and weighing up his most inner thoughts...

It is the inner thoughts - or subconscious - which will affect the surface i.e. the flesh vehicle. If the flesh was not dependent on what the Being who 'owns' it thinks, it would be ok. But unfortunately, those inner thoughts have a deteriorating effect on the flesh of the owner, if they have not been sorted out or weeded out of the system.

Yes, it can start from childhood, as all children have worries and some also still recall their 'previous' lives, which adds to the burden of the inner thought baggage! So, the notion of trying to sort out inner thoughts of the subconscious may be extremely daunting because one does not always know one has them!

The 'secret' is to sit often and tune in to oneself, to *find out how one feels at the moment, what one dreads in life, what one longs for and whether there are conflicting emotions.*

FEARS constantly build themselves up in people's Minds; so they really need to be eradicated - but this is *to be done during the wide awake state*, away from the sleeping time, otherwise there will be an overlapping and the creation or visual appearance of all that troubled you! This is only a suggestion but it should be a useful and effective one.

As the Mind settles down to do that task of 'sorting out' and weighing up, the necessary inspiration will come from your own Higher Self to sieve the important information, from not so important- therefore you will feel what is 'right' and 'wrong', what is really 'bugging you' and what is not so essential.

Then you could be helped to come to terms with the problems if you tune in to your Self and your Higher Self and your 'Guiding Helper'. How can you do that? Like one does when one tunes in. Simply sit quietly and *feel* the expansion of your Self, your centre, your Mind or rather your Consciousness. Let it 'spread' and expand and most of all WISH for the understanding and the solution to manifest themselves.

When you come to terms with, say, big problem 'A' - which possibly has even been dormant for ages at the back of your Mind (but still does exists for you, since you are thinking of it!) - then ACCEPT that problem 'A' is a hitch and concern and decide to tackle / analyze/ it separately.

One problem at a time. Then your Mind will carry less burdens and will settle better. Everybody has worries and concerns which are muffled up or pushed back to the bottom of one's 'thoughts container' - the big box where you dump the million of thoughts swamping and flooding your Mind daily!

That's why a mental spring cleaning is ever so useful, urgent and even essential.

Mind you, some people do not like doing that, because it makes them face the very things that they have wanted to burrow at the back of the 'garage' of their Minds... A kind of vicious circle — But all this is worth doing.

So for the gentleman in distress: ask him to try and follow these directives. All he is experiencing is the rehash of many bottled up, muffled up, smothered emotions, which have the bad habit of popping up.

Therefore, as the body of Energy (which is made of those emotions too) leaves the flesh and feels free when 'out'... the moment he is coming back or is close to the flesh vibrations, there is the turmoil of not wanting to face the Earth life which is the cause of those disarray and dissatisfaction and concerns.

This is all very simple, really – but not pleasant for whoever does not want to find himself in between the "*I want to stay free*" and the "*Those bugs are still clogging my Mind and its peace and freedom; get rid of! get rid of!*" That's what the whole being is screaming for!

If the gentleman is feeling 'squashed under a weight' it is not his own fault. He is not making it up, he is not imagining it. It is a real feeling he has, caused by the imaginary weight but *felt weight* of his concerns. This is simply how things work, my dear, it is no good doubting, because it won't solve your problem of answering his queries.

BR- I was not doubting, I was just surprised!

334

If he has a lot on his Mind (whether he realises it or not), there is bound to be a *release mechanism* for this 'weight'/ this concern to be let loose somehow, at some point. If there was not, it would drive him mad with intense inner stress, or he'd be frustrated in his daily life and he would possibly not know why.

So, that's the weight that holds him down. The fear this brings is not helpful either because from one incident to another, he will be dreading it each time he has to go to bed and sleep.

Therefore the best thing to do is face the fact those things happen, because the Mind has too much to bear - whether one acknowledges it or not- it's there!

The fact he feels paralyzed is linked to the previous answers, as 'inner paralysis' is an outer representation of the conflict going on inside, below all possible 'visibility'. This is therefore an application of the 'rule' that all emotions are reflected in the flesh body and the flesh body is a replica of the emotions felt and endured.

BR- Why did his body "shake violently"?

Remember: His body is made of flesh, his Mind is in charge and reflected by the body. Whatever the problems, cares or concerns and whatever their sizes, even minimal—the **inner struggle of the Mind is reflected by the flesh,** as the ups and downs of emotions, or doubts, or hesitations, or unfulfilled longings and wishes, show there in the flesh—where they have been buried deeply within for a long time, even if he does not remember it! But **childhood fears could still be buried deeply within the subconscious** and none of you would remember... because they are from childhood days—and because they have consciously been *buried by the subconscious who knows what it is doing*, in order to bring some peace and quiet in the daily life of the adult nowadays.

So all that trembling and shaking underneath is like an earthquake or tsunami suddenly revealing there are tremors

335

deeply within, which no one had paid attention to or even knows about. All in all the same as the rest given above earlier.

That's all we can say for now. If you want to type it to tell the gentleman you can do so now. We have finished our 'sermon'!

HOW TO IMPROVE YOUR AND OTHERS' LIVES

You may recall us mentioning the importance of the Power of Thought over and again. This is never to be forgotten because this is what you have to use when you are here - you may as well be used to it and have practised a tool you will have for Eternity if you wish to stay here!

We are only joking about this because you will have it **wherever you go**, whether on Earth, elsewhere, or in our world: all is needed is to **use one's thoughts to make things happen.** They may happen in different ways, but they will happen, whatever the 'Matter' of the environment is at that 'time 'or 'place'.

You see, we do not give details of 'places' because there are so many possibilities of dimensions. You all need to **understand there isn't one single place or case where you would not need or use your Mind.** So why not get accustomed to using it? It is and will be up to you, as your wishes and desires for exploration and experimentation will create them or take you there.

So, we were saying: the Power of your own Thought is extremely and exceedingly enormous: that's what we need to develop both as a theme and as a tool.

As explained before, if you want to be able to progress, you will all have to learn the process of relaxing, focusing, **intensifying the direction of your thoughts and maintaining that focus with an increasingly powerful desire** deep within yourself.

You need not and SHOULD NOT WORRY about the outcome! Because if you worry or doubt, you will decrease the intensity of your desire for success and create some negativity which is never conducive to success!

WHAT IS SPIRITUALITY?

The pattern to follow is always the same i.e. know what you want, know it is for your or someone's good. You cannot want something bad, whether for yourself (which is rare!) or for others out of nastiness or pettiness, jealousy etc! It is essential you wish it for the good of others and self, otherwise it will not work and the negative energies you sent out will bounce back and return to you as a hundred fold power to knock you off your paltry pedestal!

When a Soul sees another one in danger or peril, it should be its natural reaction to want to help. That is what the Law of Spirituality is about. **Spirituality is Life Energy made 'concrete', expressed into various deeds.** So the very fact of wanting to help means you have Spirituality within you, your Inner Core is responding to others' needs. Therefore that is what you should always listen to.

If you wish for something with the same inner desire to help, the same strength and intensity or even more, you will find the right path and focus to maintain the inner flame burning for success to present itself.

You'll have to want it so badly, so much, so intensely, that nothing else counts in your world - **then you'll see results.**

Make sure you maintain a calm enough Mind during this process, because a sea of waves of emotions will not be conducive to the unilateral direction for the creation of your goal and wishes. You need to keep at all times a clear Mind and a calm body too, so that your whole Being is focused on that one goal and desire, to help it on its way to being materialised in your Earthly world. And that's all there is to it!

337

We know you may find it difficult but it will be and is feasible, if only you try to do so regularly, with attention and great focus. Having said that, we hope you will start practising, for the more you do it, the more you'll get results - then you'll feel encouraged by your own efforts.

"Nothing that I can do will change the structure of the Universe. But maybe, by raising my voice I can help the greatest of all causes: Goodwill among men and Peace on Earth."

Albert Einstein

RECAP & CONCLUSION

You can trust the veracity of what is taught as we have done a lot of research and have received a lot of genuine facts, which means we can pass them on to you! Surely you don't think we would bother giving useless or incorrect information! **This is a book for the totally uninformed public.** Not for scientists or pseudo-scientists thinking they 'know it all', even though what they look at is only seen from within the physical Universe, with NO hope of viewing it properly like we all do here from an unbiased perspective!

It is true indeed that **we link up with—and ourselves are channelling—information provided Minds to Minds by those Beings involved in reconstructing and maintaining the Universe you live in** and many others. Those are **Beings who have never been on Earth** or in any 'physical worlds' as such because they are much more interested in the creation of such worlds.

BR- Wouldn't they want now and then, over millennia (or even 'billiennia'?) to sample what they are creating?

It is not necessary, though some may have of course. But what matters to you Humans is to **understand HOW you have become what you think you are, yet are not!** This is the crux of our teachings, the focal point: you are not your physical bodies, you are not 'just Humans'—which in fact is a disguise, a false appearance, a trick of the eye! **You are Beings of Energy who chose to be involved in the activities of the created Universe**.

This Universe did not construct itself, it did not 'come from nowhere' - it was actually built up piece by piece to produce what you see and kind of know, as of course none of you really and properly know much about the rest of your Universe, never mind all other Universes and levels of Mind!

Since we are dictating our books to help you all grasp that, we have to simplify the explanations so that our readers get the overall picture and some basic understanding.

We had thought of calling it "Make your Mind up about the world you live in", but we know it may be too long a title for you all. *(BR- NOTE- That comment came out of the blue, unrequested!)* So, you may want to condense it to something shorter.

BR- I don't think that title gives a clue regarding what your book is about: it could be politics!

We are sure you'll find something good. It had not been decided as such because it is not so urgent; we have to first give you the information to publish.

BR- Do you wish to dictate more info or is your book finished?

What we'll have to say is simply to wrap it up and remind and summarize one last time! Sorry if you think we are repeating ourselves but we have to! It is **so vital to drill it onto all Humans' heads**... Please keep in mind the fact that you are all Beings coming from BEYOND this Earth of yours. Moreover **you are not simply originating from the 'Spirit World'** but even 'BEYOND' that 'Spirit World'! Not in physical distances but through layers of concentration and realization that you are an eternal Being consisting of Mind Energy!

That means: As you think more deeply and consider 'what' you are, rather than 'who' you are (which restricts it to Human personalities in your Mind), you'll see that the important point is: keep your Mind open, ready to receive, ready to absorb, ready to grasp more and more information enlightening your Inner Self with even more new knowledge— or reactivating and reminding you of knowledge already acquired at different mental levels.

This leads us to emphasising the fact that you are constantly thinking, constantly creating all around yourself and within yourself. This is why you are continuously building and rebuilding and **'destroying' yourself** with your own thoughts and mental attitude!

This is valid at any level but especially at the Human level, because in that world your body of flesh reflects your Mindset. And Mindsets are particularly powerful, nearly insidious we could say, because unless you are constantly aware of what goes through your Mind, **you are easily damaging your own physical structure with your mental tools!** Isn't that extraordinary? You are making yourself ill!

Isn't that terrible if you don't realize you are continuously doing it? This is why we go to great lengths to point this out and drum it into your heads: think but be wary of what and how you think and feel!

The 'extraordinary news' to some of you, that **you and we are all Energy Beings who exist BEYOND what you think of 'heaven' or 'Spirit World',** is an intrinsic part and aim of our teachings. This is all you need to ponder about and grasp, because then, it will reduce all your little Earthly activities to mere kids' games, and your fights and arguments to puny tantrums etc. You all need to see everything on a far larger picture!

You are not of this Earth, you are not even of the 'Spirit World', when it comes to the inner points!

You are all **constantly creating your own world, your imaginary worlds, your imaginary selves**—which appear ever so real to you now—until one 'day' when you step out of

341

each of those flesh disguises and look back from a long 'mental distance'! Then you realize that you have wasted your Energies on pathetic matters and topics which were all ethereal and short lasting... just like dreams.

This of course will only be viewed that way when you have all progressed individually at your own pace beyond the Human way of thinking.

DON'T PANIC!

Now, we are aware that our stating this may make many of you panic and even reject what we are saying, because all you want it "to be happy and have fun on Earth" - then 'fun' at your own level of the 'Spirit World' where you hope and expect to meet up with all your loved ones! **Yes, you will meet them. Yes, they are or will be waiting for you**. That is not a problem - you will enjoy being reunited, learning new things, possibly together if your Minds are alike. And we must point out that any feelings of love and affection never disappear, is that clear? **Those feelings create a bond** between you, an affinity, a like -mindedness, a caring towards each other. So, no matter what happens over 'centuries' of your imaginary Earthly 'Time', **you can keep that bond**—even if the Earthly label in this current life is 'mum/ dad/ child/ pet'.

Hoping this reassures you, we could then point out that anyone you have loved that way (as well!) in **other** Earthly existences 'before' as you call it, are no longer in your Mind as mum/ dad/ lover etc. Yet you had loved those people, hadn't you? BUT the bond, the affection, the admiration, the link is still there and will still exist. Such Energy never disintegrates.

This is why you may meet some 'stranger' in this current life of yours and you are amazed by the feeling of affinity with them, you easily bond with them. That is probably because you have known them in a positive way 'before', during some experience of your other facets, i.e. the other aspects of your Oversoul/ Higher Self/ Real You. The 'echo' of those ancient links still resonates....

If you, reader, can understand this, then you may be prepared to open your Mind and understand that this kind of process stretches out throughout the levels of experience Beings of Mind go through. Reminding you that you are a Being of Mind Energy first and foremost. So are your loved one whether in this current life or 'past' ones...

You all mingle as various creative Energies, all enjoying and discovering what you can achieve with your power, sharing it or simply savouring it for yourself. It is a continuous but exciting journey on a gigantic scale, unimaginable for a Human to grasp as one picture, but so rewarding and fulfilling!

So please enjoy the fact and the thought that, though you currently see yourself as a two-legged person on Earth, **you have far more potential and creativity within you**, waiting to explore even more, all the time! And 'time' is no limit because you are all searching and discovering and playing with the fabulous creative powers of your Higher Selves which are continuously creating... and recreating and juggling with possibilities, just for the joy and fun of it all!

That is what '**existing forever' means. And you and your loved ones still have plenty to discover** over aeons ahead—at your own pace. Isn't that exciting?

(An aside to me, BR) We think that will be enough for this current book. We hope you can publish it soon...Thank you!

"Aspire to Inspire before you Expire"
Eugene Bell Jr.

343

THE PERFECT GIFT

Poetic prose entirely dictated to me in one fast flow, without any hesitation, by my Spirit Teachers, in 1998. Having now read this book, their 'poetic piece' may make even more sense to readers?

Creation… Creation…Wonderful Creation!
The joy of putting together
The most exciting forms to express Life:
Millions of flowers, millions of plants,
Millions of animals, millions of birds,
Millions of little creatures, larger ones too...
The joy of thinking: "What the next one?"

The scenery to act the play,
The play of Man on Earth,
Had been designed for Joy,
For Health, for Food.
But the Fun is on our side:
Creating the World and its facets,
Like a diamond for You,
For those who'd appreciate...

But not all understand!
Many just look, not even looking!
All is left is dust, death and drought!
Why spoil this World of Colours, Sounds and Smells?
Why ruin this Beauty, this Jewel, this Pearl?
How could you be blind to what had been given?
This World is priceless, nowhere is the same.

You have machines, you have toys,
You have tools, you have homes;
But you have no means of creating this:
A Tree... a Cat... a Fish... a Bird...
You can't make a sea, you can't make a sky,
You can't make fire out of nothing,
You can't make a leaf or a flower!
Where are your tools, your machines, your pride?

You have nothing, you think you are All;
Your pride is trivia... you face a Marvel!
Why waste it, you mere Humans?
After all, WHO made you?
Not you... We did.

Respect what you are given,
Respect the signs of Life
Which are shown in myriads
Of shapes, sound and scents.
You are crazy! The woods are magic,
Oceans priceless, the sky is awesome!

Open your eyes...your Inner Eye,
And see what truths are shown
In the wonderful world of Nature alone!
The search for God, the search for Life,
The Search for Cures, the search for Health,
The need for more... will be no more,
As all is given in the World you own!

© *Brigitte Rix*.1998

Please visit my website for further knowledge:
www.italkwithspirits.com

Recommended Reading
for further understanding

I'm Not Dead: I'm Alive Without a Body - Vol 1
(channelled by Brigitte Rix) ISBN: 9781898680574

I'm Not Dead: I'm Alive Without a Body - Vol 2
(channelled by Brigitte Rix) ISBN: 9781898680611

Truths, Lies & Distortions: Hidden Truths Revealed (Spirit
Teachers - channelled by Brigitte Rix) ISBN 9781898680604

Dying to be me My journey from Cancer, to Near death to
True Healing (Anita Moorjani) ISBN 9781848507 838

Proof of Heaven A neurosurgeon's Journey into the Afterlife
(Dr Eben Alexander) ISBN: 9780749958794

Soul Survivor (Andrea and Bruce Leininger)Authenticated
case of reincarnation in the 21st century. ISBN: 9781848502192

In Pursuit of Physical Mediumship (Robin P. Foy)
ISBN: 9781857566628

Witnessing the Impossible (Diary of 'the Scole Experiment')
(Robin P. Foy) ISBN 9 780956 065 100

Extraordinary Journey (Memoirs of Physical medium
Stewart Alexander) Saturday Night Publications -
ISBN 9780955705069

Seth Teachings Books *sethlearningcenter.org (Channelled* by
Deep Trance medium Jane Roberts)

My Biographical INTRODUCTION

Of "I'm NOT DEAD: I'm ALIVE without a body!"

Understanding: Who? What? When? Why? How?

"It's amazing! Whenever we lose anything you are likely to find it! You must have a gift!" How often throughout my childhood I heard Mum say this to me! I used to think I probably looked more carefully than the others. I knew nothing about Sixth Sense in those days…

I used to attend a French Catholic grammar school in Algiers, North Africa. I recall being about 15 years old when during a Religious Education lesson, the teacher was going on at length about Hell, that 'terrible place filled with flames, gnashing of teeth and gnawing pain'… Suddenly I heard very clearly someone saying to me: *"Hell is **not a place**, it is **a state of mind,** a state of immense remorse."*

I nearly jumped out of my skin, as there was no one behind or near me and we were on the second floor! At that time I realised something strange had happened, yet I didn't really understand where the voice came from.

"You are a bit like Joan of Arc, you hear voices!" Mum joked when I told her about it, *"but what you heard makes sense, doesn't it? One can feel one is in 'Hell' even while still on Earth. If someone does something horrendous and realises, later on, how much harm this has caused to somebody else, they'll regret deeply that they cannot erase the bad deeds! So it will be far worse if they are in the Spirit World, as it would be difficult or impossible to make amends! Remorse gnaws at you day and night, that's why the Church talks of flames burning you, agonising pain etc. these are symbols, allegories, to explain what will befall nasty people".*

I soon forgot this small incident which was to be, without my realising it, a forerunner of the development which began twenty-four years later...

Meanwhile, I was lucky to have parents who brought up my three brothers and me well, teaching us to do good and avoid harming others, but without imposing religious dogmas. They believed in an Afterlife, though it was probably rather nebulous in their minds...

My Catholic school exposed me more to this religion, I did not know any other. Yet from a very young age, I felt frustrated to be obliged to learn things which seemed to me, illogical and at times unfair - why couldn't a baby 'see God' and only be able to go to 'limbo', simply because it had not been christened Catholic before dying? It was not its fault!

Why were the Catholic Church and even some Popes involved in atrocious wars, such as the Wars of Religion in France, against the 'Protestants'?

What about the horrors of torture during the Inquisition? What about the massacres of indigenous Indians of the Americas, on the pretext of imposing Christianity when in fact it was just a good excuse to steal their gold and precious stones... Why? Was that what their Jesus had taught?

I used to pray dutifully, but I did not know exactly to whom I was praying. That invisible, all-powerful 'God' did not seem able to prevent criminals from doing evil deeds... and nothing seemed to improve around us! Indeed, we used to live in Algeria during the 1954 - 62 so-called Independence War. Yet we had Arab friends. Among others, an orphan, a young Arab teenager whom my Father (who was a civil engineer and designed a large number of Algerian roads) had met during his trips around the country. Dad brought him back home! Mum must have had a shock but said nothing and quickly found ways to create a room to shelter and help 'Abd' as we called him. Father, who had his office at home, introduced him to the other employees and trained him as a draughtsman too. The young man eventually earned an excellent salary and set up his own home in Algiers.

The majority of French people got on well with the Arabs. It was politicians and a handful of hooligans and ex-convicts who triggered this 'war', for their own reasons and benefits, having received weapons from elsewhere... Nobody wanted to leave this beautiful country, which was one of France's 'départements'! Yet in 1962 General De Gaulle gave it away to the 'fellaghas' rebels, thus abandoning Algeria and all its crude oil wells and vineyards, among many things!

As this gave a free hand to criminals, not only French people but also a very large number of Arabs too, felt obliged to leave because they did not feel safe. Therefore we were forced to flee our country, huddled like sheep and packed like sardines on the deck of an overfilled ship. Our only luggage - a suitcase in each hand... For our family it was destination Nice, where I was to spend only a few years before setting off for England.

Why England? Because ever since I was young I always had this inexplicable desire to go there. I studied for and obtained a degree in English at Nice University, including a compulsory one-year stay in the South of England, as an 'assistante' to improve my language learning... and my fate was sealed: I met this kind and intelligent young man, teacher of Russian, in the English school where I was making pupils practise conversation in French: Dave Rix, whose eyes were as soft and gentle as his voice...

One year later, I asked for my position as 'assistante' to be renewed - if I could remain at the side of this young linguist who could speak four languages and had asked me to marry him, I wanted to stay in this green and pleasant land. I was happy for England to be my new Motherland.

After I completed all my studies, we got married. Dave was posted to Leeds, in the North of England, where he became Director of the Russian section of The Nuffield Foundation Project (in those days, spearhead of language audio-visual teaching), then he was appointed Lecturer in Russian at the University of York where he became, over the years, Director of the very modern Language Teaching Centre.

We had two children: Jim (James Christopher) and Anne-France. Life was very busy. I too started teaching again eventually. It was for me the beginning of decades of teaching French in Higher Education - not only at Adult Education classes, but at the University of York. Then, as my reputation spread, also at Ripon &York St John College which became York St John University.

Moreover, in 1989 Nestlé took over the famous York confectionery factory, Rowntree Macintosh. Nestlé's HQ being in French speaking Switzerland with many branches in France (and the whole world), York staff had to become bilingual in double-quick time! So I was appointed to teach French at all levels, in all departments, from top executives to secretaries and receptionists! This went on for several years.

One thing lead to another and to the famous BBC 'Worldwide' asking me to write one of their future publications for tourists, '*Get by in French*' published in 1998. Later, when the publishers Arnold/ Hodder-Stoughton approached the University of York about a new series of language courses, I was asked to write the French course.

This overview of my teaching life and work is only to help you, the reader, understand who I am and show I have my feet firmly on the ground...

On top of, or between, those years of language teaching, I also trained in, then taught, modern dance and 'shape up to music'. Another experience came along later, when I became Fund Raising Organiser in Yorkshire for the Royal National Institute for the Blind.

As my children were growing up, I was then able to *discover another side of life*, which I had not had much time to learn about while they were little. For a long while I had 'done some research' via reading, to try to solve a problem stirring within myself: there were far too many reports and stories of well-documented incidents experienced by intelligent and trustworthy people such as doctors, pilots, mathematicians etc,. telling of their 'supernatural' experiences, their encounters with so-called 'ghosts'. These reliable people would not lie, therefore it must be true: something existed which I felt had been kept secret from me, which was hidden from all of us, the Public! My quest for '**THE** Truth' as I called it, had started!

I became acquainted with the wonderful knowledge of the Incas and the Mayas.

I dived into dozens of books such as 'Supernature' by Dr. Lyall Watson and Colin Wilson's work 'the Occult', as well as Dr. Carl Sagan's research and H.Bergson's works; also fascinating studies on telepathy by Russian scientists and F. Capra's 'Tao of Physics'. I tried to grasp Albert Einstein's Quantum Theory in order to endeavour to find a link with what seemed to me, a very scientific idea particularly relating to physics: the fact that those so-called 'ghosts' or invisible spirits must be a kind of energy. After all, what did the celebrated scientist Lavoisier say? Basically: nothing disappears and nothing creates itself out of nothing. Energy cannot be destroyed, it simply changes shape, that's all.

I pondered on ultra-sounds which humans cannot hear, yet animals can! Therefore, the very fact we are no longer aware of something does not mean at all it does not exist!

It is obvious we are all made of energy, our thoughts and emotions are intangible energy, so, I told myself, **they** cannot disappear when the flesh body and flesh brain turn into dust! Where do they go? Where indeed does that energy go, which was part of our personality, which was 'us'?

351

Finally, what definitely opened my eyes was my encounter, through reading, with authors such as F. Marion who had fantastic extrasensory gifts and was backed up by Dr Wiener of the London Institute for the Study of Parapsychological Phenomena.

Then I read the psychiatrist Dr Raymond Moody's reports in his books on *'Life after Life'*, telling of 'near death experiences' had by several hundred people. They died temporarily during an accident or an operation, flew out of and above their physical body, left the room or the vehicle, and could **prove** they had been witnesses of facts happening far beyond reach of their ears or eyes! Whatever their race, profession, religion or lack of, they all went towards a 'light', met somebody, often deceased loved ones, and they all wanted to stay in this superb new world; but they were told they had to go back into their flesh body, for it was not yet their time to leave. The majority somehow felt they were asked: *"How did you use your Earth life? Did you learn anything? Did you show compassion towards others?"* Upon returning to Earth they all realised they had experienced something extraordinary which changed their attitude and their life down here.

Then Doris Stokes appeared in my life, the wonderful medium who had filled the largest auditoriums in the world, whom I had the pleasure to watch at Leeds Town Hall (after reading her biography *'Voices in my Ears')* proving beyond all doubt that the so-called dead are still alive!

Eventually I also discovered there was a Spiritualist Centre in York itself!

I had reached my goal - THE Truth about the existence of 'Spirits'. They **do exist**, they can communicate, they are people without a physical body but their mental energy, their personality, their emotions still live on with them.

This awareness was not the end of my road but the beginning of an even more fascinating phase and of the rest of my life!

The year 1981 turned out to be very formative. Besides meetings at the Spiritualist Centre, I attended the amazing 'Silva Method' courses: they taught me superbly how to reach a calm and receptive state of mind, in order to develop the sixth sense and use the latent abilities we all have. Once in that state of inner peace, you can really **use your 'Thought Power'.** You learn to improve your health, stop pain, attract beneficial situations to you and finally to work at developing the gift of 'second sight' - 'know', 'see' and 'sense' at a distance. Incredible but true! I was able to do this at the end of a 4-day course, me who thought I would be totally incapable of such a feat! I must add that José Silva's organisation generously offers to refund your course fee, if you can sincerely say you have not obtained any results, which happens extremely rarely from what I saw and heard!

I also found out that in 1930 the Kirlians, a Russian couple who were scientists, had invented a photographic method to prove the existence of the **energy field which emanates from everything living** and **cannot be destroyed**. Modern technology has at last made it possible to photograph and film, in colours, this energy field, also known as 'the aura,' which spreads out of and around our physical body and changes constantly with our emotions and our state of health.

It has even been possible to take photos of this 'energy body' escaping from the physical body, at the time of death...

Among many others who took me on long journeys of discovery, Dr Richard Gerber's fascinating masterpiece, 'Vibrational Medicine', enlightened my way through the most refined systems of Human Energy. All this fascinated me!

There was I, who long ago would have loved to read Physics at University but disliked Maths too much, now beginning to discover Metaphysics, a science far more advanced than that taught by colleges! Feeling encouraged, I carried on developing this sixth sense, as I had the intense desire to learn THE Truth, learn everything there is to know and, it seemed, had been kept hidden from me...

I also wanted to be eventually able to speak to scientists in the Hereafter as I guessed their knowledge is far superior to some scientists' on Earth who refuse to have an open mind!

Do not think for a moment that I was and am gullible and 'swallow' everything and anything I see or hear, particularly at the Spiritualist Churches! Nay! Not I! Cartesian logic implanted in my French blood and my analytic mind, have always empowered me to approach any subject using good common sense... Therefore I observe with an open mind but am ever ready to analyse objectively, in case there was another reason for the amazing demonstrations of evidence that death of the physical body does not kill the real person.

To be fair, of course, one must recognise that, as in all professions, some people are better than others. Moreover, mediums are human beings, so there may be days when they feel below par. But in the majority of cases, time after time, over months and years, not only other members of the congregations but myself and my own family and friends, have had remarkable proof that our loved ones have survived and still live on, therefore everyone survives so-called 'death'!

What is the link making the communication possible? Friendship, admiration, respect, affection, love. A medium cannot 'summon' someone from the Other Side: his/ her task is to be the channel, the link, the telephone line between the two worlds and to transmit as precisely as possible information provided by the departed.

So, one does **not** 'wake up' the so-called dead: it is **they who choose to come and communicate**, the medium is only their telephone!

One must not forget that those 'departed' in fact still live on. They are alive in a world where telepathy is the means of communication, since there, one uses one's thought power and one can receive and read the thoughts of those around you.

354

The operation is quite tricky, if you think about it somewhat - if those 'survivors' want to be able to convey some information to the Earth world, they must learn to control their thoughts and direct them with clarity, one at a time, towards the person they want to transmit them to. This implies necessarily an adjustment of vibrations! Moreover, the recipient must also be at least clairaudient, i.e. hear clearly, but perhaps also clairvoyant (clear seeing) and clairsentient (clear sensing).

So, 24 years after hearing a mysterious, supernatural voice during a grammar school lesson defining 'Hell', there was I, now guided to develop this gift, shelved for so long! Various mediums told me:

"You have a guide (like everyone has; some call it 'guardian angel' but I could never grasp this idea of a being of light with feathered wings!) *who is waiting patiently for you to open the door of your mind to him"*. Easier said than done when one has a brain like mine, faster than a racing car... If I don't practise regularly the Silva Method exercises, as it often happens, I get very rusty, my busy life wins with all its worries, so the inner calm is choppy!

Around that time, I made the acquaintance of Kay R. who became a dear friend and who renewed her own skill at 'Automatic Writing' (an invisible hand guides the pen to form words). After many a conversation with her guide, via Kay's pen, one day

I sighed: *"How I wish I could do this!"*

Her guide replied: *"Get on with it! Relax, take a pen and try!"*

Very surprised and most unsure whether I would be able to, I thought: *"It will take me at least 6 months... but let's try!"*

On that Monday, morning and evening, I sat quietly alone at home, after a short prayer, just in case, asking for protection against any possible mischievous clown who may have wanted to play tricks on me, because I was new to this.

I had a piece of paper and held a pencil on it, asking aloud: *"Anyone there wants to speak to me?"* Just in case, to prevent my brain possibly interfering and thus risking to influence what might come, I kept it busy by looking at the wall opposite me and repeating aloud: *"Wall, wall, big wall, plain wall..."* - I did not look at the paper.

The little zigzags beginning to appear? I ignored them, assuming it was probably blood pressure or muscle tension or some other anatomical reason! Throughout that week, twice a day, I repeated the experiment, determined to let the pen write on its own, **if** that was meant to happen! The zigzags changed shape but did not mean anything to me.

Five days later, on that Saturday morning, 29th January 1983, after my usual question I felt the pen move, without my looking at it, but I realised somehow it felt different... When I looked down, there was one single word: *"Yes"*... As I had not watched the pen, the letters had overlapped a little but it was very legible - it was far from the original little zigzags resembling an electro cardiogram! I was flabbergasted, excited and incredulous at the same time! *"Who are you?"* I asked, 'emptying my brain' as best as I could, thinking only of the bare wall facing me.

The writing started again very slowly and carefully. I had absolutely **no idea** what was being written. When it stopped, I looked: there were several letters all linked up, in fact two words linked up. I deciphered: 'Silver Arrow'. A few moments of confusion, then I dimly remembered, one or two years earlier, a medium saying to me: *"Your guide calls himself Silver Arrow, though it does not necessarily mean he was an Indian. Names given can be symbolic too."*

Ah! So it was my guide at the other end of the pencil? Yet I had **not** thought of him at all, nor of his name!

I asked another question, I forget now, to which he answered yes. So, delighted, I very naïvely told myself I was going to be able to find out all sorts of information, acquire great knowledge such as the origin of the world etc. (!) Therefore I asked and waited for the revelations! The pencil started off very slowly, wrote a bit more than before and stopped suddenly.

I looked and read: *"Very tired, bye"* followed by a downward stroke caused by the drop of the hand and the pencil. So much for the flood of great knowledge!

"Just a minute, please, please, stay a little longer?" I begged, but despite my efforts to get the pencil going again, not a single zigzag, not a single letter! Not even a 'message from my subconscious' in case some people imagine that's what was communicating with me!

I dashed to Kay's to show her. She pointed out that I had pressed the pencil down too hard on the paper, which explained the slowness of the writing... and the burning up of my poor guide's energy! In fact it is better to use a ballpoint pen.

Of course, that evening I tried to 'tune in' again. He came back more easily but was firm, though kind too. His answer to my requests about 'out of the ordinary facts' was: *"We shall teach you what **we** judge suitable, all in good time!"* (And he was right, for what they taught me over the years to come has been more and more complex, as my comprehension was gradually able to expand and learn).

Anyway, that week he also adapted his communication means - I soon **started hearing his thoughts** as they were written! He explained it was easier for him than manipulating the pen! He was blending his mind with mine - telepathy! At the beginning I panicked as I was wondering whether it might be the famous 'subconscious' interfering and I gave my communicator a hard time to prove to me it was and is indeed him!

357

After all these years, I know and can state categorically without any doubt whatsoever, that the various people who spoke and speak to me are indeed alive in the Hereafter, a fact confirmed many a time by numerous mediums who did not know anything about me.

A few weeks after crossing my 'Sound Barrier' by learning to successfully tune in to the Great Beyond, one day, unexpectedly, my conversation in English (as usual) with my guide changed suddenly... and I heard French spoken! I asked why it changed language. The voice replied: *"Because I always spoke French to you, my darling daughter, and anyway I can't speak English!"*

As I had not realised there had been a switch of communicator, I was taken by surprise! Imagine the shock to speak to someone I actually knew well, my own Dad—this happening about 3 or 4 months after his departure from the Earth. That evening, he told me of the joyful welcome he had received when he arrived on the Other Side, his impressions, his sadness to be parted from us, but also his joy not to suffer any longer, his regrets etc. I could hardly believe my ears, I was biting my fingers to check I was not dreaming... It seemed to amuse Dad. Our first conversation lasted a very long time! Mum was surprised but also moved to learn he had managed to communicate with me, all the more since he had asked me to pass on a (private) message to her.

Over the years to come, my conversations with my guide and helpers became more and more interesting, educational and revealing. From time to time, Dad would come in for a chat and share his 'discoveries', especially about physics, because it intrigues him, seen from another world! Not only in our correspondence but also when I went on holiday to my Mum's, in Nice, I made her discover and understand as well as possible what my Friends from Beyond were teaching me. She seemed to accept it on the whole.

Not only had she often had premonition dreams herself which turned out to be correct, but sixty years earlier, she was very impressed by a lady who had the gift. This person made several detailed predictions for Mum's future, every one of which proved to turn out to be amazingly correct!

As I uncovered, discovered and learnt more myself about the Afterlife and developed my own psychic gifts, I was careful not to tell anyone about it (certainly not 'in passing' during small talk) apart from those who understood the subject. This for a good reason: unless one has a lot of time to explain in factual details, with examples, the **scientific side** of communications with the World Beyond, and to reply to questions or 'objections', what's the point of risking to be labelled 'mad' or 'a danger to the public for dealing with the devil', as some ignoramus could imagine it to be (especially if they've been brainwashed by a narrow minded religion!)?

Moreover one does not know what other people picture in their mind if, for example, one talks of mediums or of hearing voices! Because they saw some stupid horror films, some imagine some idiocies and lies such as thinking a Spiritualist Church spends its time having 'frightening séances in the dark', or that horrendous apparitions come to 'attack' people, or that hearing voices means one is ready for the straight jacket and the lunatic asylum! All this is completely wrong.

How many people, gifted with a good sixth sense and with second sight, must have been, and may still be nowadays, incarcerated by some doctors or psychiatrists who are either ignorant, or closing their mind to **the reality and facility of communication between the two worlds!**

On the other hand, people who know me well, professionally and in private too, will testify that I have my feet firmly on the ground. They think that I have some common sense, am sensible and reliable. I say this as modestly as I can, in order to explain why I realise I have a **good reputation as being levelheaded**. People I know (even only on a professional level, without being 'friends') to whom I gradually reveal my other facet, are amazed *'not to have noticed before'* (Noticed what?) and are surprised I had said nothing on the subject throughout all these years! Basically, they all said to me:

*"I believe you for I know you well. If anyone else talked to me of 'voices, visions' etc I'd think she is potty! But I know you are so sensible, absolutely normal, in good physical and mental health, educated and you approach things in a rather methodical, rational and let's say 'scientific' way. So if **you** believe in all this and can do it, well... there must be something true in it! Tell me more."*

Of course, I must point out as well that Mum who is also down to earth, intelligent and with good sense, never had her head in the clouds, so she would have shaken me and told me off if she had suspected that I was 'losing my mind' or was filling it with nonsense! All the more since her motto was: *"Don't ever waste your time!"* Yet she never said it about my delving in After Life communication!

As can be understood by reading the chapters to follow, my guiding Friends from Beyond and my 'deceased' loved ones have indeed helped, warned, guided, taught and given me proof of their existence since we started communicating a quarter of a century ago. Now I do NOT BELIEVE in an Afterlife, I KNOW it exists!

An example my guide reminded of, in Sept. 1999:

*"We are all here to help you help others learn as much as possible about our world. So, there is no reason why we could not give you good results, is there? You must trust us, of course, but you know we have given you beautiful and good **proof** of our sincerity towards you, whether to do with your Mum's departure or the details of her arrival or the very fact you wanted us to warn you etc..."*

How true! Indeed many years earlier, **long before** my Mum's sudden demise, I had sent a fervent prayer to the Spirit World, asking whether my guide could warn me when the fatal day I was to be deprived of her was approaching. I would indeed be eternally grateful, if it was possible to **give me a clue** that the end was near (as I live far away in UK). I also wished I could be helped to be near her, at the time of her 'departure' - if possible several days before, so that she would know I was there!

When I make wishes, I pile them on!

During one of my ensuing conversations with my guide, he announced, in those far-off days, that my request would be fulfilled, even though that day was certainly not yet on the horizon! So I replied:

"Just a minute! You are very kind to say this but... do not rush making promises, as I know that 'the Future' is very flexible and difficult to foresee. Besides, I'll have in writing what you have just told me... So I could reproach you if it did not happen as you said! Therefore you can go back on this promise now, I'll understand perfectly". But he insisted and repeated his announcement. So, on the cover of that notepad I wrote: '**THE** Promise!' not to lose track of it.

Years later, in June 1999 everything happened as promised!

In January 1999 as if by chance, in the course of a chat with the Spirit guide of E.C. (A good medium, then in trance), his guide implied I should do my utmost to go and spend some good time with my Mum in France, as that would "do us both a lot of good"… and that the Spirit World was sending me plenty of healing energy as they wanted me strong for things to come… So I went to Nice (France) as soon as I finished teaching for the Easter break. I found Mum in better shape than she had been for a long time, as she had treatment for her thyroid in January; even my brother noticed it. Those weeks together in April/May were very pleasant, we chatted a lot and exchanged ideas. Then I had to return to the UK because of my teaching.

About 6 weeks later, on June 14th, via the excellent medium A.W, whom I happened to be consulting only about my job, Dad came to speak first and I received an unexpected piece of news, without my asking about Mum!

He did not want to sadden me but he wanted *"to prepare me and warn me, he said, that the 'process' had started and was inevitable"* as far as Mum was concerned, and he would be there to receive her... What a shock!

*(NOTE- It is essential to understand I have been warned **because** my dear Spirit guide KNOWS that I WANT and NEED to be told of such news in advance, to prepare myself. Otherwise no genuine medium would tell you such thing).*

I asked if it was possible to get an idea when it might happen, as I lived so far away. The **only response** the medium got was being **shown a wintry scene** - a very snowy landscape. On the left, white trees, a path covered with snow. On the right, large drifts of snow blocking the door of a house.

The description was very precise but I could not think of such a house. I reckoned since Nice (French Riviera) does not get this quantity of snow, it must mean 'in the middle of winter'. So because it was June then, I'd have 6 months to 'prepare' myself. After that, I was given other messages relating to my work etc.

Five days later, on June 19th, at dawn, I received a phone call from my brother in Nice: the night before, he had found Mum struck by a stroke and paralysed on the left side! I just had time to pack a case quickly, reserve seats on trains and plane and shoot off to catch my flight to Nice!

I was then able to spend a week on a chair, at Mum's bedside at the clinic, taking no heed of any visiting time rules, disappearing just in time when doctors were due to visit. Mum knew I was there, **just as I had been promised** by my Spirit Guide! During what turned out to be her last days on Earth, the shameful inefficiency of some nurses of the L.II clinic (who on top of that went on strike, all day long, on the Thursday) resulted in them not noticing Mum was suffering! They were practically laughing at me when I drew their attention by saying I knew she was in pain! It's because I did insist so much, that on the Friday they realised, at last, that Mum's bladder had been nearly completely paralysed and she had a very painful kidney infection! So a doctor had to give her a powerful painkiller.

Eventually I was told they could not do anything for her and we should go home. Her blood pressure dropped next day, on that Saturday morning, June 26th, her fingers were blue... I was told she could still hear me despite the drug, if I spoke to her. Therefore I was telling Mum she'd soon go back home and would see her beloved cat and that I hoped she had heard what I said... when suddenly she opened her eyes, stared in front of her looking surprised and inquisitive, gave two sighs and she fell asleep for ever... I really was not expecting her to die there and then!

Yet *as promised by my Guide, I was in fact also with my Mum right until the very last moment!*

I only understood the clue of the snow scene after leaving her bedroom, a few minutes after her 'death', when I let the staff see to her body (as Mum had donated her body to Science—I am also an Organ Donor).

Instead of scurrying down the corridor as I had done, day and night, for a whole week, I stayed near her door and leant against the wall. That's when I saw the small painting on the wall near her bedroom... Until that day I had never had enough time to notice it, as I was shooting past! It was the **very snowy scene** my Dad had *shown to the English medium,*

12 days earlier: the description was 100% correct! I was so flabbergasted that I spoke aloud (in English, whereas all week I had been speaking French!) repeating the words I remembered her saying.

That picture was to show me Mum was not going to come out of this place alive, whereas, over the years, she had stayed in many different hospitals and had come out. It was me who had wrongly interpreted Dad's clue, thinking he was talking of 'winter'! *But my Friends from Beyond had kept their fantastic promise, made years earlier, to the very last detail!*

So, how did I come to write this book you are reading?

The beauty and marvel of it all is that **I did not write it** myself! I only typed the manuscript of what had been said to **me** by my Mum herself over several years, during our numerous full-length conversations! Nothing magic about that... Except she started to dictate it about 26 hours **after** the **death** of her physical body, as she'd arrived in Spirit World, in Paradise, whatever the name given, in that very real world where we shall all go one day!!

This book is the journal, the report of this 'new arrival' full of wonderment, enthusiasm and emotions: sadness to have 'abandoned' her family but also joy to find, in the Other World, loved ones and old friends again, and never to be in pain again. Throughout her conversations with me and answering my questions without any hesitation, Mum describes how she left her physical body without even noticing she was doing so (*"I played a dirty trick on myself to 'die' without warning myself"* she jokes), how she learnt, so quickly, to communicate with me still on Earth. Also the surprises she had, her astonishment and bewilderment at first, as it is a world where thoughts take shape in front of you, since the main 'tool' of the residents in the Hereafter is the Power of Thought.

Then we follow her progress as she is determined to learn more and more, to adapt to her new life and to share with us her fantastic, mind-boggling discoveries! Several interesting communicators joined in too and, tragically for us, eventually my husband (who left his flesh body a few years later) described his own passing and settling down too...

I made the error of not realising the extent and magnitude of what was going to be gradually revealed to me, nor the time it would take me to type it neatly on the computer. I started, unfortunately, quite late to get round to typing neatly (and translating into English!) those hundreds and hundreds of handwritten pages which were written at high speed as I heard the words clairaudiently, some starting in 'Automatic Writing' at times!

It is the firm but kind calls to order from my guide and even from Mum and Dad, which opened my eyes. My life was very hectic, then once more, struck by another tragedy in the family, but I had to organise myself better to dedicate some time to try to catch up with lost time...

Why so much effort? Just to show my brothers that our Mum lives on and Dad too?

No, not just for them, the revelations are too superb. I had never read elsewhere, nor heard of, many of the facts my communicators talk about, the extent of knowledge is so wide, that I could not keep all this for us! I had to share it with all those who, like me 30 years earlier, look for 'the Truth'!

$$SSS$$